Prospects for Constitutional Democracy

Prospects for Constitutional Democracy

Essays in Honor of R. Taylor Cole

Edited by John H. Hallowell

Duke University Press • Durham, N.C. • 1976

Table of Contents

Contributors   vii

Editor's Preface   xi

Publications of R. Taylor Cole   xvii

Zelman Cowen • The Way We Live Now   3

Barry Cooper • Culture and Anarchy: The Politics of Matthew Arnold   21

J. A. A. Lovink • Prospects for Democratic Control   36

J. A. Corry • The Prospects for Constitutional Democracy   53

Samuel H. Barnes • The Dark Side of Pluralism: Italian Democracy and the Limits of Political Engineering   75

Helmut Kuhn • Germany—Divided Once More   101

Francis Canavan s.j. • The Prospects for a United Ireland   118

Howard A. Scarrow • Participation Through Decentralization: The Case of Britain   134

J. Harris Proctor • Communal Representation in the Republic of Malawi   146

Ralph Braibanti • Context, Cause, and Change   165

Emmette S. Redford • Watergate: A Test of Constitutional Democracy   183

Contributors

Samuel H. Barnes is a professor of political science and program director, Center for Political Studies, Institute for Social Research, at the University of Michigan. He has taught at the University of Michigan since completing his doctoral dissertation at Duke University under the direction of Professor R. Taylor Cole. He is the author of *Party Democracy* and *Representation in Italy* as well as of articles on the politics of Italy, France, Germany, Belgium, the United States, and Canada. He is currently coordinator of a cross-national survey project on Expectations and Political Action in eight advanced industrial democracies.

Ralph Braibanti, born in Danbury, Connecticut, in 1920, is a James B. Duke Professor of Political Science at Duke University. He has been consultant to several governments, including the Ryuku Islands, Japan, Pakistan and Saudi Arabia and a consultant to the Ford Foundation, the U.S. Department of State and the United Nations. A former president of the International Studies Association–South, he was chairman of the Development Administration Panel of SEADAG and is currently the first president of the newly organized American Institute of Pakistan Studies. His published works include *Research on the Bureaucracy of Pakistan* and editorship and coauthorship of *Asian Bureaucratic Systems Emergent from the British Imperial Tradition* and *Political and Administrative Development*.

Francis Canavan, s.j., received the doctorate in political science from Duke University in 1957. He subsequently taught at St. Peter's College (Jersey City), served as associate editor of *America*, and since 1966 has taught at Fordham University where he is a professor of political science. He is the author of *The Political Reason of Edmund Burke* and of articles which have appeared in the *Journal of Politics*, the *Review of Politics* and the *American Journal of Jurisprudence*. In 1973–74 he was a visiting professor in the Dublin branch of the National University of Ireland.

Barry Cooper was born in Vancouver and educated at the University of British Columbia and Duke University. He has taught at Duke,

Bishop's, and McGill Universities and is presently teaching political science at York University (Toronto). He has translated *History and the Dialectic of Violence* by Raymond Aron and he is the author of articles on Canadian politics and political theory in the *Canadian Journal of Political Science, Journal of Canadian Studies, Political Science Reviewer, International Philosophical Quarterly, Eglise et Théologie,* and other journals.

J. A. Corry holds the L.L.B. degree from the University of Saskatchewan and the B.C.L. from Oxford University. He taught law at the University of Saskatchewan from 1927 to 1936 and political science at the same university from 1936 to 1961. From 1961 to 1968 he served as principal of Queen's University. He was a visiting professor at Duke University in 1974. In addition to being the author of *Elements of Democratic Government* he has written extensively on legal and political subjects and on university government. Professor Corry is a Fellow of the Royal Society of Canada and Companion of the Order of Canada.

Zelman Cowen was born in Melbourne, Australia, in 1919. He was educated at the University of Melbourne and at Oxford University. From 1951 to 1966 he was dean of the University of Melbourne Law School and from 1967 to 1970 vice-chancellor of the University of New England (N.S.W.). Since 1970 he has served as vice-chancellor of the University of Queensland and is now an emeritus professor. Since 1949 he has frequently served as a visiting professor and lecturer at law schools in the United States. He has written extensively on law and social issues. Among numerous books he has authored are *The British Commonwealth of Nations in a Changing World* and *The Private Man.* He is a member of the board of International Association for Cultural Freedom, Fellow of the Royal Society of Arts, and president of the Australian Institute for Urban Studies.

Helmut Kuhn was born in Lüben, Silesia, in 1899. He was educated at the Universities of Breslau, Innsbruck and Berlin. From 1930 to 1937 he was a lecturer in philosophy at the University of Berlin. He was professor of philosophy at the University of North Carolina from 1938 to 1947, at Emory University from 1947 to 1949, at the University of Erlangen from 1949 to 1953 and at the University of Munich since 1953. He is now professor emeritus. Among his numerous books and articles are *Freedom: Forgotten and Remembered,*

Encounter with Nothingness, and *Begegnung mit dem Sein.* For several years he was rector of the Hochschule für Politik in Munich.

J. A. A. Lovink is professor of political studies at Queen's University. He studied at McGill University, the University of Western Ontario, and Duke University (Ph.D., 1967). His teaching, research, and publications have been in the field of Canadian and comparative politics. He is currently on a two-year policy advisory assignment with the government of Canada.

J. Harris Proctor is Charles A. Dana Professor of Political Science and chairman of the Department of Political Science at Davidson College. He graduated from Duke University in 1948, earned his Ph.D. from Harvard University and was a member of the Duke faculty from 1958 to 1970. He has also taught at the Massachusetts Institute of Technology, the American University in Cairo, the University of Nairobi, and the University of Dar es Salaam. He has conducted research in Kenya, the Gambia, Botswana, Lesotho, Tanzania, Swaziland, and Malawi. He has published numerous articles on African politics in professional journals.

Emmette S. Redford was born in San Antonio, Texas, in 1904. He was educated at the University of Texas and at Harvard University. He has taught political science at the University of Texas since 1939 and since 1964 has held the Ashbel Smith Professorship of Government and Public Affairs. Since 1970 when the L. B. Johnson School of Public Affairs opened, Professor Redford has divided his time between that school and the Department of Government. In 1960–61 he served as president of the American Political Science Association. He has written numerous books and articles including *Democracy in the Administrative State, Ideal and Practice in Public Administration,* and *Public Administration and Policy Formation.*

Howard A. Scarrow was born in Detroit, Michigan, in 1928. He holds both the A.B. and Ph.D. degrees from Duke University. Since 1968 he has served as professor of political science at the State University of New York (Stony Brook). Previously he taught at Michigan State University. He is the author of *Comparative Political Analysis, Canada Votes,* and of numerous articles in professional journals.

Editor's Preface

The self-complacent assurance that characterized a great deal of thought in the nineteenth century has given way in many quarters in the twentieth century to a deeply rooted despair. Most men seem to oscillate between the poles of optimism and despair. It is the rare man who steers the middle course refusing to yield temperamentally to either extreme. The man whom we honor in this volume of essays, however, is such a man. Temperamentally a man of moderation, an eclectic in philosophy, he is remembered by several generations of students as the restless questioner who, for the sake of getting at the truth of the matter, frequently asked them to consider another point of view or another set of facts. Taylor Cole has fulfilled the role of moderator not only as a teacher but as a scholar, as an editor, professional leader, and university administrator. To all these tasks he brought the Aristotelian virtue of prudence, and by his example has often inspired others to appreciate the practical wisdom of moderation.

Robert Taylor Cole was born on November 3, 1905, in Bald Prairie, Texas, the son of Robert Wiles and Elizabeth Taylor Cole. He attended the University of Texas and received the A.B. degree from that institution in 1925, the M.A. degree in 1927. While a graduate student he taught political science at Louisiana State University from 1926 to 1929 and again from 1931 to 1933. In 1930 he went to Harvard University to study for the doctorate and served as an instructor in Government there from 1930 to 1931 and again from 1934 to 1935. At Harvard he studied with, among others, Professor Carl J. Friedrich, and one of his first books, *Responsible Bureaucracy*, was written in collaboration with Professor Friedrich. He received the Ph.D. degree from Harvard in 1936. While at Harvard he married Anne C. Berton, who is affectionately known to her friends as Nan.

In 1935 Taylor came to the then relatively new Duke University as an assistant professor of political science. Except for a one-year appointment as the Ford Research Professor at Harvard and a leave of absence during World War II, Taylor has given forty years of loyal service to Duke in a variety of capacities. During those years of service, Duke University has grown in academic stature and international reputation—its growing reputation for excellence due in no small part to the contributions of Taylor Cole.

Taylor consistently and persuasively urged the university to widen its concerns to include those of Europe, Asia, and Africa. It was through his initiative that the British Commonwealth-Studies Center, one of the first interdisciplinary programs, was founded. Under its auspices many Commonwealth students come for graduate study, and many distinguished Commonwealth professors from a variety of disciplines have taught at Duke. The British Commonwealth-Studies Center sponsored through its program a large number of distinguished scholarly studies published by the Duke University Press. A new program of intensive Canadian studies directed by Professor Preston of the History Department is an outgrowth of this early program.

Taylor Cole's scholarly writings reflect these interests. He has concentrated upon the problems of bureaucracy and federalism and has had a long-time interest in the politics of Germany, Italy, and Canada. In recent years he has turned his attention to some of the newly emerging nations of Africa, especially to Nigeria and Tanzania. As a result of his experiences as a university administrator, he has also concerned himself in recent years with problems faced by universities in western Europe and Canada. The phenomenon of Italian fascism and German national socialism has long engaged his scholarly interest, and it is his intention to return to a study of national socialism in the near future. His wide-ranging scholarly achievements received recognition when he was appointed a James B. Duke Professor at Duke in 1953.

During the war years Taylor served as a member of the Office of Strategic Services at first in Washington and later, from 1942 to 1945, as a Special Assistant to the United States Minister in Stockholm, Sweden. Taylor is reticent about these activities, but they were significant enough to merit the award of the Medal of Freedom in 1945. Following the war Taylor served during the summers of 1948 and 1949 as a consultant to the United States Military Government in Germany.

Throughout his career Taylor has been an active member of both the Southern and the American Political Science Associations. He served as president of the Southern Political Science Association in 1951–1952 and as president of the American Political Science Association in 1958–1959. He was also the editor of the *Journal of Politics* from 1945 to 1949 and of the *American Political Science Review* from 1950 to 1953. He is an active member of the International Political Science Association. He has been a long-time member of the Social Science Research Council and served from 1955 to 1969 on its Committee on Comparative Politics.

In 1960 Taylor accepted appointment as Provost of Duke University, a post which he held until 1969. This turned out to be one of the most turbulent decades in American higher education. Despite the persistent attacks on the traditions of civility, Taylor proved not only equal to the tasks which confronted him and the university but managed during these difficult years to keep the university's attention focused on its long-range educational goals. His career as provost was marked by loyalty, courage, and unruffled attention to the details that keep a university functioning. Duke was fortunate to have him in this position of academic leadership.

His experience as a university administrator has been drawn upon by numerous institutions. He has served as a consultant to a number of foundations and wrote a report for the Ford Foundation on American studies abroad. Since 1964 he has been a member of the Council of Ahmadu Bello University in Nigeria. He has been a member of the Overseas Liaison Committee of the American Council on Education.

It is appropriate in recording some of the details of Taylor's professional career to mention the role of his wife, Nan Cole. Nan has extended the gracious hospitality of her home to several generations of students, university colleagues, and guests from all parts of the world. The warm welcome she extends to all who visit in her home is remembered with appreciation. Nan has accompanied Taylor on his numerous trips to Europe, Canada, and Africa and been everywhere received as an ambassador of goodwill.

This volume of essays examines problems and countries with which Taylor has long been concerned as a scholar and teacher. It represents but a few of his many former students, colleagues, and friends who wish to pay tribute to his influence as a teacher, scholar, and friend. The essays fall into three categories: (1) those which aim at examining the moral and institutional health of constitutional democracy in a general way, (2) those concerned with the problem or problems of constitutional democracy, in particular, states of western Europe and Great Britain, and (3) those which review cases of social and cultural problems of developing countries in which ethnic, racial, and cultural problems affect the constitutional order. The concluding chapter on Watergate focuses attention on the constitutional crisis through which we have so recently passed.

In the first category Professor Cowen examines that ancient pillar of constitutional democracy which we identify as "the rule of law." He notes that "the law has entered upon troubled times and along with other social and political institutions is beset by malaise and self-doubt." He explains why this is so. Barry Cooper reminds us through an analysis of the political thought of Matthew Arnold of the danger of regarding "freedom" as some self-sufficient end in itself, that when freedom is without any guiding purpose or sense of reason it literally becomes anarchy. J. A. Lovink examines the meaning of "democratic control" from the perspective of a political scientist and with reference to a growing professional literature both in Canada and the United States on that subject. It is a problem that is dealt with in other essays and contexts. J. A. Corry asks whether constitutional democracy can survive without some "unifying collective purpose." Is that purpose "really within the reach of political systems that are held together, in great part, as someone has said, 'by compromise, ambiguity, and contradiction?' "

Turning from general considerations to more specific cases, Samuel H. Barnes seeks to explain, with the aid of social science methodology, the instability of the Italian political system. In doing so he contributes not only to our understanding of Italian politics but to the phenomenon of pluralism that is found not only in Italy but in other democracies as well. Helmut Kuhn suggests that constitutional democracy in Germany today may be endangered not only by the political division of Germany into two Germanies but by the emergence of a militant New Left that divides generations, families, friendships, schools, and political parties. The so-called "rebellion" of youth, he points out, is not confined to Germany. He suggests that the older generation may in some sense have failed them and that "their rejection of our world is a judgment . . . on ourselves." In a very different context and in the light of its own peculiar historical past Francis Canavan looks at the prospects for a united Ireland. His analysis suggests that while there are universal characteristics of all political systems yet each has its own peculiar history and culture, which those seeking political understanding can never ignore. It is difficult to conceive that Great Britain, the mother of parliaments, should be upon the brink of a constitutional crisis. Yet that seems to be the case. Howard Scarrow analyzes an aspect of that problem by drawing our attention to the two conflicting conceptions of authority that exist within British political culture.

The problems of developing nations, while analogous to the problems of developed nations, have their own peculiarity. The attempt, sometimes too rapid, to adopt Western institutions or to graft them on to existing institutions has had revolutionary consequences and promoted an anxiety of self-identity. Harris Proctor documents some of the difficulties which one small African nation has had in seeking to implement a parliamentary system of government and to achieve economic growth amidst the tensions of a multiracial society. Ralph Braibanti suggests that it is a "moral imperative for a system adopting a new technology to do so with extreme caution and only after assessing its own traditions for acculturated equivalents and using them whenever feasible." There is, he says, "a moral responsibility to preserve man's psychic continuity with his past. This psychic continuity is typically fostered through religious and familial institutions which must be respected. What I suggest is a new balance between the moral imperatives of change and psychic continuity."

The volume closes by bringing us back to our own peculiar problems. As Emmette Redford says, "Watergate constitutes, among other things, a test of a particular system of constitutional democracy." We return to the themes of our introductory essays, the rule of law and the consent of the people.

The contributors to this volume represent a variety of methodological perspectives which accurately reflect the breadth and eclecticism of Taylor Cole's work both as a scholar and teacher. They are indicative of his own versatility and wide-ranging professional interests.

John H. Hallowell

Publications of R. Taylor Cole

Books

The Recognition Policy of the United States Since 1901. Baton Rouge: Louisiana State University Press, 1928.
Responsible Bureaucracy (with C. J. Friedrich). Cambridge: Harvard University Press, 1932.
Government in Wartime Europe and Japan (with Harold Zink). New York: Reynal and Hitchcock, 1942.
The Canadian Bureaucracy. Durham: Duke University Press, 1940.

Books Edited

European Political Systems. New York: Alfred A. Knopf, 2d ed., 1961.
The Nigerian Political Scene. Durham: Duke University Press, 1962.
Post-Primary Education and Political and Economic Development. Durham: Duke University Press, 1964.
A series of political science monographs and textbooks for Appleton-Century-Crofts during the years 1957–1963 while serving as Political Science Editor for that publishing company.
Special publications of the Southern Political Science Association and of the American Political Science Association when editing the journals of those professional associations.

Contributions to Books

"Comparative Government." In *Research in Political Science,* ed. by E. S. Griffith. Chapel Hill: University of North Carolina Press, 1968.
"Commonwealth Federations Old and New: Canada and Nigeria." In *A Decade of the Commonwealth, 1955–1964,* ed. by W. B. Hamilton et al. Durham: Duke University Press, 1966.
"New Dimensions of West German Federalism." In *Comparative Politics and Political Theory,* ed. by Edward L. Pinney. Chapel Hill: University of North Carolina Press, 1966.
"The Ministerial System in Tanzania." In *Festschrift für Gerhard Leibholz.* Tübingen: J. C. B. Mohr, 1966.
"Comment on Productivity, Administrative Reform and Antipolitics: Di-

lemmas for Developing States." In *Political and Administrative Development*. Durham: Duke University Press, 1969.
"American Studies in Western Continental European Universities." In *Theory and Politics: Festschrift for Carl J. Friedrich*. The Hague: Martinus Nijhoff, 1971.

Articles

[*On Fascism and Post-Fascist Problems*]

The Evolution of the German Labor Front. *Political Science Quarterly* 52 (Dec. 1937):532–58.
Italian Fascist Bureaucracy. *American Political Science Review* 32 (Dec. 1938):1143–57
The Italian Ministry of Popular Culture. *Public Opinion Quarterly* 2 (July 1938):425–34.
Current Appraisals of German National Socialism. *Journal of Politics* 1 (May 1939):195–205.
Comparative Organization of the Third Reich. *Review of Politics* 2 (Oct. 1940):438 ff.
National Socialism and the German Labor Courts. *Journal of Politics* 3 (May 1941):169–97.
Labor Relations in Western Germany. *OMGUS Visiting Expert Series* 2 (1948).
Neo-Fascism in Western Germany and Italy. *American Political Science Review* 49 (March 1955):131–43.
The Role of the Labor Courts in Western Germany. *Journal of Politics* 18 (Aug. 1956):479–98.

[*On Federalism*]

The West German Federal Constitutional Court: An Evaluation After Five Years. *Journal of Politics* 20 (May 1958):278–307.
Functional Representation in the German Federal Republic. *Midwest Journal of Political Science* 2 (Aug. 1958):256–77.
Three Constitutional Courts: A Comparison. *American Political Science Review* 53 (Dec. 1959):963–84.
The Independence Constitution of Federal Nigeria. *South Atlantic Quarterly* 60 (Jan. 1961):1–18.
Federalism in the Commonwealth. *Public Policy*, 1965, pp. 355–79.
The Canadian Bureaucracy and Federalism, 1945–1965. University of Denver Monograph Series, 1966, pp. 1–35.
Universities and Federalism in Post-Civil War Nigeria. *South Atlantic Quarterly* 70 (Sept. 1971):449–66.

The Universities and Governments under Canadian Federalism. *Journal of Politics* 34 (May 1972):524–53.

[*On Bureaucracy*]

Wartime Trends in the Dominion Civil Service in Canada. *Public Administration Review* 6 (Spring 1946):157–67.
The Democratization of the German Civil Service. *Journal of Politics* 14 (Feb. 1952):2–18.
The Reform of the Italian Bureaucracy. *Public Administration Review* 13 (Autumn 1953):247–56.
Lessons from Recent European Experience. *Annals* 292 (March 1954): 65–75.
Bureaucracy in Transition: Independent Nigeria. *Public Administration* 38 (Winter 1960):321–38.
Public Administration Training Program in Nigeria. Multilithed for distribution by the Committee on Education and Human Resource Development of EWA, 1966.

[*Miscellaneous*]

The Police Jury of Louisiana. *Southwestern Political and Social Quarterly* 11 (June 1930):55–85.
A Suggested Research Strategy in Western European Government and Politics. *American Political Science Review* 49 (Dec. 1955):1042–49.
Bibliographical Material on Political Parties and Pressure Groups in Australia, New Zealand, and South Africa. *American Political Science Review* 51 (March 1957):199–219.
The Bundesverfassungsgericht, 1956–1958: An American Appraisal. *Jahrbuch des Öffentliches Rechts der Gegenwart* 8 (1959):29–47.
Die Unabhängigkeits-Verfassung des Bundesstaates Nigeria. *Jahrbuch des Öffentliches Rechts der Gegenwart* 11 (1963):417–59.
African Studies and Training in West Germany. *African Studies Bulletin* 6 (March 1963):14–21.
Federalism and Universities in West Germany: Recent Trends. *American Journal of Comparative Law* 21 (Winter 1973):45–68.

[*Special Reports*]

American Studies Abroad, with Particular Reference to the American Council of Learned Societies Program (with Craufurd Goodwin and Bernard Baylin). Mimeographed, Ford Foundation, 1969.
An Assessment of Graduate Studies in Political Science in the Universities of Ontario, Canada (with Alan Cairns and Peter Waite). Mimeographed, Council of Ontario Universities (1974).

Prospects for Constitutional Democracy

Zelman Cowen • The Way We Live Now

The Way We Live Now is the title of one of Anthony Trollope's most important novels, and in it he was concerned with some of the social issues of his own time. As it happened, and I did not know it when I chose the subject, the book first appeared in serial form in 1874, exactly one hundred years ago. Trollope began to write it in 1873, and it was published in book form in 1875. Trollope, I would suppose, is generally remembered as a comfortable novelist, as a prolific writer whose themes were those of a stable, assured, and ordered society.

The Way We Live Now does not fit this description. As one of Trollope's biographers writes, in this book his vision darkened, and he wrote at great length of the collapse of standards and the decay of social morality. The English society which he depicted was in the grip of corrupt transforming powers. International financiers like August Melmotte who became the central figure of the book—I say *became* because it is apparent from Trollope's preliminary sketches that this was not intended—had settled in England. There was a fever of speculation, and noblemen and embarrassed country gentlemen lent their names to Melmotte's schemes and corrupt enterprises; they scrambled for his favors and for the gift of shady directorates bestowed by him. In his heyday he commanded assiduous attention and a seat in the House of Commons. It was a world of fraud in which people rushed to attach themselves to a man whom they knew to be corrupt and whom they abandoned only when the fraud, which they knew to be associated with his enterprises and activities, was about to be publicly exposed.

Trollope first wrote the book and then gave it its title. There are many memorable passages. We read of the successful and wealthy Sir Damask Monogram that "he had really conquered the world, had got over the difficulty of being the grandson of a butcher and was now as good as though the Monograms had gone to the Crusades." Of Sir Roger Carbury, one of the few figures of old-fashioned integrity who belongs to the world with which we normally associate Trollope,

This essay was originally delivered as the Sir Richard Stawell Oration before the Australian College of Surgeons at Melbourne on May 1, 1974. It has been published in the Australian Medical Journal *and is reprinted here by permission of the author.*

he wrote in characteristic style that the "condonation of antecedents which in the hurry of the world is often vouchsafed to success, that growing feeling which induces people to assert to themselves that they are not bound to go outside the general verdict and that they may shake hands with whomsoever the world shakes hands with" had never been acceptable to him.

The book suffered at the hands of the reviewers; Trollope was rebuked for gross caricature. The *Spectator* did not mince words. Its reviewer supposed that there is "somewhere a world like that which he describes, and so somewhere among the marshes there is a sewage farm and we would as soon go there for a breath of fresh air as to 'The Way We Live Now' for entertainment." Critics at that time made their points robustly. The *Times*, it should be told, had a different point of view. While it expressed a minority viewpoint, it praised Trollope for his candor and judged the book "only too faithful a portraiture of the manners and customs of the English in the latter half of the nineteenth century. For all its exactitudes, however, it is neither a caricature nor a photograph, it is a likeness of the face which society wears."

One commentator observed that Trollope wrote *The Way We Live Now* soon after his return from travels in Australia where, it was said, he met healthy men and assiduous women (whatever such an adjective may mean), people who were honest and hardworking, and this contrasted sharply with the character of prevailing English society. That is a very comforting comment on the character of our forebears if, improbably, it was true.

We certainly had our share of rogues in high places in Trollope's time. And *The Way We Live Now* would, I fear, evoke many a responsive nod of recognition from contemporary Australian readers. In our recent past we have seen the rise and fall of our own Melmottes, courted in the day of their success (with all the asides of whispered suspicion and distaste) and abandoned, just as Melmotte was abandoned at the time of collapse. What Trollope saw as unpleasing and corrupt in the English society of his time is commonplace in our day. Only the other day I read a comment that in our own unpleasant century we are mostly displaced persons and may feel tempted to take flight into the nineteenth century as into a promised land and to settle there like illegal immigrants for the rest of our lives. Of course it is impossible, and it is interesting to think that Trollope, at least the Trollope of *The Way We Live Now*, would not have thought it a very good choice of time. The evils, the corruption, the sycophancy which Trollope portrayed, are nothing new in our day. For a long time they have been part of the way we live now. There is little for our comfort in the evocation of it in Trollope's great book.

It is an interesting speculation to ask what Trollope would have said about the way we live now, if we could have brought him out of the shades to write of our time. One reasonable possibility is that he would have responded with a quick "no thanks" to our invitation, followed by a rapid retirement into those comforting shades. What then, to restate the words of the *Times* critic of *The Way We Live Now*, is the likeness of the face which our society wears? Even the nasty world of Trollope's book had a spaciousness, a style, a face which marks it off as very different from anything recognizable in our current situation. What is so characteristic of our time is the rapidity of change, which leaves so many of us deeply confused, disturbed, and uncertain. Few of us, I believe, have been able to take in what has happened within the space of the last decade, perhaps even fewer years. It has been said that during the sixties, and particularly the second half of the decade, we moved, in our world, into a period of almost continual hysteria. There has been frantic growth and frantic change. For one like me who has spent much of his life in universities, and since the latter part of the sixties has had substantial responsibility for the general administration of two of them, the truth of this is abundantly clear. In a symposium on universities and higher education published towards the end of the sixties, it was aptly said that a book written about higher education early in the decade could not be printed at its end without major alteration. And moving only a few years beyond 1969, the picture has changed very much again. And it may be that there are new and sharp changes imminent.

In the early 1960s, it could be said that in the universities, or at least in the great universities, there was a shared consensus on what was important and what was not important, on what the standards of achievement were, and how one ranked individuals in terms of those standards. Intellectual distinction and scholarly achievement were what counted, and with this general consensus on values there was also a general acceptance of the system for measuring achievement of those values on the part of both students and faculty. I have little doubt that these words will be well understood and appreciated by many in this audience. But a few years later, it was certainly not an accurate description of the situation. In the second half of the sixties, the state of higher education was described as suffering from "a complete collapse of any generally shared conception of what students ought to learn," as moving from one fashion to another in the constant pursuit of something new, without any consensus on goals.

A few years earlier, in a celebrated essay, Lord Snow warned us of the breakdown of communication between men, intellectual and learned men, in differing disciplines. It was substantially different, I believe, in Trollope's time. Bleak though the way we live now may have seemed to him, there was a common discourse among educated men and scholars, a common set of educational standards, and a belief in the capacity of the educated man to understand most things commonly accepted as important.

In a remarkable essay, Lionel Trilling has reminded us that when John Stuart Mill's *Principles of Political Economy* was published in the mid-nineteenth century, it provoked great public debate and discussion, it entered into the general culture of its time, and it was an object of the general intellect of the nation. In our day no work comparable in completeness to Mill's could be similarly received; the contemporary economist writes in terms so technical and abstract that his subject is placed at a hopeless distance from laymen and indeed from others professionally expert in the social sciences.

Lord Snow provoked a great controversy when he argued about the two cultures. As he wrote, "in our society we have lost even the pretence of a common culture. Persons educated with the greatest intensity we know can no longer communicate with each other on the plane of their intellectual concern." That, you will recall, was written in the context of a discussion of the science and the non-science based cultures. With the vast growth and complexity of knowledge, it is not surprising that it is so, though Snow's arguments have been subjected to sharp criticism. It is true, however, as Robert Oppenheimer once said, that there has been a thinning of common knowledge. There is an overwhelming predominance of things that are new over things that are old, and I believe this has had a great impact on the patterns and character of our culture, our intellectual institutions, and in particular on their coherence.

It has been said of our universities that they have lost identity, that they have become disaggregated, and, perhaps in caricature terms, that the university serves only as a bookkeeping convenience for its members. Size compounds the problem, though it does not wholly explain it. The Robbins Committee report on higher education in the United Kingdom in the early sixties spoke of a major role of the universities as the transmission of a common culture and common standards, and I would suppose that few then would have questioned this proposition. Less than ten years later another British university report considered these words of Robbins and proposed a substantial reframing, observing that they gave expression to a doubtful philosophy at a time when, all over the world, social notions were in a state of rapid and explosive change. This in effect questioned the very assumption of a cohesive and common culture.

The themes of this last decade have been those of crisis, tumult, violence, and uncertainty. There is a widespread rejection of what was eloquently expressed in times not long past as the permanence and certainty of social institutions as something which not only civilize man, but add a dimension of significance to his otherwise brief and insignificant life. As the mobs have marched and protested, as tumult has succeeded tumult, as passionate causes have waxed and waned, it is hard to picture, to recall a world in which such notions have much meaning.

It has been an unhappy, uncivil, untrusting time, and at the same time, what has been asserted has been a romantic utopianism, an assertion of the impulse life against what is seen as bare cognition and as hypocritical moral codes. Equality and togetherness have been asserted against meritocracy, and meritocratic systems have been seen as divisive, as pitting person against person in undesirable competition, as setting up and identifying undesirable and undesired elites. Lionel Trilling, in a deeply disturbing passage, has spoken of a complex tendency in our contemporary world, our life and culture, to impugn and to devalue the very concept of mind.

In all of this, attitudes toward law have undergone significant change. There has indeed been a strong and insistent challenge to the authority of law. In a thoughtful essay, Edward Levi, former president of the University of Chicago and now Attorney General, has said that whether we like it or not—and in varying degrees many do like it—we find ourselves in a period of instability, disruption, and violence. The times question the idea of law and its administration. Law has not prevented the basic unrest, it has not prevented the acceptance, popularity, and frequent effectiveness of tactics of disorder. I have no doubt that this is so, and you will have seen evidence of it in these streets and in the wider world.

In society at large, there is open dissent against authority, voiced not simply by criminals, but by public figures. In the university, the authority of teacher and constituted authority is battered, parental authority is questioned, and in the relationship of the sexes, male authority is under spectacular and much publicized assault. The Church has faced a sharp and insistent challenge to its authority; government faces confrontation and opposition on a variety of issues and too often responds uncertainly, quixotically, and unevenly. Unions seeking to achieve political and social objectives employ the weapons of boycott and strike action in matters quite unrelated to their historic missions. There are clashes with police, not the clash of individual gunmen or gangs, but the clashes stemming from mass, and not infrequently violent, resistance of people protesting about various political and social issues.

None of this is now unfamiliar to any of us. Of course the questioning of law, or perhaps better, of laws, goes far back into history. Men have long asserted the right, and some have asserted a duty to disobey the law in particular circumstances. Socrates declared that he loved his city, but that he would not stop preaching what he believed to be true. The classic concept of civil disobedience was disobedience to formally binding law without challenging the validity of the law or the legal system, the incidental disobedience of general law which was itself neither challenged as invalid nor disapproved. This incidental disobedience was resorted to in the course of agitating for a change in public policies or social conditions which were regarded as bad on grounds of moral or political principle. There is a classic statement of this position by the late Martin Luther King.

> The devotees of non-violent action . . . feel a responsibility to obey just laws. But they recognize that there are also unjust laws . . . an unjust law is one in which people are required to obey a code that they have no part in making. . . . In disobeying unjust laws we do so peacefully, openly and non-violently. Most important, we willingly pay the price whatever it is. . . . In this way the public comes to re-examine the law in question. . . . We believe that he who openly disobeys a law, a law that conscience tells him is unjust and then willingly accepts the penalty, gives evidence thereby that he so respects the law that he belongs in jail until it is changed. An appeal is to the conscience.

Civil disobedience in this sense may be effective, and historically has been effective in achieving reform in various fields. This gives it legitimacy. In more recent years, however, the character of civil disobedience has changed. In the first place it is no longer seen as a principle of last resort. In the second place it is associated with violence and sometimes with gross violence. And third, and very significantly, it denies legitimacy to the law; it rejects the obligation to obey altogether. The change was taking place when Martin Luther King was stating the principle I have quoted. In his latter days he was indeed scorned by some as an Uncle Tom. Why the change should have come about, it is not easy to say. It may be that over a period of time, civil disobedience was resorted to increasingly as one issue followed another—civil rights issues, Vietnam—as masses were increasingly involved and there was an increasing resort to violence. What is significant in the new attitudes is that the binding force of the law has been repudiated. It was not only the action of mobs and masses; individuals have asserted and laid claim to a right to act free of penalty and authoritative constraint. Another aspect of the same thing is an attitude to gross breaches of the law which sees the violator as an innocent victim, perhaps even more as some sort of hero.

By way of example, a modern American historian said of the man who planted a bomb in 1970 in the University of Wisconsin Mathematics Research Centre which killed one and wounded four, "To condemn Karl Armstrong is to condemn a whole generation. His intentions were more significant than the unanticipated consequences of his action." The mind boggles. I heard a similar thing on a television debate recently: an argument in defense of Charles Manson, who, with his grotesque tribe, was convicted of multiple murders in California some time ago. He was, it was said, the victim of a society from which he was alienated; the blame and the shame lay with society and not with him. He is to be defended against the law. To be sure, the causes of criminal behavior are complex, and a man is what he is and does what he does by reason of many factors, and guilt rubs off on all of us. But attitudes of this sort are still shattering. Yet another aspect of this is exemplified by the Ellsberg case. Ellsberg made public the Pentagon Papers to which he had access by virtue of his confidential employment. His asserted justification for doing this was his profound moral opposition to the Vietnam War and his consequent obligation to take steps to bring it to an end and to expose related governmental actions. Ellsberg's justification for his act won a substantial measure of popular support. Whatever one may think of the issues of Vietnam, it is extremely troubling that the justification of conscience comes so easily and so readily.

Of course, the answer is not crystal clear in all cases. A man in the course of official duty may be forewarned of appalling genocidal or other gross acts proposed or perpetrated by his government and his sense of duty to disclose may be overwhelming. We know that there is always the possibility of such a case, and the pressure of overwhelming obligation to act to prevent such evil from being done may be great, but Ellsberg's act was not of that order and in practical terms did not achieve that. His threshold was too low. It was an assertion of the right to be his own judge of his conduct, free of penalty, a judgment in my view taken far too lightly in our times, and what is more to the point, supported by very many who shared Ellsberg's view on the substantive issues of Vietnam. It is possible, very possible, to condemn both the Vietnam War and such action as that taken by Ellsberg.

We see also new formulations of principle in which scholars construct arguments in support of exempting certain types of lawbreakers from liability for their breaches. Not long ago, the Professor of Jurisprudence at Oxford published a lengthy argument in favor of not punishing those who refused to comply with the obligation to perform military service. These were not conscientious objectors; they were draft resisters. I do not propose to canvass his arguments at length; they are based ultimately on moral arguments, though they distinguish between moral objections to different kinds of law, in a way which I find quite unacceptable. Some are said to be excusable, others not, though the moral intensity may be equally great. I find this sort of argument very troubling and unacceptable, but it has to be said that it commands not unsubstantial support.

More recently still, I have read a very interesting book by Mortimer Cadish, *Discretion to Disobey*, which explores these arguments at length and canvasses questions which bear on what is called "legitimated disobedience." One point made in this book, in a discussion of decisions of postwar German courts, is that the implications of the decision of the immediate postwar Nuremberg War Crimes Tribunal have been taken into account by those courts. It will be remembered that the tribunal denied to those charged the defense that they were acting in accordance with the laws of Nazi Germany and pursuant to the direction of those laws. It was said that if such laws contravened international law, the actor might properly be answerable before an international tribunal and punishable for his actions. I find this a very troubling doctrine. The laws of Nazi Germany under the authority of which these men acted were grotesque and utterly wicked, but it is a formidable thing to say to a man whose defense is "I obeyed the law" that he may be punished for doing that. It is not without significance that some of those who are making the challenge to law which I am describing here have invoked this Nuremberg principle in their support. It is a very worrying thing, perhaps not fully considered at a time of understandable recoil from Nazi evil, and we do well to ponder on the long-term implications of such a doctrine.

The attitudes toward law which I have described have, in turn, provoked the reaction of "law and order," an assertion that there is an unqualified obligation imposed on the citizen to comply with the mandatory rules of the state; it is not for the citizen to judge the law, but to obey it. This has become a rallying cry in recent years for those who urge the rigorous and forceful suppression of crime, political and nonpolitical, with single-minded disregard of countervailing considerations. It is at times a gross reaction to gross excess and in some respects it may have contributed to the general weakening of respect for law.

Among those who most loudly proclaimed the inexorable obligation to comply with law, were the men deeply involved in the complex of scandals we know as Watergate. Some of those in the highest places in American government have been shown to have no respect for and a readiness to break the law when it stood in the way, while with their public faces they vociferously proclaimed the obligation to obey it. Over an extended period in the United States the executive power of the American presidency grew virtually unchecked and what Watergate showed so clearly—the whole complex of acts under that umbrella title—was that the executive and its minions were contemptuous of legal constraint. The summum bonum—the highest good—was the achievement of the president's goals, his reelection, the discrediting of his opponents, the effectuation of his policies and purposes including, incredibly, the discredit of Ellsberg by engineering (ineptly as it turned out) the theft of psychiatric records in the rooms of his medical adviser. The shattering thing is that some of the highest officers in American government and those who served them saw no wrong in all of this. As a former attorney general of the United

States has put it, the values exhibited by Watergate are "lawless, truthless, and violent values that seek to seize power, to curb opposition, to have their way." It may be as Professor Alex Bickel, an American constitutional authority, has said, that great need, the imperative demands of national security, may lead a president to take extra-legal action in justifiable invocation of the precept *salus populi suprema lex*, but the threshold must be high. "In a paroxysm of paranoia," he writes, "to state the case as indulgently as possible, the Nixon administration lowered the threshold." There can be little doubt that such banner carriers for law and order have done great damage to and have corrupted the values of law.

Watergate, of course, has not produced the changing attitudes toward law about which I am speaking, though it compounds the problem. Those events lend support to those who raise the cry of pervasive corruption. The fact is that the law has entered upon troubled times and along with other social and political institutions is beset by malaise and self-doubt. In seeking to explain what has been called the breakdown of law, it may well be that we have to look to a deeper breakdown of the underlying order on which law is based. Law, it is clear, cannot depend for its ultimate acceptance upon the presence of the policeman. In the marginal case he is important and necessary, but the law is obeyed ultimately not because of the force of the sanction and the fear of detection, but for deeper reasons which relate to a consensus: some general acceptance of the social order and the rules necessary to maintain its integrity and coherence. Specifically, in the area of law, there is a general agreement that certain behavior cannot be tolerated, that groups with legitimate interests to advance are nonetheless seen by society as lacking any legitimate right to disrupt. Today, as I have said, that consensus appears to be threatened. Bernard Levin, in a recent article in the London *Times* looking at a variety of events—bomb attacks, hijackings, industrial militancy—has said that a crisis has come about because various groups have realised that the restraints on their power that have in the past operated to limit the use they could make of that power are, and probably always were, imaginary—self-imposed fetters that depended on an acceptance by the wearers of certain assumptions which they are no longer willing to make. The moment they abandoned their willingness to make the assumptions (assumptions about the nature of the society in which they lived and their relations with others in that society and outside it) the fetters fell from their wrists. Nor is it any use pointing out that power requires responsibility and freedom involves obligations; those concepts are among the assumptions that are no longer made.

If this be the way we live now, and I believe that there is much evidence that it is so, there is reason for great concern, at least on the part of those of us who cherish the values and the rules of a civil, liberal society. It is profoundly disturbing that there should be a pervasive tendency to idealize men, women, and groups who set themselves against the law and seek to achieve their ends through direct action. In great universities there have been occasions when speakers with unpopular views have been denied the right to present those views, and in some cases they have suffered personal assault. There are to be found in the universities teachers who will support the doctrine that some views should not be heard.

In our day, there is persistent advocacy of violence. We have seen it in many parts of the world and in many forms. Violence has differing faces and degrees: the shooting down of people; the burning, smashing, and bombing of property and valuable equipment; air piracy and acts of terrorism; the swarm of body force which has become almost a commonplace in our age.

I have no doubt that in all of this there is a real danger to the institutions which I, certainly, cherish. There is a limit to the amount of defiance that a legal system can tolerate. Where and when the cracking point comes, it is not possible to say, a priori. There are occasions when the sensible course is to turn a blind eye, and the doctrinaire exponent of law and order does not lead us to a satisfactory resolution of the problems. The silliness and triviality of some acts will be recognised as such if they are ignored, and it does not follow that disregard of any breach of the law will encourage more and worse. The contrary may be true. Be that so, the system is under heavy strain, because disrespect for the law, depicted and magnified by a formidable media technology which can and does provide for instantaneous transmission of existing and tumultuous events thousands of miles away, is contagious, highly contagious. There is much force in Hannah Arendt's warning that "the practice of violence like all action changes the world, but the most probable change is a more violent world."

I ask a familiar question in the context of these attitudes to law: why is it so? and I quote at some length from the essay by Edward Levi to which I have already referred.

Law does have to achieve through fear, favor or the persuasion of process or ideals of justice, a widespread willingness to submit to its governance. The necessity for voluntary submission emphasizes the pernicious effects upon the whole system when a habit of violation is permitted or encouraged. Many aspects of our present system encourage this habit. Statutes which are misleading or which for one reason or another carry a high level of unenforcibility, failures of enforcement with as high a level of crimes unsolved as we now have, the willingness to isolate areas of life, as in the ghettos, where a different standard is used—all these are enemies of law's legitimacy. The failure of law to make good its assertion of sovereignty and the effects are long with us. And this is true whether the acts of violence are lynching or are regarded as justified by good motives or an inevitable part of social conflict. The danger for law as a whole is increased when a high moral value is placed upon the violation, within groups where members violate in concert, or where an individual through one of the most serious oddities of our law is encouraged or in some sense compelled to establish a significant legal right through a personal act of civil disobedience. The distinction between such acts and ordinary violations becomes more fragile in a period of turmoil. The failures of agencies of government to acknowledge or to conform to the processes of law ... increases the moral assurance with which private citizens in other matters also disregard the law. In important ways the operations of our legal system have contributed to basic unrest and to tactics of disorder.

Every word in this statement merits the most careful attention. For the state of affairs he describes, governments must carry a share of the blame. They must not enact laws as part of a game of bluff. Without conducting a debate on the merits of particular laws, it has to be said that if they are written deliberately into the statute book they must have credibility so long as they are there.

If, except in the case of trivial breach, it be said that the course of political wisdom is to lie doggo, the costs in terms of the standing of the law are high, because the disease of disregard and defiance is very contagious. This is not simply saying "law and order"; it says rather: use your law-making machinery wisely and sparingly, with adequate thought, foresight, with awareness of what you are at, and with intestinal fortitude. If you are not going to enforce the laws you have enacted, they ought not to be there. Disregard or capricious and partial application of the law is a very unwise course; it corrupts the whole fabric of the law. University administrators with fragile authority are sometimes charged with weakness and indecisiveness, and while I do not want to embark on a game of recrimination, let me say of all Australian governments that their record measured by reference to what I have just said is far worse.

I believe that the law has suffered through overexposure, overuse. In our times there has been a massive resort to law to regulate many areas of economic and social life. It may well be that there is an overuse, too much of a disposition to resort to law to regulate too much of our lives. It has been said, fairly I think, that a healthy society requires that there be considerable play in human relations, a degree of trust in the good faith of others, confidence that things can be worked out tolerably, a willingness not to insist on every right one may think one should ideally possess, and a large amount of individual self-reliance. The attempt to define all the rights of individuals and to enforce them by legal processes signifies the elimination or disappearance of those virtues. We write them down too much.

The overuse of law puts power at times into dangerous or at least unfit hands; it is productive of corruption in that it vests authority in people who have ignoble standards, it frustrates initiative, it allows of minor and not so minor tyrannies. If government would encourage respect of the law, it must show proper respect for the proper use and procedures of the law. I do not think that there is much doubt that the individual feels increasingly hemmed in, increasingly the victim of injustice, if not oppression. There are few of us, I would suppose, who have not felt resentment arising out of some episode, small or large, in which he has been a victim of official arbitrariness, whether it be a departmental dealing, a concern that some exercise of discretion has not been wholly aboveboard, a resentment at the indifference or insolence of some functionary to whom we must go for some purpose. The state, the liberal democratic state certainly, must take steps, on grounds of principle and particularly if the law is to command respect, to assure as best it can that the legitimate complaints of citizens in face of state power can and will receive adequate investigation and hearing. The demand for ombudsmen—now gaining increasing recognition in some parts of Australia, including this part—is an expression of this discontent and the need for remedy.

The ombudsman is seen as the "people's guardian against the government," and I believe that it is fair to say that where ombudsmen have been appointed, an enhanced esteem for government and for the law is likely. The governor-general designate, Sir. John Kerr, as chairman of the Commonwealth Administrative Review Committee in his report in 1971 recommended the appointment of a general counsel for grievances who would serve as a federal ombudsman. Action to appoint an ombudsman has already been taken in this state. Sir John Kerr's committee also proposed reforms of the present law relating to review of governmental administrative action. The law in this area has developed a complexity and a serious inadequacy and has, I believe, failed to provide appropriate remedies in the courts in respect of complaints and claims against public bodies and authorities. We need a comprehensive review and reform of procedures in this field to give citizens and affected bodies speedy, cheap, and effective remedy in the courts, be they ordinary courts or specially designed administrative tribunals.

In other areas, the state of the law contributes to its poor standing in our time. I would commend to you a very interesting and provocative book, *The Honest Politician's Guide to Crime Control* by Norval Morris and Gordon Hawkins. Mr. Hawkins writes regularly in the columns of the press and teaches in Sydney, and Norval Morris once taught with me in the Melbourne Law School and now occupies a distinguished chair in the University of Chicago. The book was published in America, but its argument is relevant to our situation. It deals specifically with the criminal law; it tells us to look at our calendar of crimes and warns that if we expand it too broadly we do harm. We impose overgreat burdens on the police by preventing them from doing effectively what they should be doing to protect us from offenses against persons and property, we encourage contempt and disregard for the law, we may in fact encourage and increase crime because the things we forbid are still done and are done by organized criminal groups who earn rich profits from doing them. As the authors put it, referring to the laws relating to narcotics, gambling, and prostitution,

> the criminal law operates as a crime tariff which makes the supply of such goods and services profitable for the criminal by driving up prices . . . this leads to the development of large-scale or-

ganised criminal groups which as in the field of legitimate business tend to extend and diversify their operations, thus financing and promoting other criminal activity . . . the high prices which criminal prohibition and law enforcement help to maintain have a secondary criminogenic effect in cases where demand is inelastic . . . by causing persons to resort to crime in order to obtain the money to pay those prices. . . . The proscription of a particular form of behaviour (such as homosexuality, prostitution, drug addiction) by the criminal law drives those who engage or participate in it into association with those engaged in other criminal activities and leads to the growth of an extensive criminal subculture which is subversive of social order generally. It also leads, as in the case of drug addiction, to endowing that pathological condition with the romantic glamour of a rebellion against authority or of some sort of elitist enterprise. The expenditure of police and criminal justice resources involved in attempting to enforce statutes in relation to sexual behaviour, drug taking, gambling and other matters of private morality, seriously depletes the time, energy and manpower available for dealing with the types of crime involving violence and stealing which are the primary concern of the criminal justice system. This diversion and over-extension of resources results both in failure to deal adequately with current serious crime and, because of the increased chances of impunity, in encouraging further crime. These crimes lack victims, in the sense of complainants asking for the protection of the criminal law. Where such complainants are absent it is particularly difficult for the police to enforce the law. Bribery tends to flourish; political corruption of the police is initiated. It is peculiarly with reference to these victimless crimes that the police are led to employ illegal means for law enforcement.

This is a powerful statement, and although it is made in an American context, it is relevant to our case. The argument is not a permissive one in favor of many things that we find repugnant; it urges, in the context of the criminal law, that we should think carefully about what we are doing and think of costs and implications for the fabric of the law generally. We should look to the calendar of crimes: there may be all the difference in the world, so far as the criminal law is concerned, between pushing and drug taking. Drunkenness may be an inconvenience in public places, but the use of the criminal law to deal with it costs a good deal in manpower, energy, and resource and may strike disproportionately at particular and disadvantaged groups in the population, such as aborigines. The point is that we need to take a long, hard look at the reach of our criminal laws and make proper enquiry into costs and consequences, and above all into the impact on the fabric of the law generally.

A number of these things which impair the authority and the standing of the law we can do something about, if we have the energy and the will to do so, and the capacity to move government which may have its eye on other priorities. On a wider, perhaps even a world-wide scale, the problems which underlie the breakdown of consensus are formidable. I have spoken of Bernard Levin's statement that all over the world we see the outbreak of violence, the disappearance of self-imposed fetters on behavior which depended on an acceptance by the wearers of certain assumptions which they are no longer willing to make. He follows this up by pointing to the great disparities which exist in the world between the resources of the developed and the poor countries, between classes and groups within countries. The grievances which flow have already found expression in the rejection of constraints on behavior and action hitherto accepted, but no longer countenanced. As with the emperor, so with the law; it is seen that there are no clothes. And for society, international and national, the prospects are chilling. Levin points out that out of the disorder which is an expression of the discontent there could come solutions or attempted solutions which would involve the extinction of freedom in the form of some sort of Maoist totalitarianism, as the price of equality. He says, however, that he hopes a better solution can be found, one which secures social and economic justice in a society as free as ours is today. He says further that this is necessary if our society is to remain free. I think he is right.

For a long time past, I have been concerned with some of the problems which beset the liberal society. A few years ago, in the A.B.C. Boyer Lectures, I spoke of the "Private Man," of the problems of protecting and assuring a decent privacy for people in our society and in our time. I like to think that what I said then gave some a greater awareness of those problems. In speaking on the way we live now, I would like to raise further questions in a different and, I think, even more serious context. When an Australian national paper can write in a recent editorial that "the fact is that the level of violence in western society has escalated to the point of an undeclared war . . . [we are probably at] the end of the era when it could be assumed that only the exceptional maniac would threaten sensational public violence and [at] the beginning of a period in which the greater part of organized western society must think it is in the middle of a civil war with those forces which wish to overturn it," we must pause to ask whether this is absurd extravagance or whether we are faced with a gross threat to the security and integrity of liberal society and its values. I believe that we are faced with such a threat.

We find ourselves in a world which was always ugly for many, but which is now grossly disordered. There is impatience with rule, a contempt for means, a continuing and a mounting hysteria, and in varying degrees many have virtually a love affair with violence. For some, perhaps many, this is compounded by the belief that we face a situation in which finite resources, proliferating pollution, and the press of human numbers pose terrible threats to the life of the planet. So much of this has come upon us, as so many things have, with dizzying rush and intensity during the last decade. It has furnished new occasion and new ground for confrontation. In many ways the society in which we make our lives has become a dark, threatening, dangerous, and uncivil place, with daily and pervasive contempt for rule, order, and authority—and there is a more immediate reality to the Hobbesian description of man's condition, outside the embrace of *Leviathan* as solitary, poor, nasty, brutish and short. It seems to me that government acts indecisively and with great uncertainty in its response to the multitude of challenges which daily confront it. They are so many and so difficult that the fragility of the consensus, upon which liberal democratic society inevitably depends, often stands nakedly exposed.

We are at sea on so many important issues and questions: on the meaning and standing of law, as I have said, and on such issues as the principles and purposes of punishment we hear all manner of extravagant propositions on every side. The word extravagant perhaps best characterizes many responses, positions, values, standards in the way we live now, and I think that there is great danger in all of this. In a world of extremism and polarization, liberal values and standards have little chance of survival and if, as Hobbes says, only

Leviathan, totalitarian authority, can save us from the danger and menace of our fellow man, we are in for a poor time and the prospect is dismal.

Between the wars, W. B. Yeats wrote some disturbing and deeply pessimistic lines:

> Things fall apart; the centre cannot hold;
> Mere anarchy is loosed upon the world,
> The blood-dimmed tide is loosed and everywhere
> The memory of innocence is drowned;
> The best lack all conviction, while the worst
> Are full of passionate intensity.

I certainly do not share Yeats' political philosophy, but I do have a sense of foreboding. Is this the way we live now? One of the wisest of the academic leaders among us, President Theodore Hesburgh of Notre Dame, wrote during the aftermath of widespread university troubles:

> I doubt that anyone would be able to label our age, although it might be called the age of frustrated expectations, the age of protest against almost everything, the age of unlimited possibilities and disappointing results. It is an age that can put men on the moon yet create an impossible traffic tangle in every metropolitan centre. It is an age of unbelievable wealth and widespread poverty. It is an age of sensitivity to human dignity and human progress, yet one in which there is relatively little of either, despite the available resources. It is finally an age where the hopes, the expectations, and the promises of humanity have been more rhetorical than real. . . . There is a wide gulf between the blueprint and the reality, the word and the deed. One is often reminded of Charles Dickens' opening statement in *The Tale of Two Cities*: 'It was the worst of times; it was the best of times . . .' We can survive the worst, if we achieve the better or, hopefully, the best.

We have to find the way, or at least a way. Despite our massive skills and our incredible command of technology, we have neither clear minds nor clear directions.

Barry Cooper • Culture and Anarchy: The Politics of Matthew Arnold

The name of Matthew Arnold for most contemporary political scientists is associated with a handful of widely anthologized poems. Most of us can quote approximately the line from "Dover Beach," about ignorant armies clashing by night, but the rest of his work, especially his prose, remains relatively unknown. This selective memory may have surprised Arnold's contemporaries, for according to one of his most balanced critics, "a successful writer upon educational, political and theological subjects—who had once written poetry which nobody read, and who from time to time wrote literary criticism which not very many people read—that, I think, would be a fair description of Matthew Arnold as he appeared to his contemporaries."[1] That Arnold's political writings are so little remembered may well be because they contain so few positive doctrines.

Literary critics and others have passed the most varied judgments upon Arnold's political writings. George Saintsbury said he had "no 'ideas,' no first principles, in politics at all,"[2] while according to Henry Sidgwick he was no more than a fop, "shuddering aloof from the rank exhalations of vulgar enthusiasm, and holding up the pouncet-box of culture betwixt the wind and his nobility."[3] For T. S. Eliot he was an imprecise rhetorician, at best a "forerunner of humanism."[4] McCarthy and Lippincott are agreed that Arnold was antidemocratic, Barker said he was an authoritarian, Brown said he was a reformist, and Harvey called him a collectivist.[5] Lionel Trilling argued that *Culture and Anarchy* was an "indirect answer" to Mill's *On Liberty*; Super called it a "sequel," and Alexander was of the

1. H. W. Garrod, *Poetry and the Criticism of Life*, The Charles Eliot Norton Lectures, 1929–1930 (Cambridge: Harvard University Press, 1931), p. 80.
2. *Matthew Arnold* (Edinburgh: Blackwood, 1899), p. 152.
3. *Miscellaneous Essays and Addresses* (London: Macmillan, 1904), pp. 57–58.
4. *Selected Essays*, 3rd ed. (London: Faber and Faber, 1951), pp. 431–32, 434.
5. Patrick J. McCarthy, *Matthew Arnold: The Three Classes* (New York: Columbia University Press, 1964), p. 168; B. E. Lippincott, *Victorian Critics of Democracy* (Minneapolis: University of Minnesota Press, 1938), pp. 93 ff; Sir Ernest Barker, *Political Thought in England, 1848–1914* (Lonnon: Butterworth, 1915), pp. 198–99; Charles Harvey, *Matthew Arnold, A Critic of the Victorian Period* (London: Clarke, 1931), p. 211; E. K. Brown, *Matthew Arnold, A Study in Conflict* (Chicago: University of Chicago Press, 1949), pp. 156, 175 ff.

opinion that Arnold and Mill had the same purpose in their writings, "to prepare their culture for its imminent democratization."[6] Sometimes the same writer has trouble concluding just how Arnold should be classed: within the short space of twelve pages Walcott characterized him as a democratic reformer, a conservative, and as a benevolent, rational authoritarian.[7]

This range of opinion is not solely a result of the whims of critics, and one of the objectives of this paper is to clarify some of the ambiguities in Arnold's political writings; a preliminary task is to justify our concern with him in the first place. Political philosophy (as I understand it) is the reasoned consideration of the whole of man, what Aristotle called *peri ta anthropina*, in his relation to the order of the whole of what is. Prima facie, therefore, there is no reason why political philosophers should not look to literary criticism, comparative religion, classical philology, philosophy of history, or a dozen other specialized disciplines for significant contributions to their own concerns. Moreover, if Germino's generalization, that "the period from the French Revolution to World War II was one which witnessed the ascendancy of ideology and the near eclipse of political theory,"[8] is correct, then the contingencies of our historical situation are such that we may not be amiss in looking outside the so-called mainstream of political ideas, which in Victorian England means political economists such as Marx, Bentham, and Mill, for insights into the problems of a nascent industrial and technological society.

If, then, it be accepted that political theory is not only justified but perhaps compelled to look beyond the realm of "political thought" in some narrower sense if we are to find a reasoned discussion of human affairs, the next preliminary question must be: why Arnold? This paper is intended to provide a more lengthy answer, but briefly one may point to the following considerations: there seems to be a consensus among literary critics, whatever they make of him, that Arnold's criticism "was not merely of literature in the narrow sense—for Arnold literature has no narrow sense—but of politics and social

6. Lionel Trilling, *Matthew Arnold* (New York: Norton, 1939), p. 260; R. H. Super, "Vivacity and the Philistines," *Studies in English Literature*, 6 (1966) p. 633; Edward Alexander, *Matthew Arnold and John Stuart Mill* (London: Routledge and Kegan Paul, 1965), p. vii.

7. Fred G. Walcott, *The Origins of Culture and Anarchy: Matthew Arnold and Popular Education in England* (Toronto: University of Toronto Press, 1970), pp. 116, 117, 128; cf. Trilling, *Matthew Arnold*, pp. 278, 284 ff.

8. Dante Germino, *Beyond Ideology: The Revival of Political Theory* (New York: Harper and Row, 1967), p. 15.

structure, and of religion and every yearning of the human spirit."[9] More important, we have his own testimony as to the way he experienced his own times, an experience for which in our own day echoes are not hard to find. "These are damned times" he wrote to Clough, "everything is against one—the height to which knowledge is come, the spread of luxury, our physical enervation, the absence of great *natures*, the unavoidable contact with millions of small ones, newspapers, cities, light profligate friends, moral desperados like Carlyle, our own selves, and the sickening consciousness of our difficulties."[10] The experience of spiritual disorder that was expressed in this and other letters of the period as well as in his poetry and religious writings has been noted often enough by literary critics;[11] the most superficial reading of *Culture and Anarchy* makes plain the political dimension of his response.

We would add two notes of qualifications so that our purpose is not misunderstood. First, we shall not deal with Arnold's writings on ultimate reality; broadly speaking, that is, we shall not be concerned with his religious opinions even though they had some influence upon his political judgments, save to say that Arnold was not hostile to religion in general, nor to Christianity, nor to philosophy, but to dogmatic religion, dogmatic Christianity, dogmatic philosophy. And second, we are not focally concerned with the sources of his ideas or his place in the history of ideas.[12] Arnold's ethical analyses, no less than his proposals for reform, were intended to be practical and to have real consequences. Even so, it makes sense, for purposes of our analysis, to distinguish his diagnosis of moral decay from his more pragmatic analyses of the drift of events and his recommendations to ameliorate their more undesirable consequences. There was no doubt in Arnold's mind, however, that the unedifying politics he described was a consequence of a decline in morals, and that, in the end, as

9. Carleton Stanley, *Matthew Arnold*, The Alexander Lectures, University of Toronto (Toronto: University of Toronto Press, 1938), p. 136.

10. *The Letters of Matthew Arnold to Arnold Hugh Clough*, ed., F. H. Lowry (London: Oxford University Press, 1932), (Sept. 1849), p. 111.

11. An excellent treatment of this level of Arnold's writing is J. Hillis Miller, *The Disappearance of God: Five Nineteenth-Century Writers* (Cambridge: Harvard University Press, 1963), pp. 212–69.

12. For such treatments, see R. Williams, *Culture and Society* (Harmondsworth: Penguin, 1961); Trilling, *Matthew Arnold*; R. H. Super, *The Time-Spirit of Matthew Arnold* (Ann Arbor: University of Michigan Press, 1970); D. G. James, *Matthew Arnold and the Decline of English Romanticism* (Oxford: Clarendon, 1961); Otto Elias, *Matthew Arnold's politische Grundanschauungen* (Leipzig: Mayer and Muller, 1931); Basil Willey, *Nineteenth-Century Studies: Coleridge to Matthew Arnold* (London: Chatto and Windus, 1961).

with Aristotle, politics and ethics were but two aspects of a single reality.

II

The various terms and concepts which recur in[13] Arnold's most famous prose work, *Culture and Anarchy*,[14] such as "culture and its enemies" and "authority and anarchy," suggest by themselves the area of Arnold's preoccupations. We shall begin, therefore, by tracing, mainly from this work, what Arnold meant by "culture" and its relationship to authority and anarchy.

We should not expect to find a rigorous definition of culture because, as Arnold said, "what we are concerned for is the thing, not the name; and the thing, call it by what name we will, is simply the enabling ourselves, by getting to know, whether through reading, observing, or thinking, the best that can at present be known in the world, to come as near as we can to the firm intelligible law of things, and thus to get a basis for a less confused action and a more complete perfection than we have at present" (V, 191). Culture is not just a smattering of Latin and Greek or a taste for French novels and Italian art. Nor is it mere intellectual curiosity but includes as well "love of our neighbour, the impulses toward action, help, and beneficence, the desire for removing human error, clearing human confusion and diminishing human misery, the noble aspiration to leave the world better and happier than we found it,—motives eminently such as are called social" (V, 91). It has its origin in "the love of perfection; it is a *study of perfection*" and becomes effective "by the force, not merely or primarily of the scientific passion for pure knowledge, but also of the moral and social passion for doing good" (V, 91). That is, culture is the tension of seeing and doing, "which consists in becoming something rather than being something" (V, 95).

Adopting Swift's formula, culture is a passion for "sweetness and light" but, Arnold added, culture has an even greater passion, that sweetness and light should prevail, and prevail everywhere. Thus, for Arnold, the men of culture are tied to no class and no social or political status; they are "the true apostles of equality" (V, 112–13).

13. For details see S.M.B. Coulling, "The Evolution of *Culture and Anarchy*," *Studies in Philology*, 60 (1963): 637–68.
14. R. H. Super, ed. *The Complete Prose Works of Matthew Arnold* (Ann Arbor: University of Michigan Press, 1961–). Hereafter cited as *Prose Works* or by volume and page number in text.

The "equality" involved was not, to be sure, an equality of one man/one vote but an equality implied in what Arnold called our "best self." We habitually live in "our ordinary selves, which do not carry us beyond the idea and wishes of the class to which we happen to belong" (V, 134). In our ordinary self there is neither equality nor reason but both could be developed, he said, by culture. Our "best self" embodied the authority of "right reason," a capacity to think that, beneath ordinary class prejudices, all men possess in virtue of their common human nature (V, 134, 143, 155). Culture, therefore, was effective in society only through persuasion or, more specifically, through an appeal to the rational element in men's souls.

At other times Arnold called "the thing" civilization, "the humanising, the bringing into one harmonious and truly humane life, of the whole body of English society."[15] Love of perfection may help us answer the question of how to live, but the context of question and answer is practical and political. "The true and noble science of politics is even the very chief of the sciences, because it deals with this question for the benefit of man not as an isolated creature, but . . . for the benefit of man in society."[16] Culture, in one sense, is Aristotelean political science.[17] Thus Arnold argued that simply by trying to see things as they are (III, 258) and because of its appeal to reason, culture "is surely well fitted to help us judge rightly . . . the qualifications and titles to our confidence of these three candidates for authority [i.e., the aristocracy, the middle class, and the working class], and can thus render us a practical service of no mean value" (V, 124). In other words, while the ultimate purpose of culture is persuasive, to transform society in order to make possible the diffusion of sweetness and light, its immediate practical significance is that it enables us to judge soundly the politics of the day and the various claims to political authority.

In his concept of "authority" Arnold sought a middle term between culture whose effectiveness depended upon an appeal to our "best self," and the state, which could enforce the conduct of our "ordinary self" as well. Force and the external "mechanical" apparatus of administration was a necessity—at one point Arnold said it was "sacred" (V, 223)—but the state in this most primitive sense was not necessarily authoritative. The genuine, authoritative state is "the nation in

15. *Irish Essays and Others* (London: Smith, Elder, 1882), p. 118; see also *Prose Works*, VIII, 286, 370.
16. *Irish Essays*, p. 149.
17. *Nicomachean Ethics*, 1094a 28, 1095b 6; *Politics*, 1282b 16–17, 1324a 23–25.

its collective and corporate character, entrusted with stringent powers for the general advantage, and controlling individual wills in the name of an interest wider than that of individuals" (V, 117).[18] A genuine state is not the embodiment of the idea of any particular class but of the whole community. Moreover, the relationship between the genuine, authoritative state and culture is reciprocal. On the one hand such a state, informed by principles of reason,[19] would be the result of a collective and conscious choice prepared by the persuasion of culture. And on the other, "some public recognition and establishment of our best self, or right reason" was "indispensable to that human perfection which we seek" (V, 162).

One may summarize Arnold's argument so far by the observation that culture, in its aspect as the study of perfection, yields standards for judgment that, if acted upon in the political realm, would result in a genuine, authoritative state, which in turn is a necessary condition for the fullness of culture as the well-ordered existence of men in society.

Now let us consider "anarchy." By this term Arnold did not mean just the riotous behaviour of workingmen in London or in the northern manufacturing towns of England,[20] although, as has been pointed out recently, the Hyde Park demonstration that so annoyed him was a genuine test of strength between the state, albeit merely the external state, and one class.[21] By anarchy Arnold first of all meant moral anarchy, the "diseased spirit of our time" (V, 191). The political expression of the "diseased spirit" was "our preference of doing to thinking" (V, 163). More specifically, it was the "mechanical" or unreflective "worship" of freedom, "without enough regarding the ends for which freedom is to be desired" (V, 117). In practice, such freedom was literally an-archy, action without any guiding purpose, sense, or reason.

This "superstitious" belief in freedom was justified in terms of "an

18. Arnold attributed the phrase to Burke (*Prose Works*, II, 26, 294) but, as one commentator observed: "Arnold uses [this] phrase some sixteen times in his essays. Although Burke uses both the words *collective* and *corporate* in describing the State, he nowhere uses the exact phrase Arnold credits him with here." See R. C. Tobias, *Matthew Arnold and Edmund Burke* (Ann Arbor: University Microfilms, 1958), p. 173n. Quoted in *Prose Works*, II, 377.

19. *Irish Essays*, p. 149.

20. See *The Letters of Matthew Arnold*, ed. George W. E. Russell, 2 vols. (London: Macmillan, 1901), 14.12.67 (I: 438); 9.11.70 (II, 50–51); 22.12.80 (II, 217).

21. Royden Harrison, "The 10th April of Spenser Walpole: The Problem of Revolution in Relation to Reform, 1865–1867," *International Review of Social History*, 7 (1962): 368–69.

Englishman's right to do what he likes; his right to march where he likes, meet where he likes, enter where he likes, hoot as he likes, threaten as he likes, smash as he likes" (V, 119). "At the bottom of our English hearts," he said, we have "a very strong belief in freedom and a very weak belief in right reason" (V, 121) so that, consequently, the appeal to right reason and the authority of our better self is quickly checked by the appeal to a man's freedom to do as he likes. Arnold made clear that the belief in doing as one likes was not a matter of class: the Hyde Park demonstrator was an embarrassment to society not because he was exercising the same love of freedom that the aristocratic and middle classes had long enjoyed but, Arnold said, because he was so raw and rough in his manner of doing as he liked. Most importantly, however, in order for the aristocratic and middle classes to do as they like the lower orders must remain submissive (V, 122–23).

This inconsistency in aristocratic and middle-class outlook led Arnold in some of his most amusing and ascerbic writing to show the variety of behavior that a desire to do as one likes manifested among the "barbarians, philistines, and populace," and concluded that the present earnestness of doing, or "Hebraising," must be tempered by a delicacy and flexibility of thinking, or "Hellenising." "What is most wanted by us at present," he said, is "the development of our Hellenising instincts, seeking ardently the intelligible law of things, and making a stream of fresh thought play freely about our stock notions and habits" (V, 190).

There are, no doubt, ambiguities in Arnold's categories: what is the relationship of the authority of culture to the authority of the state? Who are the cultural authorities that discriminate the best that has been thought in the world from the second best? What does he mean by perfection? Does he think that men may be perfected? If Arnold were creating a system whose most important feature was internal consistency such questions would have some kind of contextual sense. But he is not the creator of a system.[22] If the texts we have cited in this section are understood as a blueprint for a utopian society, the sense of them will be missed entirely, for Arnold was concerned with elaborating a paradigm, variously termed culture, humanization, and civilization, that could be apprehended by "right

22. Walter J. Hipple, "Matthew Arnold, Dialectician" *University of Toronto Quarterly*, 32 (1962): 6 ff. deals with the argument of some literary critics who are impatient with Arnold's seeming inconsistency.

reason" and so serve as a standard by which to understand the "damned times," the "diseased spirit of our times," the moral anarchy of his fellow citizens. It was precisely understanding, not blueprints and action, that the times so sorely lacked.

III

T. S. Eliot's opinion, that "Arnold represents a period of stasis; of relative and precarious stability, it is true, a brief halt in the endless march of humanity in some or in any direction,"[23] however well it fits his own view of the times, was not shared by Arnold. We are entered, Arnold wrote, upon "an epoch of dissolution and transformation" (III, 288); "undoubtedly we are driving toward great changes" (II, 29); "we are on our way to what the late Duke of Wellington, with his strong sagacity, foresaw and admirably described as 'a revolution by due course of law' " (V, 135–36). As with all such times, "the action of individuals becomes more distinct, the shortcomings, errors, heats, disputes, which necessarily attend individual action, are brought into greater prominence" (III, 288), and the great question was whether such changes could be wisely guided. Here we touch upon the more practical side of culture. In common with most men of his day, Arnold spoke freely of wisely guided change as "progress," but he meant something more than material improvement or the secular "meliorism"[24] of so many of his contemporaries. "Human progress consists in a continual increase in the numbers of those who, ceasing to live by the animal life alone and to feel the pleasures of sense only, come to participate in the intellectual life also, and to find enjoyment in the things of the mind" (VIII, 169). Progress could be measured, as it were, by the extent to which culture in fact informed the structure of society and the deeds of public men.

We noted earlier that Arnold's advocacy of culture was a form of persuasion, and persuasion, even if it consists of an appeal to reason, is a form of action. Indeed, Arnold said that his writing constituted an "indirect" political act.[25] He also knew that the persuasive force of his writings on culture, our best self, on right reason and the genuine state, was impaired because such terms were too abstract for

23. *The Use of Poetry and the Use of Criticism*, 2nd ed. (London: Faber and Faber, 1964), p. 103.

24. See Howard R. Murphy, "The Ethical Revolt Against Christian Orthodoxy in Early Victorian England," *American Historical Review*, 60 (1955): 800–817.

25. *Letters*, ed. Russell, 17.10.71 (II, 77); *Prose Works*, III, 118, 280–81.

many of his readers: "When one is not a man of genius, and yet attempts to give counsel in times of difficulty, one should be above all things practical."[26] What was wanted, therefore, were observations on specific features of this "period of transformation" so that, discerning clearly their own condition, men might "adapt themselves honestly and rationally to its laws" (II, 29). Arnold's analysis of the "laws" of this transformation centered upon the dynamics of the three classes.

The days of aristocratic tenure were fast drawing to a close: "The English aristocratic system . . . must go."[27] It had been a great use and had done great things, "but the use is at an end, and the stage is over" (VIII, 304). It had served as a valuable example of the noble qualities of courage and honour (II, 6) but in an industrializing era it had no real purpose. It was "tempted, flattered, and spoiled from childhood to old age" (VIII, 300); its sons neglected Homer and Cicero, not in favor of Goethe and Montesquieu but the *Times* and the *Agricultural Journal* (II, 315), and the class as a whole served only to provoke the resentment of others. "Its splendour of station, its wealth, show and luxury, is then what the other classes really admire in it; and this is not an elevating admiration" (VIII, 303). The aristocracy was doomed most emphatically, however, because of its inherent conservatism. In a time of change, new ideas are needed: but the aristocracy was not only set against novelty but was impervious to ideas (III, 121; V, 124; VIII, 301).[28] "No," he said, "they are not Jerusalem" (II, 222).

What may have offended so many critics among our own contemporaries and provoked them to call Arnold an antidemocratic reactionary is that, in his view, the proletariat were not Jerusalem either. The working class was "raw and half-developed, . . . half hidden amidst its poverty and squalor" (V, 143), "brutalized" (VIII, 303), and, "pressed constantly by the hard daily compulsion of material wants, is naturally the very centre and stronghold of our national idea, that it is a man's ideal right and felicity to do what he likes" (V, 118). Moreover, the most organized and articulate members of the working class simply sought power and recognition for themselves. They may not have been as brutalized as their inarticulate brethren but they were equal in the vulgarity of their aspirations

26. *Irish Essays*, p. 77.
27. *Letters*, ed. Russell, 12.5.56 (I, 57); *Prose Works*, III, 390.
28. See also *Irish Essays*, p. 66, and A. Whitridge, ed., *Unpublished Letters of Matthew Arnold* (New Haven: Yale University Press, 1923), p. 48.

with the middle class above them. One may see what was missing from the English working class, he said, by a comparison with their French counterparts. Both may be ignorant, but the French at least have a wit, tact, and delicacy, a "civilisation" wholly missing from the English (VIII, 290–91). And the reason for this discrepancy was the great inequality of classes and property inherited from the middle ages, which "has the natural and necessary effect, under present circumstances, of materialising our upper class, vulgarising our middle class, and brutalizing our lower class" (VIII, 299).[29]

The wealth and leisure of the aristocracy had been squandered on trivial indulgence; the laborers suffered too greatly beneath the sting of poverty to aspire much beyond its relief through material plenty. Clearly, if culture was to relieve the aridity of the times, its work must be done within the middle class. But as it was neither poor nor educated to grasp much beyond the satisfaction of "animal life," it was self-satisfied (II, 307), the great center of Philistinism: "On the side of beauty and taste, vulgarity; on the side of morals and feeling, coarseness; on the side of mind and spirit, unintelligence—this is Philistinism" (III, 390). Even though "stiff necked and perverse" (V, 140), the middle class "with all its faults is still the best stuff in this nation." But it must be transformed (VIII, 347).[30] As the aristocracy against which it was built, the "prison of Puritanism" had served its course (III, 121; VI, 390; VIII, 201, 294) and now only perpetuated complacency and baseness. The age was one of "expansion" most notably in the growth of an industrial manufacturing economy; it was characterized by "industry and intelligence" (V, 126), forces that were dissolving the power of the aristocracy, forces that the middle class was naturally in harmony with (II, 12–13, 318; III, 269; V, 123–24, 320–21; VIII, 371–72). Daily the industry of the middle class was on display, but lacking intelligence, expansion was warped and distorted.

Unlike Carlyle, Arnold did not look towards an "aristocracy of nature" to overcome the Philistinism of his contemporaries; unlike Bentham, he was aware that Philistinism and all it stood for was narrow, intolerant, and petty; unlike Marx he refused the temptation of placing his sociological observations in an eschatological context. The middle class had replaced the aristocracy; it was vulgar and base;

29. See also, *Prose Works*, VIII, 302–3, 345; *Irish Essays*, pp. 120–21.
30. See also *Irish Essays*, p. 141; *Letters*, ed. Russell, 16.2.64 (I, 264).

it would not be replaced by the proletariat for a long while to come (if at all). "Ousted they will not be, but transformed" (V, 255). Transformation meant, of course, a growth in culture, civilization, humanization. Then, he said, "we may find, not perhaps Jerusalem, but, I am sure, a notable stage toward it" (II, 322).

IV

We have presented Arnold's paradigm of a well-ordered society and have suggested that its actualization would depend upon the success of an appeal to right reason; we have also examined his description of the social dynamics of Victorian society. If the "epoch of dissolution and transformation" were in fact to consist in "a revolution by due course of law" then a legal "civilising" agent was called for. If the middle class were to "perfect" itself it must be done, initially at least, from without. There was little point in appealing to right reason until a sense of right reason had been awakened in the Philistine— and in doing this, the first step of his transformation to culture would have been taken. To break the circle of barbarian-aristocratic materialism and middle-class vulgarity, Arnold called upon the state (II, 3, 16ff), at first merely the external state but in time, perhaps, a genuine one. If the state could act upon the middle class, it would eventually raise the brutalized laborer as well to a vision higher than comfort and self-satisfaction.

Two areas in particular were appropriate for state action. The first would revitalize the Church of England by introducing greater breadth of vision to Puritanism, the narrow, and cramped religion of the Philistines. It would also unfreeze the dogmas of the Establishment and loosen the bonds between the Church and the aristocracy. As the force of Arnold's civil theology turns upon the coherence of his natural theology, we must leave consideration of his views for Church reform to another occasion. The second area was education.[31] That he was concerned with educational reform should surprise no one: he was, after all, an inspector of schools and the son of a famous head-

31. A good deal has been written on Arnold's recommendations for educational reform. See W. F. Connell, *The Educational Thought and Influence of Matthew Arnold* (London: Routledge and Kegan Paul, 1950); Walcott, *Origins of Culture and Anarchy*; Peter Smith and G. Summervale, eds., *Matthew Arnold and the Education of the New Order* (Cambridge: Cambridge University Press, 1969); G. H. Bantock "Matthew Arnold and Education," *Journal of Education*, 87 (1955): 443–46.

master of Rugby. Our concern here, however, is not so much with the details of his proposals as with his arguments for advocating the state as the instrument of culture.

Middle-class education was, at the time, widely financed by middle-class voluntary subscription. This method of educational organization he held to be inadequate on two counts: first, it lacked "unity of plan or coherence of operation" (IV, 11), but more importantly, as its schools lacked any meaningful standards, as they were ordered according to what Dickens called Gradgrindery, they could not provide a good education: "right reason would suggest that, to have a sheer school of Licensed Victuallers' children, or a sheer school of Commercial Travellers' children, and to bring them all up, not only at home but at school too, in a kind of odour of licensed victualism or of bagmanism, is not a wise training to give these children" (V, 154). The results of such schools would simply be the production of more and more Philistines who had attained neither satisfactory intellects, nor manners, nor sense of beauty. It was perfectly understandable for the aristocratic and professional classes to be reluctant to give up their places at Eton and Harrow or even Winchester and Rugby so as to make room for children of the middle class. Yet even the privileged classes must see that "our civilisation is maimed by our middle class being left as it is, and that the whole country, the whole English nation, suffers by it" (VIII, 369). Since the whole nation was injured by the bad education of the middle class, action on behalf of the nation, state action, was clearly required.

The great center of resistance to state action was not as one might expect, in the aristocracy, which feared the dissolution of their own order and their own control of government (II, 303–4), but in the middle class. There were obvious reasons why they had looked unfavorably upon the state. Historically, state action for the middle class was associated with acts of religious, political, and economic repression by the aristocracy, so the state was distrusted. But historically as well, repression had been successfully resisted, so the state was not respected (II, 20, 306). Times had changed, Arnold said, and middle-class attitudes ought to change with them, first of all with respect to the state: "we can give it what form we will. We can make it our agent not our master" (II, 309). All that could be gained by a persistence of traditional middle-class attitudes was the maintenance of "the aristocratic class in its preponderance, and the middle class, their own class, in its vulgarity" (VIII, 215). Specifically, the middle class could move beyond its "ordinary self" and begin the road towards culture only through state supported education.

The era of medieval endowments of public schools and university colleges was over; these endowments were, in effect, public aid, and middle-class subscription schools could be no adequate substitute (II, 286). Eton and Harrow, and Oxford and Cambridge had done well in educating the British aristocracy, but a new form of public aid was required for a new educational need. "For public establishments modern societies have to betake themselves to the State. . . . Education is and must be a matter of public establishment" (II, 294–95). The middle class most sorely wants "largeness of soul and public dignity" and, with the older establishments closed to them, they could learn these clearly political virtues only in "great honourable public institutions" (II, 292–93). That such results could be achieved Arnold knew from his inspection tours of continental schools and universities, and he invariably said as much when submitting his reports to the government.

He felt he had reason to hope that a "notable stage" towards Jerusalem might be taken with educational reform as it was so clearly in the interests of the middle class (II, 323). It is not an easy task to judge whether his hopes were well founded, for it is not at all clear that the triumph of "meliorism" in the contemporary welfare state betokens an increase in culture.[32] What does seem plain is that Arnold held a substantive view of education: it was not an empty technique but a means by which younger generations could be civilized, humanized, and taught civic virtues that were broader than aristocratic conceptions of honor and more lofty than middle-class notions of wealth.

V

Arnold wrote on other political topics as well, most importantly on the "Irish question."[33] As with his recommendations for reform in education and his analysis of the changing structure of English society under the impact of industrialization, his remarks on Ireland and other less pressing matters attempted to be free of what he called "stock-notions." For example, he supported altering the inheritance

32. Consider, for example, the remarks of F. R. Leavis, in *Nor Shall My Sword* (London: Chatto and Windus, 1972).
33. For details of Arnold's views on Ireland see William Robbins, "Matthew Arnold and Ireland," *University of Toronto Quarterly*, 17 (1947): 52–67.

laws not because of the "supposed natural rights" of younger children, a "stock-notion" of liberal members of Parliament, but because the "present system does not work well now at all, but works altogether badly."[34] Likewise, agricultural laborers should be enfranchised not because "there is either any natural right in every man to the possession of a vote, or any gift of wisdom and virtue conferred by such possession," but because "it is well for any great class and description of men in society to be able to say for itself what it wants, and not to have other classes, the so-called educated and intelligent classes, acting for it as its proctors, and supposed to understand its wants and to provide for them. They do not really understand its wants, they do not really provide for them."[35] But was not his own advocacy of educational reform an attempt to provide for the middle class something that, in their satisfaction and complacency, they did not want? Is there, then, some justification after all for the charge of illiberality and antidemocratic authoritarianism?

Arnold might have answered the charge by distinguishing between a "proctor" that is, a paternal technician who knows what is best for agricultural laborers, middle-class licensed victuallers, or anyone else, and a man of culture who wished not that others conform to his idea of perfection but that they consider whether their own ideas are adequate. And this meant an appeal to one's "best self," to right reason that all men possess even if all men seem not to actualize. Arnold said it was impossible to attain perfection and that its study must always be the task of a few. At the same time "progress" could be measured by an increase in their number. He summarized this seeming contradiction in a speech, famous in its day, delivered before an American audience: "If we are to enjoy the benefit . . . of the comfortable doctrine of the remnant, we must be capable of receiving also, and of holding fast, the hard doctrine of the unsoundness of the majority, and of the certainty that the unsoundness of the majority, if it is not withstood and remedied, must be their ruin."[36] The remnant may live a life of culture and may evoke the spark of right reason in the majority, from time to time, by persuading them of the soundness of their proposals. The remnant may counsel resistance to the ordinary self within all men, but it cannot act as "proctor" because it

34. *Irish Essays,* pp. 120–21.
35. *Irish Essays,* p. 147.
36. "Numbers; Or the Majority and the Remnant," in his *Essays in Criticism, Second Series, Contributions to* "The Pall Mall Gazette," *and Discourses in America* (Edition de Luxe), (London: Macmillan, 1903), vol. IV, p. 309.

cannot truly understand the wants of the majority. Arnold knew this, and in an age when political and social thought was turning increasingly to technical calculation and efficient implementation, or abandoning responsibility to an hypostatized "history," it was an important achievement.

In one sense Arnold was not a great or profound political thinker: *Culture and Anarchy* is not a text to be considered with the *Republic* or *Leviathan*. His recommendations were hardly startling—after all, what did they amount to but that education was the means to civilization and culture? It may be allowed however, that his analyses showed common sense and his recommendations were moderate and practicable. From his therapy we are referred back to his diagnosis of the source of spiritual disorder in the "moral anarchy" of doing as one likes and to his own "sickening consciousness of our difficulties." His own view of himself was clearer than we are often led to believe: "I am a liberal, yet I am a liberal tempered by experience, reflection, and renouncement, and I am above all, a believer in culture" (V, 88). He declared himself to be a politician "but a politician of that commonwealth of which the pattern, as the philosopher says, exists perhaps somewhere in heaven, but certainly is at present found nowhere on earth,—[I am] a liberal, as I have said, of the future."[37] Arnold did not, of course, mean that heaven would come to earth at some future date. Rather, like Plato's commonwealth, whose paradigm was *en ourano* and also *en logois*, in the very discussion that comprises his *Republic*, so Arnold's culture could serve as a rational standard for political judgment as well as a motive for public conduct. He was, in short, concerned *peri ta anthropina*; in his resistance to the "damned times" Arnold was a political theorist, one worth our attention today.

---

37. *Irish Essays*, p. 144.

J. A. A. Lovink • Prospects for Democratic Control

Although political science has long ago given the group theory of politics its deserved burial, it is nonetheless a commonplace among students of modern democratic politics that nonelected powerholders of all kinds typically exercise a major influence in the definition and implementation of public policy.[1] Up to some hard-to-define point, and assuming that all sectors of society are equally represented, such political participation has its positive aspects. Both the responsiveness and the effectiveness of public policy stand only to gain. But beyond that point, where influence burgeons into veto power, obvious democratic objections present themselves, all the more so since equality of mobilization and access for all sectors of society do not obtain anywhere.

Regrettably, political science cannot tell us whether the contemporary political process in the modern democracies has reached (or has perhaps exceeded) this limit of democratic acceptability. Neither our theoretical and conceptual apparatus nor our empirical data and capacity for measurement are up to the task. The reasons are easy to grasp: one need only consider the intimidating difficulty of (1) specifying theoretically how much political influence for nonelected powerholders is too much (a question raising, among other conundrums, the unresolved "intensity" problem in democratic theory);[2] (2) measuring that influence over the whole range of public policy and administration; and (3) comparing such measurements from polity to polity and over time. Although one cannot therefore precisely identify the relative political influence of elected and nonelected powerholders, the impression is nonetheless widespread that this relationship

I am very grateful to Edwin R. Black for his incisive criticisms of an earlier version of this essay.

1. The term *nonelected powerholders* is used here to encompass the most senior levels of the public bureaucracy, the judiciary, and all private interests that seek to influence the formation and administration of public policy.

The leading modern exposition of the group theory of politics may be found in David B. Truman, *The Governmental Process* (New York: Knopf, 1951). For a good brief critique, see Roy C. Macridis, "Interest Groups in Comparative Analysis," *The Journal of Politics*, 23 (1961): 25–45.

2. For a brief discussion of this problem, see Robert A. Dahl, *A Preface to Democratic Theory* (Chicago: The University of Chicago Press, 1956), ch. 4.

has been undergoing a secular change, one that implies a significant weakening in the power of the politician.

The main purpose of this essay is to offer some thoughts on the future evolution of this power relationship, and on the scope for redirecting the expected path of change by deliberate intervention. As a preliminary to that discussion, it is essential to describe very briefly the apparent trends to date, and to define the meaning of democratic control as it is here to be used.

Given the wide variety of ways in which both democracy and control have been interpreted, the term *democratic control* is obviously not self-defining. Reasonable men may disagree about the conditions which a decision must satisfy to lay claim to the adjective *democratic*—at what point the basic requirements of liberty and equality have been satisfied sufficiently that each member of the society (or his representative) has had as equal an opportunity as possible to shape the outcome, and to what extent the outcome itself must respect and promote the values of liberty and equality that justify the democratic method in the first place.[3] Where direct democracy is impossible, further dispute may rage about the democratic legitimacy of decisions arrived at on Burkean versus populist principles of representation. Use of the term *control* raises similar spectres of confusion and misunderstanding. After all, control, like power and influence, is a relational concept, so that its disciplined use requires a careful delimiting of the actors and scope of action to which it is being applied, and of the associated frequency and extent of compliance.[4] It follows, therefore, that a speculative discussion of the prospects for democratic control might reasonably adopt a wide variety of approaches, depending on the aspect and interpretation of democracy selected, and on the actors and issues chosen for study.

In this essay, I propose to use the term *democratic* to describe any act of government (or any "authoritative allocation of values for the whole society," in David Easton's terminology) which corresponds to the wishes of the majority of the legislature. It will simply be assumed that this will of the majority respects all the values that democracy seeks to promote, and that there is no conflict between the wishes of the legislative majority and the preferences of the ma-

3. For a valuable discussion of the relationship between liberty, equality, and democracy see George H. Sabine, "The Two Democratic Traditions," *The Philosophical Review*, 61 (1952): 451–74.

4. See Robert A. Dahl, "The Concept of Power," *Behavioral Science*, 2 (1957): 201–15.

jority of the voting public. By control, I shall mean the capacity to exercise the effective final say in all choices of public policy, or to reverse any choices delegated to others, with the freedom and knowledge to do so in accordance with one's own preferences, albeit within limits set by objective, impersonal constraints. Democratic control will therefore be thought to exist to the degree that the majority of the legislature (or its elected leadership) controls the acts of government in the manner just described.[5] The question before us, then, is whether the apparent decline in democratic control (as here conceived), is likely to continue, and if so, what corrective action offers hope of success.[6]

The politician's competition in the political power stakes comes from two main directions: the governmental bureaucracy and the broad array of organized interests found in every modern society. In some countries, important competition also comes from politicians at other levels of government, but any losses or gains on this front do not, strictly speaking, affect the extent of democratic control. Such competition has therefore been ignored in this essay. So has the competition offered by the judiciary and the communications media, in the former case because this role of the judiciary varies too much among the western democracies to permit generalization, and in the latter case purely for convenience. Any full-scale analysis of the prospects for democratic control would certainly need to encompass trends in the role of the communications media as well.

There is no mystery about the reasons for the major influence on public policy exercised by present-day government bureaucracies and organized private interests. Unquestionably, its principal source has been the staggering extension in the "reach" of modern government, itself a response to the vast range of new needs created by the process of rapid social change in the past three or four decades. For reasons that are well understood, the politician has coped with this

5. This paper ignores the fact that in some countries legislative majorities exercise political control more directly than in others. To avoid unduly complicating the analysis, it is simply assumed that in the more disciplined legislatures there is no conflict between the policy preferences of leaders and followers, so that the political control exercised by the legislative elite commands true majority support and thus qualifies as democratic control. In reality, of course, the problem of securing such harmony between leaders and led is an important hurdle in the search for democratic control.

6. Although the point has already been made in the introduction to this paper, it does no harm to stress again that the exact extent of democratic control remains everywhere an unknown variable. This section merely attempts to summarize the present understanding on this subject.

expansion in his formal responsibilities by delegating all but the most vital decisions to the public bureaucracy, to regulatory bodies of all sorts, and to the judiciary. This has been accomplished without derogating from his continuing political responsibility by enacting enabling legislation whose ends and means are specified only in general terms. While formal political responsibility thus remains the politician's, much de facto power of legislation passes to others. As for the most vital political decisions, even here the politician's former relative autonomy has been undermined by his substantial dependence on the knowledge and judgment of others, inputs that inevitably influence his analysis of problems, his definition of the practical alternatives, and his selection among them.[7] All of which is not to argue that the politician has ceased to be a major policymaker. If framework legislation is interpreted contrary to his intentions, he can provide a remedy, either through bureaucratic command or through legislative amendment. If the advice he gets proves wrong, or tainted by uncongenial values, he can change his advisers. And the final choice among the policy alternatives that reach him remains his. Still, it is only by exception that he can ascertain the need to use these controls, and only to the most far-reaching or politically salient policy questions that he can apply his political judgment. With all other decisions, there is only the hypothetical assurance that the preferences of the majority of legislators are being served.[8]

Even more dangerous for democratic control, the expansion of government has given private interests a powerful incentive to mobilize their collective political resources, both for self-protection and to harness government to their own ends. Many of these organizations

---

7. Government bureaucrats being human, one cannot expect their advice to be wholly disinterested. See Anthony Downs, *Inside Bureaucracy* (Boston: Little, Brown, 1966), for a set of stimulating hypotheses about the ways in which bureaucratic interests may find expression in policy making.

8. Discussion of the role of the government bureaucracy in policy making is complicated by the notorious ambiguity of the distinction between policy making and administration. Some clarity emerges, however, if we follow Raymond Bauer in conceiving of policy making as "parameter-shaping." It may then be posited that the scope of policy making at any given bureaucratic level is a function of the specificity of the parameters laid down by the level immediately above, and of the effective opportunity for appeal and redress against decisions made at the lower level. In these terms, the major policy-making role of contemporary bureaucracies can be traced in part to the growing impossibility of legislating in detail, and to the practical difficulty of reviewing the mass of statutory instruments for their fit with the legislature's (often obscure) intention. See "The Study of Policy Formation," in Raymond Bauer and Kenneth Gergen, eds., *The Study of Policy Formation* (New York: Free Press, 1968), p. 2. See also J. E. Hodgetts, "The Civil Service and Policy Formation," *Canadian Journal of Economics and Political Science*, 23 (1957): 467–79.

command substantial political resources (such as a legitimacy, prestige, economic power, and strategic social location) allowing them to visit severe sanctions on the rest of society if their demands are slighted. What is more, their unique command of essential information has made them into indispensable partners in formulating public policy, while their subsequent cooperation is often essential to implementing it efficiently, or at all. Between them, these political resources give many groups a powerful claim on governmental responsiveness. The growing signs of pluralist stagnation and political deadlock evident in many Western democracies can probably not be understood without reference to this pluralization of political influence.

The political influence of modern interest groups has also been linked to two vital ideological underpinnings. One is a growing tendency throughout the West to see society from a quasi-corporatist or syndicalist perspective—as an amalgam of occupational and vocational groups each having such unique interests as to require direct political representation and a large measure of self-government. As a corollary of this outlook, it is in many places becoming a key criterion of the legitimacy of any public policy that the interests most directly affected by that policy have had an adequate voice in its formulation. Thus, in Britain the belief is reportedly widespread that producers' groups "have a 'right' to take part in making policy related to their sector of activity; indeed, that their approval of a relevant policy or program is a substantial reason for public confidence in it and conversely that their disapproval is cause for public uneasiness. It is in short an attitude reflecting the widespread acceptance of functional representation in British political culture."[9] Similar attitudes are believed to prevail in many other countries.[10]

9. Samuel H. Beer, *British Politics in the Collectivist Age* (New York: Knopf, 1965), p. 329.

10. For the United States, see, for instance, Theodore J. Lowi, *The End of Liberalism* (New York: Norton, 1969); for Canada, Robert Presthus, *Elite Accommodation in Canadian Politics* (Toronto: Macmillan, 1973); for Norway, Harry Eckstein, *Division and Cohesion in Democracy* (Princeton: Princeton University Press, 1966), and Stein Rokkan, "Norway: Numerical Democracy and Corporate Pluralism," in Robert A. Dahl, ed., *Political Oppositions in Western Democracies* (New Haven: Yale University Press, 1966), pp. 70–115; for Sweden, Nils Stjernquist, "Sweden: Stability or Deadlock?" ibid., 116–46; for the Netherlands, Arend Lijphart, *The Politics of Accommodation* (Berkeley: University of California Press, 1968). By contrast, however, I could find no reference to such attitudes in Jean Meynaud, *Les groups de pression en France* (Paris: Colin, 1962), or in Joseph LaPalombara, *Interest Groups in Italian Politics* (Princeton: Princeton University Press, 1964). It should also be noted that none of the sources cited in this or the preceding footnote offers direct, survey evidence

A second ideological underpinning for modern pluralist politics may be found in what Samuel Beer has called "the basic attitudes of modernity, rationalism and voluntarism."[11] This spirit has manifested itself, among other ways, in the growing modern impatience with restraints of all kinds and in the evident diminution in respect for authority, two approaches to life that appear congruent with an expanding universe of active interest groups. Ideological change thus appears to have contributed vitally toward bringing modern interest groups to flower by enhancing their legitimacy and by supplying a major source of drive and militancy.

In turning now to the prospects for change in the political role of nonelected powerholders, I shall at first make the strong assumption that all apparent relevant trends will persist. On that basis, one would expect, among other things, to see a continuing expansion in the scope of governmental intervention in the economy and society. The main push for this expansion is likely to come from a growing public awareness of the so-called externalities of economic activity and development—from environmental pollution and the social costs of dislocation and overcrowding to the need for massive new social overhead expenditures. To respond to the attendant insistence that economic investment be governed by a broader calculus than in the past, governments would ineluctably be drawn into much more advanced social and economic planning than is now common.

Although the exact form of this intervention is impossible to foresee, its implications for the distribution of political influence seem clear. On the governmental side, the brunt of this new policy making burden will undoubtedly fall on the bureaucracy. In a field as complex as this, it seems inconceivable that politicians could do more than set some very general guidelines and priorities. It is also likely that they would actively avoid undue involvement, partly in acknowledgment of their own technical inexpertise, and partly to escape direct responsibility for potential fiascos. On the private side, the potential threat to established economic interests seems bound to generate unprecedented defensive activity. If the past is any guide, this defense may well succeed in minimizing any real loss of private

of public attitudes to, or awareness of, interest group participation in policy making. This gap cries out for further research, especially in view of the apparently widespread perception that the established interests command undue political access and preferred treatment.

11. *Modern Political Development* (New York: Random House, 1973), p. 119 and passim.

economic control, for as E. P. Herring has pointed out, "The greater
the degree of detailed and technical control that government seeks
to exert over industrial and commercial interests, the greater must
be their degree of consent and active participation in the very process
of regulation, if regulation is to be effective or successful."[12] Indeed,
Samuel Beer has taken this generalization one step further in suggesting that "ironically, a pluralizing and decentralizing of power is
a likely result of the attempt to centralize it."[13] Taking an overview
of the probable consequences of the expected expansion in government for the distribution of political influence, one may thus reasonably posit that the prime gainers will not be the politicians but the
public bureaucracy.

If we continue to assume that apparent present trends will persist,
the prospects for democratic control should also be dimmed by a
further weakening of party loyalties. This trend has been especially
marked in countries formerly afflicted by deep class, ideological, and
religious antagonisms. As rising affluence and progressive secularization have gradually reduced the intensity of these cleavages, the
electoral support of parties with sharply defined ideological or sectarian appeal has diminished, stimulating some of them to transform
themselves into parties of the "catchall" or brokerage type.[14] Within
limits, this Americanization of many major European parties[15] is
likely to be a self-reinforcing process—with a drop in ideological or
sectarian commitment promoting a convergence of party appeals, a
consequential rise in the heterogeneity of party support, and a further
resort to catchall appeals—and may well continue for some time. As
a result, the commitment and stability of party support is likely to
exhibit a secular decline.

In the United States, the major political parties have long been
of the catchall variety, but strong voter identification with one or
the other major party has nonetheless been widespread. For reasons
that are not entirely clear, however, party loyalty among Americans
also appears, in the long run, to be in a decline,[16] a trend that may

12. *Public Administration and the Public Interest* (New York, 1936), p. 192;
quoted in Beer, *Modern Political Development*, p. 53.
13. Ibid.
14. Otto Kirchheimer, "The Transformation of the Western European Party
Systems," in J. LaPalombara and M. Weiner, eds., *Political Parties and Political Development* (Princeton: Princeton University Press, 1966), pp. 177–200.
15. Cf. Hugh G. Thorburn, "Towards a More Simplified Party System in France,"
Canadian Journal of Political Science, 1 (1968): 204–16.
16. W. D. Burnham, *Critical Elections and the Mainsprings of American Politics*

or may not be reversed by a recent upswing in the proportion of voters professing to see significant policy differences between the parties.[17] In Canada, party loyalties among the electorate are already relatively feeble, and appear to have been so for decades.[18] Recent declines in party identification in Quebec should probably be seen as part of the larger process of *rattrapage* (or "catching-up") which that province has been undergoing.

As Otto Kirchheimer has suggested, this gradual crumbling of the politician's base of committed electoral support presents a serious threat to his political control. Increasingly, other powerholders can be counted on to respond to this weakness, and to the typical vagueness of the politician's electoral mandate, by firmly rejecting as lacking in popular support any major policy initiatives not consistent with their interests. Kirchheimer continues:

How does the catch-all party in governmental positions treat such conflicts? Will it be satisfied to exercise pressure via the mass media, or will it try to re-create a militant mass basis beyond the evanescent electoral and publicity levels? But the very structure of the catch-all party, the looseness of its clientele,

---

(New York: Norton, 1970), and by the same author, "The Changing Shape of the American Political Universe," *American Political Science Review*, 59 (1965): 7–28, and "Theory and Voting Research: Some Reflections on Converse's 'Change in the American Electorate'," ibid., 68 (1974): 1002–57, including comments by Philip Converse and Jerrold G. Rusk, and reply by Burnham. See also Philip Converse, "Change in the American Electorate," in Angus Campbell and Philip Converse, eds., *The Human Meaning of Social Change* (New York: Russel Sage Foundation, 1972), pp. 263–337.

17. G. Pomper, "From Confusion to Clarity: Issues and American Voters, 1956–68," *American Political Science Review*, 66 (1972): 415–28; see also David RePass, "Issue Salience and Party Choice," ibid., 65 (1971): 389–400. The possibility must be considered that the sharpening of the perceived policy differences between the parties has served not to strengthen identification with one or the other, but to create alienation from both. See Arthur H. Miller, "Political Issues and Trust in Government: 1964–70," ibid., 68 (1974): 951–1001, including comment by Jack Citrin and reply by Miller.

18. An elaborate listing of the many writers on Canadian politics who have perceived party identification in Canada as relatively weak is given in Paul M. Sniderman, H. D. Forbes, and Ian Melzer, "Party Loyalty and Electoral Volatility," *Canadian Journal of Political Science*, 7 (1974): 268–88. Sniderman et al. make a valiant attempt to overturn this "textbook theory," but the data they present are too incomplete and ambiguous for this debunking to succeed. Their main accomplishment, in my view, is to show that the relative weakness of party identification in Canada should not be exaggerated: it does remain a useful explanatory variable. The suggestion that party loyalties have been relatively weak in Canada for a long time is based on the finding that the considerable instability of party electoral support at the constituency level in Canada has remained virtually constant since 1925. See J. A. A. Lovink, "Is Canadian Politics too Competitive?" *Canadian Journal of Political Science*, 6 (1973): 341–79.

may from the outset exclude such more far-reaching action. To that extent the political party's role in Western industrial society today is more limited than would appear from its position of formal preeminence.[19]

Here, then, would be a further reason to expect a continued decline in democratic control.

These prospects are unattractive from at least four perspectives. First, they spell a further erosion of the democratic credentials of public policy, already weakened by the existing obstacles to democratic control and by the social and economic biases of interest group representation. Second, this course of events will tend to make democratic politics even more opaque than it already is by enlarging the proportion of policies arrived at through closed bargaining between government bureaucracies and interest groups, by diminishing the issue content of election campaigns, and by accentuating the tendency to justify public policy not in terms of its consistency with general abstract objectives, but purely in terms of the participatory process followed in its adoption. The ensuing rise in the incomprehensibility of public policy would create new grounds for political cynicism, alienation, and apathy. Third, this scenario is likely to reveal increasing signs of political immobilism. The principal reason for this tendency would be the desire of special interest groups to maintain the status quo. The traditional posture of interests securely situated is conservatism.[20] Finally, the anticipated decline in democratic control may well imply a further decrease in governmental effectiveness, if by that we mean the capacity of governments to attain their declared objectives. Unfortunately, the causes of such ineffectiveness are notoriously difficult to separate and weigh. It is difficult to know, for instance, to what extent the rather indifferent performance of many contemporary governments in coping with such problems as inflation, unemployment, poverty, or environmental pollution is due to a resistance to change by established interests, to a lack of popular support for the measures required, or to an inability unilaterally to control key relevant variables, like the international money market. Clearly, the answer will differ from problem to problem. The forces

19. "The Transformation of the Western European Party Systems," p. 200.
20. These last two drawbacks of organized pluralism run amok are discussed in detail in Lowi, *The End of Liberalism*. For a study that treats control of the environment as the key objective in politics, see Neil McDonald, *The Study of Political Parties* (New York: Random House, 1955).

discussed in this essay should therefore affect the effectiveness of government differentially, largely as a function of the domestic controllability of the causal factors at play.

It is now time to drop the assumption that present trends will continue undisturbed, and to consider the possibility that evolution might take some other course, either naturally or by deliberate redirection.

The most plausible natural source of change, it seems to me, would be the emergence of new conflicts of ideology or interest that would provide politicians with new bases of appeal and support. Such cleavages might arise, for instance, from already changing perceptions of the costs and benefits of economic growth, and from disagreement about how this process should be controlled and its burdens and advantages distributed. But new bases for political conflict do not necessarily increase the scope for democratic control. To do so, the resulting divisions in the electorate need to fit (or be amenable to) dual representation, be it through two parties or through party coalitions. Failing that, the potential of such new cleavages as the means of mobilizing the stable majority essential for democratic control clearly diminishes. From this same standpoint, any new basis for political cleavage also needs to be linkable, in one way or another, to existing issues of public policy. There will be no difficulty in establishing this linkage if the new conflict finds ideological expression. After all, ideologies are by definition vehicles for integrating a diversity of concerns into some coherent whole. If, in contrast, new issues are treated as sui generis, and merely add another dimension to the existing kaleidoscope of conflict, then the political support derived from them will do little to strengthen the politician's hand in other policy "arenas," leaving the existing scope for democratic control largely unchanged. It is this latter pattern that appears to fit many major issues that have arisen in the past two decades—like racial equality in the United States, *deux nations* in Canada, and the Common Market in Britain—on which attitudes have displayed remarkably little congruency with preferences on other issues. Finally, it has to be considered that a rise in political conflict may endanger other values. For example, the economic growth issue posited earlier might well divide some countries along regional lines, thereby reinforcing possible existing tendencies to regional nationalism and creating a critical threat to national unity. A decline in consensus is likely to enhance democratic control only in certain circumstances, and may in any event be attended by undesirable side effects.

Turning now to the prospects for change through deliberate reform, one finds that modern political science offers little cause for optimism. In general, political scientists tend to see political life as a complex system of interrelationships in which it is difficult to intervene successfully piecemeal. To succeed, it is generally held, reform must proceed on many fronts simultaneously. The obstacle to that, of course, is that normally the chances of maintaining majority support diminish with every expansion of the reform program, a difficulty that confines major effective reforms to times of crisis, when opposition may dissolve before necessity or before a general loss of faith in "the system" as it stands. Consistent with this general conception, many political scientists regard modern political parties as largely dependent variables, molded by the attitudes of their clienteles and by the established arrangement of political institutions, and possessing relatively little reciprocal formative influence.[21] Thus, major reforms in political parties are seen as unlikely without appropriate prior changes in the political market to which they seek to appeal. Similarly, many political scientists tend to see the key constitutional arrangements in stable democracies as pretty firmly rooted in the existing structure of interests and beliefs, and thus to be skeptical of the workability of reforms that are not preceded by changes in those underlying variables.

This standard view of the limited scope for short-range "political engineering" makes much sense, but should not be distorted by exaggeration. The scope for such reform presumably varies from proposal to proposal, depending on the firmness with which the disliked behavior, institution, or power relationship is anchored in the political system and its environment.

Two common reform proposals that would contribute to greater democratic control have decidedly dismal prospects of success. One is the often heard insistence that politics ought to be re-polarized along class lines, or that the parties ought at least to clarify and differentiate their policy positions. The practical weakness of this proposal lies in its underlying premise—that the present emphasis on nonclass cleavages (like regionalism) and on vague catchall appeals

21. This view has been advanced with greatest clarity by Frank Sorauf. See his *Political Parties in the American System* (Boston: Little, Brown, 1964), and "Political Parties and Political Analysis," in W. N. Chambers and W. D. Burnham, eds., *The American Party Systems* (New York: Oxford University Press, 1967), pp. 33–55.

is not necessary to the pursuit of majority support but reflects a middle-class elite desire to suppress real opposition—a notion that seems to exaggerate grossly the capacity of parties to structure the political market as they (or their leaders) may desire.

A similar practical deficiency besets the well-known argument that the American parties should transform themselves, by one means or another, into disciplined, "responsible" parties on the British model.[22] As Austin Ranney and many others have pointed out, implementation of this proposal would bring with it a fundamental revision of the American constitution along majoritarian lines, and has no chance of being adopted until widespread public support for that larger reform can be generated.[23] Readiness for such fundamental reform is unlikely to develop until the major interests can be persuaded that the capacity of the present system to produce acceptable decisions in sufficient number has declined to the point where the ability to control those decisions no longer yields a net advantage.

A third and rather more plausible avenue to increased democratic control would be to try to stimulate political interest and participation. Not much imagination is needed to see that if the substantial sector of the population that is now everywhere politically inactive could be mobilized in even the most minimal sense, all existing coalitions would be in peril. Interests that can now be ignored with at least short-run political immunity would then need to be accommodated. E. E. Schattschneider has put his point dramatically:

[To] an astonishing extent [those who vote] are at the mercy of the rest of the nation which could swamp all existing political alignments if it chose to do so. The whole balance of power in the political system could be overturned by a massive invasion of the political system and nothing tangible protects the system against the flood. All that is necessary to produce the most painless revolution in history, the first revolution ever legalized and legitimatized in advance, is to have a sufficient

22. I accept this reform proposal as an avenue to greater democratic control because it seems to me elementary that politicians will have greater power collectively when organized into stable, cohesive groups than when coalitions have to be formed on an ad hoc basis. The latter arrangement may have some advantages from a democratic standpoint, but the creation of opportunities for the systematic pursuit of agreed objectives commanding majority support is not one of them.

23. See Austin Ranney, *The Doctrine of Responsible Government* (Urbana: University of Illinois Press, 1962), ch. 10.

number of people do something not much more difficult than
to walk across the street on election day.[24]

Out of such a new electorate it might well be possible to forge not
only a major shift in policy, but also the more polarized politics that
was dismissed above as impractical within the limits of the present
electorate. From a democratic standpoint, the advantages of this new
situation would be numerous, but not least among them would be
to strengthen the support base and mandate of the politician, and
thereby the scope for democratic control.

But how can the politically dormant section of the electorate be
awakened? What can overcome the sense of hopelessness, the feeling
of political inefficacy, and the preception of politics as almost totally
irrelevant, that feature so prominently in every explanation of political
apathy? It may be that these attitudes can be weakened indirectly,
by promoting greater worker control of the workplace.[25] In the long
term, there may also be some hope in the techniques of fostering a
spirit of community, self-determination, and political activism in
economically depressed urban and rural neighborhoods.[26] For the
foreseeable future, however, political participation seems unlikely
to expand significantly without, at minimum, a firm commitment by
a major political party to appeal directly to the interests of the politically uninvolved.

The prospects of gaining such a commitment seem unpromising.
For unless there were a radical and congruent change in electoral
preferences, a major policy shift of that kind would simply forfeit to
other major parties a large portion of the party's existing supporters.
In return, it might (or might not) gain the support of a number of
present nonvoters, producing almost certainly a net loss of support.
Here, surely, lies part of the reason, as has so often been argued, why
the apathetic are not now courted more aggressively. Regrettably,

24. *The Semisovereign People* (New York: Holt, Rinehart, and Winston, 1960),
pp. 98–99.

25. See Carole Pateman, *Participation and Democratic Theory* (Cambridge: Cambridge University Press, 1970), for an assessment of the consequences of various ex-
periments in industrial democracy.

26. In the United States, the leading exponent and practitioner of such techniques
has probably been Mr. Saul Alinsky. See S. D. Alinsky, *The Professional Radical*
(New York: Harper and Row, 1970). In Canada, most experimentation along these
lines has been in Quebec, where it is referred to as *animation sociale*. For a brief
description, see Michel Blondin, "Social Animation: Its Nature and Significance in Le
Conseil des Oeuvres de Montréal," in W. E. Mann, ed., *Poverty and Social Policy in
Canada* (Toronto: Copp Clark, 1970), pp. 400–406.

then, our third hope for improved democratic control seems also in vain.

A fourth option would be to combat the effects of the decline in the politician's committed support by heightening the emphasis, already pronounced in many places, on personal plebiscitary leadership. Such a strategy might conceivably be defended as democratic, if one carried to an extreme the elitist conception of democracy advanced in various forms by Schumpeter, Herring, Key, and most recently, by Sartori. In this view, democracy arises from a competition among elites for public favor in periodic elections, not from participation in policy making by the mass public, impossible in any event.[27] Although in this conception it is clearly intended that such governing elites should be plural in nature, little theoretical attention has been given to the minimum acceptable elite size. In a different approach, personal, plebiscitary leadership might also be defended as conditionally democratic, depending, that is, on the extent to which the leader proved open and responsive to the wishes and needs of all sectors of the public, organized or not.

Neither of these hypothetical defenses of the "white knight" as an answer to the erosion of democratic control strikes me as persuasive. Although it is true that the plebiscitary leader might command sufficient political support to get the society "moving again," as John F. Kennedy once put it, the democratic quality of such initiatives would be highly questionable. Not only would there be even less assurance than at present that the (often irreversible) changes made commanded majority support, but serious damage would also be done to the sense of mutual responsibility, the commitment to collective self-determination, and the resulting will to participate politically that a democracy ought to foster.[28] "Let George do it" would tend to become the public motto. It is debatable which among existing institutional arrangements offers the greatest potential for minimizing these adverse consequences.

A fifth way of resisting a further erosion of democratic control might be to decentralize political responsibility. From that perspec-

27. Sartori attempts to link this descriptive conception of democracy to the so-called traditional theory by adding the requirement that the governing elites admit the moral obligation to be responsive to the needs of the mass public. To qualify as democratic, leaders must exhibit the right *forma mentis*. Giovanni Sartori, *Democratic Theory* (Westport, Conn.: Greenwood Press, 1973), esp. ch. 5, 6.

28. See Pateman, *Participation and Democratic Theory*, ch. 2, for an excellent review of the participatory theory of democracy that underlies this comment.

tive, the hope would be that in enhancing local control political interest and participation might be stimulated, and that the weight of public opinion in the legislative process would rise accordingly. Whether these payoffs would materialize is questionable. Politics at subnational levels has not thus far been noted for its participatory vibrancy or weakness of interest group and bureaucratic influence. Moreover, the inevitable need for subsystem coordination is likely to introduce new problems of democratic control, arising from the difficulty of maintaining a legislative say over the executive agreements arrived at. In many federations, this is already an issue of much concern. Although in many policy fields there are good reasons for decentralization, there is thus some question whether the enhancement of democratic control is one of them.

More hope may lie in a sixth option, aimed at securing improved political control over the bureaucracy. One way of pursuing this objective would be to follow the Swedish example in opening more of the bureaucratic process to public inspection. Although there can be no question that to push this reform too far would hurt the quality of policy making, it is equally evident that at the moment the legitimate claim to confidentiality is abused very badly. Unfortunately, significant reform on this front would require political leadership of extraordinary public-spiritedness, given that the ensuing improvement in the quality of political opposition might well threaten the in-party's (or ruling coalition's) security and would further complicate life in the political executive.

As a second approach, political control over the bureaucracy might also be expanded by a program of organizational reform on several fronts: (1) by establishing machinery to allow the political executive to devote more attention to planning and priority setting, and to help in monitoring the bureaucracy's response; (2) by requiring the bureaucracy to adopt such management tools as planning, programming and budgeting systems; and (3) by ensuring, as has long been the practice in the United States, that the top bureaucratic positions are held by politically responsive individuals. All three parts of this program are currently being tried by the Trudeau government in Canada.

Opportunities for improved democratic control might also be sought along the familiar path of legislative reform. Proposals to abolish the seniority system in Congress, to weaken the House Rules Committee, and to establish limits on debate in the Senate would all benefit democratic control, as here defined. So would changes, in parliamentary systems, that would allow members to evaluate the political executive's proposals and performance more knowledgeably yet without reducing the incentives to cohesion that form the indispensable power base for the political executive in its relations with other powerholders.[29] If the past is any guide, however, confidence in rapid progress along these lines would be misplaced.

Finally, following Theodore Lowi, one might also pin part of one's hopes for better democratic control on a campaign to discredit the legitimacy of group participation in policy making.[30] Such a campaign might well succeed in breaking up overly cozy relationships between interest groups on the one hand and the public bureaucracy and regulatory agencies on the other. But in view of the powerful underpinnings of interest group influence in politics, discussed earlier, one might reasonably be skeptical that the success of a propaganda campaign would go much beyond that.[31]

By and large, this paper has presented a pessimistic prognosis. Most of the potential ways of improving democratic control that were discussed appear to have little prospect of being adopted. The remainder, while practically more promising, are either blemished by a variety of unfortunate side effects, or offer only minor progress. Yet all of these judgments are based on a simple projection of past experience into the future. As such, they may be far too deterministic, and may underestimate what can be achieved by a determined and imaginative political leadership bent on reform. Such leaders may succeed, for instance, in generating public support for major long-term policy objectives, both through political argument and debate and by practical demonstration, overcoming fears of change by incrementally modifying public policy in the desired direction. In the short term, there also seems to be considerable potential for improved democratic control in single-issue campaigns to mobilize pub-

29. For an extended argument in support of this tendentious proviso, see my "Parliamentary Reform and Governmental Effectiveness in Canada," *Canadian Public Administration*, 17 (1973): 35–54.
30. In *The End of Liberalism*.
31. Lowi explicitly rejects this skepticism as unduly deterministic. He comments, "History is much like a prison or a ghetto. It is difficult to escape, but the captive may succeed—unless he does not try. The only test of a deterministic hypothesis is whether real-world attempts to deny it fail." Ibid., p. 287. This is a useful reminder that no estimate of the prospects of change in human affairs, including those made in this paper, ought to be taken too seriously. Yet this general warning is of little use when it comes to assessing the probable validity of a particular hypothesis: some hypotheses are more plausible than others.

lic support for key reforms. Good illustrations may be found in the provincial politics of Quebec during the early 1960s, when leading politicians undertook extended campaigns to build public support for radical changes of policy in the natural resources field and in education. By the same token, there may also be more scope for party, legislative, and bureaucratic reform than the past suggests.

Finally, it could probably be shown that from the standpoint of democratic control both the present situation and the prospects vary substantially from one field of public policy to another. Presumably, the problem is at its most serious where producer interests are most intimately involved, and where complexity reaches a peak, as in the management of the economy. Conversely, the scope for democratic control may be relatively great where the immediate significance of policy for the average citizen is clearest, as in social welfare legislation. A careful elaboration of this differentiation, and of the key factors that underlie it, would contribute significantly to a better understanding of the problem of democratic control, and of the prospects of overcoming it.

J. A. Corry • The Prospects for Constitutional Democracy

In examining the prospects of constitutional government and democracy, I shall have the Anglo-American societies in the forefront of my attention and concern. Of the more populous and extended societies of the present day whose prospects might be examined, these are the ones with the longest mature experience with constitutional-democratic politics, and the ones most familiar to me. These are the critical instances for examination because their failure to work this form of government would likely be decisive elsewhere.

Faith in the durability of constitutional democracy, even in these societies, has been badly shaken in the last two generations. Those who can recall the bright hopes and untroubled optimism in the early years of this century find it hard to credit the decline. The sunny-minded men of that time, faced with a prophecy of the tribulations of today, would have dismissed it as the extravagant nightmare of a disordered imagination. Such things could not possibly happen in their world.

Of course not. But our world is not their world any more: it has changed beyond all recognition. Perhaps their faith held promise only in that much simpler world. So many things that could not have been foreseen, even with a disordered imagination, have happened. However, we who live in these societies and know how they have been transformed should not find the decline of faith in constitutional democracy incredible, or even surprising.

We know well enough the causes of the transformation. At bottom, it was fired by human aspirations, stirred into hope by constitutional democracy. The buttressing of individual liberty in the nineteenth century had already shown how men liberated from the constraints that had earlier confined them could better their circumstances by their own efforts. The crumbling of unwarranted privilege under democratic pressure had already sharply reduced social inequalities and gave promise, it was believed, that under conditions of general liberty the products of individual effort would be widely shared. In North America, in particular, there had long been a conviction that individual liberty and rough economic and social equality were the two sides of a single coin. The coincidence of these beliefs had already enlarged the vision of a shared common interest, composed a music nearly all could hear and march to, and unleashed mighty forces.

One fateful result was an astonishing rise in productivity which has transformed the workaday world and spawned many of the insecurities and troubles that now plague us. The energies tapped by the vision of a shared common interest were harnessed to production by ingenious and adventurous men, sufficiently freed from social control to create ever-larger forms of organization, effective in exploiting the new science and technology. The outcome was a remarkably productive system that worked successfully without any direct and open coercion and was, on the whole, staunchly supported for a generation or more by the lively sense of a shared common interest. Nothing in the experience of mankind had prepared us for this.

Nobody planned this productive system in any general concerted way: it just grew. And nobody foresaw the consequences, of which it is the necessary, if not the sufficient, cause. Rapid rises in population have made great cities in many parts of the world very crowded places. The many large organizations which sustain, and go on enlarging, productivity are exceedingly complex in their internal and external relations. (Yet these systems manage to find jobs for hundreds of thousands of new hands each year. The wonder is not that there is so much unemployment, but why there isn't more.)

The extreme division of labor and dependence on materials and resources from all over the globe have made the national structures highly vulnerable to shocks generated almost anywhere. Rival national ambitions (not new phenomena) led to two world wars which shook "the unity and married calm of states." The wars which snuffed out millions of lives and did untold damage to the survivors stimulated science and technology, accelerated inventions, new products, and new techniques including the computer with its collective memory, potent for both good and ill. They also brought new triumphs of hyperorganization, including the making of the nuclear bomb which now holds millions under suspended sentence.

The number and size of organizations, whether of corporations, governments, trade unions, or occupational associations, have grown luxuriantly. They have revealed unmistakably their inherent oligarchical tendencies, centralizing power, and often authority, in relatively few hands. They have turned large sections of the population into employees of one kind or another, making it much harder for people to translate individual liberty into mastery of their own fate than was ever contemplated in 1900. Instead, they find themselves at the mercy of decisions made elsewhere, often anonymously and, to outward appearances, often capriciously.

The cumulative effect of all these developments, and others associated with them, has changed the conditions of life. The pace of social and economic change has intensified the impact. Creatures of habit and custom, we find this at times nearly unendurable. We begin to approach the point when everybody who can afford a psychiatrist has one, if he can find him. To cap it all, in the present day, the economies, overheated in the hot pursuit of economic growth, have brought on very high rates of inflation, surely one of the most disruptive of social diseases. Constitutional democratic governments are called upon to govern this seething turmoil. Is it any wonder that there is concern about their prospects?

Of course, this is a compressed and incomplete summary of what has happened, for the most part since 1914, and perhaps almost a caricature of the very complex causation. No matter: it has been introduced here, not as a new discovery but as the context of our present discontents. Meanwhile, it is important to note that the original springs of this transformation and many of the first demonstrations of its power came in the countries that had effective constitutional-democratic systems. Subject to some honorable—and partial—exceptions, these were the countries where science and technology flourished, where individual freedom gave varied talents the best chance to express themselves, and firm public order and constitutional assurances encouraged enterprise and imagination to take risks.

It was enlarging political democracy which gave the mass of men some confidence that they would share in the gains of productivity, made them for a considerable time willing hands in the enterprise, and thus speeded development. It was the freedom to organize in spite of stiff resistance which created the trade unions and clinched for the workers thus organized some share in the gains of productivity. It was political democracy, again subject to some honorable exceptions, which ensured universal education, an indispensable support of the productive system, and which pushed persistently for the public welfare system, a system which made supportable the insecurities of working for a wage.

In short, constitutional democracy provided very effectively the political underpinnings for the great productive achievement. It was the countries which had been stabilized under constitutional-democratic forms which best survived the shocks of social change of revolutionary magnitude. However, even they have not come thus far unscathed, and the worst shocks may still be ahead. In the last ten years or so, the legitimacy of constitutional-democratic regimes has been subject to continuous erosion. Gloomy pessimism has displaced the optimism of earlier years. It has been fed by the unnerving experiences since 1914, and by the gathering intellectual doubts about the rational component in the human make-up. Yet in resisting despair, there is comfort in recalling that these regimes have shown much resilience and resourcefulness in the past. Just as no one in 1910 was able to foresee into what dangerous waters resourcefulness would take us, it may well be that we do not foresee the resourcefulness that can extricate us.

Constitutional democracy nevertheless has enemies enough, ranging from those who have no program but senseless violence through a spectrum of revolutionaries who have lost faith in all the revolutions and radical political reconstructions that have been tried—and are now seen as failures. These latter dissidents now pin their faith on variants of the past failures (associated with such names as Trotsky, Mao and Marcuse) which they hope will be found to contain the ingredients needed for success. These variants seem forlorn hopes, espoused only out of desperation.

Alarmingly enough, the desperation is there, based on a conviction that the failures of constitutional democracy are monstrous and irremediable, leaving no choice but its overthrow. It is also sustained by a millenial hope that somehow, somewhere, will be found a radically improved instrument of social order to guarantee the good life for people who would be good if their oppressors were removed.

It is important here to try to understand the source of the desperation. One of the main sources is nightmares about the overmighty subject in one or all of his garbs of great corporation, trade union, or trade association. He is seen as commanding resources and influence that are inordinate in private hands, thoughtless of the public interest, and thus irresponsible in his use of the resources he has access to. Even his loyalty is deeply suspected: the overmighty subject is always disposed to think that his extensive interests coincide with the public interest, and does not think, or care, that action to enforce this view can be treasonable.

Thus, it is believed, he plunders resources that should be conserved, loads on the public burdens that should be part of the costs of production, neutralizes, if he does not suborn, the politicians by contributions to party funds, and makes government agencies the prisoners of the private interests they were set up to regulate in the public interest. The great interests are always pressing on governments along the boundary between public power and private right. Governments buy truces by surrendering territory they should hold and protect, or by accepting fusions of public power and private right as in the military-industrial complex.

One of the reasons government was made big was to overtop the overmighty subject. These giants are now seen as making common cause. Government itself becomes greedy of power, and turns its instrumentalities to the harassment of the private citizen. There comes to be little reason to choose between constitutional democracy and the Soviet Union. Both, it is said, are horrors.

These charges and conclusions are greatly exaggerated and generally (though not always) unfair to persons in both the public and private spheres. But they are not just figments of the imagination. They are the extrapolations of tendencies inherent in bigness. Evidence is always turning up to show that there is substance in them. Desperation feeds on what substance there is, and magnifies it because of the millenial hope that there must be a surefire way to tame power.

However, hope is at least better than sheer nihilism, and it is better not to dismiss the possibility utterly. But several times bitten makes those with some shreds of prudence very wary. We have heard this story of millenial hope many times, and it has been put to the test several times and places in the twentieth century. The results have been disastrous.

The lesson of these failures seems to be the necessity for a constitutional regime that tolerates dissent and guarantees freedom to work for piecemeal amelioration of social injustices. Starting without such a regime or brushing aside one already in existence, is fatal to all the bright hopes. Desperate lunges to seize economic democracy and comprehensive social justice without securing a constitutional-democratic base seem to ensure that the worst come out on top.

The horrors of this outcome, so starkly present to our minds, warn us against panaceas, drastic courses, and extreme prescriptions. If this elementary caution is heeded, the sober alternatives are clear. We cannot return to the laissez faire of the bourgeois world. We should not fully collectivize the economy in the hands of central governments, whether national or state. This would involve throwing out the baby and keeping the bath water. It would reject the present sensitive and very effective productive system for one which produced less of material welfare and which would leave us with an all-powerful government charged with an impossible task and thus forced to drench us with tyranny. We must go on with the mixed economy and a cushioning welfare system of some sort.

Constitutional democracy has troubles beyond the scatter of outright enemies and the overmighty subjects just considered. More ominous and much more numerous are the neutrals—neither for nor against at the moment. More and more people, it appears, are bewildered by complexity, racked by the pace of change, resentful of their remoteness from the centers of decision, only dimly conscious of membership in any vital community. They are fearful, distrustful and confused, passive and apathetic. Their allegiance to democratic government and democratic processes is being eroded.

How widespread and how virulent is this affliction must be a matter of conjecture. No doubt it has many degrees of severity: almost everyone has his moments when he thinks he has no friends and that the world is arrayed against him. Our impression of its spread and severity may be exaggerated by the way the mass media thrust its symptoms on our attention: the only good news is bad news. The media dwell on the drug culture and the search for saturnalia, and on the spasms of irrational response to baneful events and to charges of manipulation and conspiracy in high places. These are measures for the malaise all right. But what else is news.

Yet one senses that the malaise is spreading most markedly in areas of dense population, populations complexly interlocked under the shadow of towering organizations. Also, it appears that, relative to the degree of hardship imposed, it is eroding confidence and allegiance more severely than did the Great Depression of the thirties. Certainly the infection did not spread as widely then among the intellectuals and the comfortable middle-class young as it does now. But caution is required in interpreting these contrasts with the thirties. Perhaps we have here one of the ironies: more people have been better educated and sense more clearly the undoubted gaps between the rhetoric of constitutional democracy and the realities. Perhaps many of the comfortable have enlarged their human sympathies and are more outraged by the gaps.

However this may be, the apathy no doubt has causes deeply embedded in our societies. Although the erosion of loyalty did not become conspicuous in its severity until the sixties, it can be rated as a delayed response to changes in economic and social structure, and to disappointments over constitutional democracy, that have been a long time in the making.

At the moment, most of the apathetic are quiescent and neutral. But unless the erosion is checked and the allegiance of many regained, the scriptural judgment will likely apply: those who are not for us are against us. In the long run, David Hume is always vindicated: "opinion is king." Constitutional democracy, more than any other form, depends on the active support of general opinion. Can that support be made more secure than it seems now? That depends on first finding the causes of the sickness.

Guessing at the prospects for constitutional government and democracy is especially difficult, because the range of the possible contributory causes of its present distresses is so extensive, and action well designed to improve its prospects so hard to prefigure. The tentativeness of so much of what has been said so far is a tendering of respect to the hazards. An effort will now be made to be more precise and specific in reference, more rigorous in analysis, and firmer in statement.

First, there is the ubiquity of bigness steadily getting bigger and more obtrusive. Bigness not only centralizes much strategic control in relatively few hands but strongly inhibits, if it does not preclude, any significant sharing in the decisions made by the many who work at the lower levels of the organizations. Because we approach the point where nearly everything is related to everything else in complex interdependence, at least the top-level decisions have to take account of a wide range of factors that bear on the choices. Also, the proliferating consequences of any choice that is to be made must be pursued outward. In many instances, the complexity of factors and consequences is impenetrable to all except those whose first duty is to grasp them, and often the task baffles even them.

The sum of the portentous decisions flowing from governments, big corporations, and trade unions drags in its wake many persons and groups not themselves enmeshed in these institutions, and sets fateful terms for many of the relationships of which the society is composed. Although many suspect sinister conspiracy by the leaders of this array (the establishment), there is no body of evidence supporting concerted design. On the contrary, each organization strives to protect itself and its clientele, and to strengthen its clout. While this struggle is an important, if somewhat messy, safeguard against wholesale domination by elites, it often involves delay in decisions and adds to the impressions of uncertainty and confusion that crowd in from all quarters.

The shape of the present-day evils of the curse of bigness emerges from the configuration just described. The big organization sets the terms of the working lives of the many who work for it. They are the managed, set off from the managers. They may be able to get consultation about what goes on on the floor of the work-place (subject to what their trade union says about it). But they have no more status in relation to top-level decisions, and perhaps middle-level decisions, than have the many outsiders who will also be affected by the decisions made. Indeed, the outsiders can raise more objections to the adverse effects than the insiders can.

However much the managed may press for sharing in lower level decisions, few of them are likely to think they have knowledge or competence for the higher levels. The only people who really want in at the high levels are those who either want to join or replace the present decision makers. But this is largely beside the point. Exclusion from a voice diminishes their sense of belonging and deprives them of an understanding of the complex and esoteric considerations that shape the decisions. The resulting decisions are often incomprehensible enough to lay minds to make them wonder what goes on at the top, to enlarge their anxiety about who has influence there, and open them to the propagandists who insinuate manipulation and conspiracy. The deplorable effects do not stop here. All the outsiders who feel themselves adversely affected by all or part of the sum of portentous decisions are exposed to similar wonders and anxieties, and to the same propagandists.

Bigness is pervasive enough for the cumulative effects to be serious. When decisions on matters of import are taken behind closed doors, proclaimed from on high, and tainted with mystery, loss of confidence and mistrust are the natural outcome. Even God himself has suffered a loss of confidence in some quarters for very similar reasons.

These effects have rightly been put down as one of the chief causes of the alienation so much talked about. It is enough to say here that this is not the only cause, as will be argued later. The consequences of alienation are far reaching. They begin with apathy but can be easily moved to resentment, irrationality, and violence. These tendencies are intensified by other developments little attended to.

In the twentieth century, men have gained an astonishing command of material forces. We can fly to the moon and grasp its substance: surely we must be able to make this solid globe yield all we want. Our expectations have risen correspondingly on the wings of fancy provided by mass advertising (which, in turn, is a reflex of the scramble for the consumers' surplus dollars). When things do not go to our particular personal satisfaction, we move just that much more easily to the conclusion that evil men somewhere are in command, turning them the wrong way.

Our rural forefathers knew there were many limits to human control. For example, the weather was both uncontrollable and unpredictable. For the most part, they faced this hard fact with patience and piety: it got them nowhere to be angry with God. Bertrand Russell once said that piety among sailors in the long ago had varied inversely to the size of the ship. But today if a moonship fails to reach the moon, we put it down unhesitatingly, and apparently rightly, to a failure of human foresight, calculation, or care. When we fail to get what we want and decide we are underlings, we don't find the fault in ourselves, or even in our stars; we pin it on unseen powerful men in the establishment. We do this because we know that someone else, equally worthy or unworthy, is getting what he wants. By contrast, the weather affected everyone within the range of vision in much the same way.

The individual in our day looks at the many obstacles in the way of doing what he wants to do on his own. When he turns to look at what he conceives to be the almost limitless control lodged somewhere in human hands, the contrast can be shattering.

The second source of distress is to be found within government itself. The bigness of governments, quite independent of burgeoning size in the private sector, is having special adverse consequences for constitutional democracy. These consequences also weaken loyalty and sap legitimacy, and most of them feed alienation. In the last forty to fifty years, the reach of government and the scope of its activity have increased enormously. There is no need to elaborate on this omnipresent fact. The writ of government, whether national, state, or local, runs to one or another facet of most of the relationships in society.

But it is important to recall how it all came about. The aggrandizement of government was itself a response to the ever-quickening tempo of economic change speeded up by the dislocations of two great wars and a great depression. With the change was coupled a decline of the capacity of—and a collapse of the faith in—laissez faire and the free market to make adequate, or tolerable, or timely enough, adjustments to dislocations. Whether or not the detailed responses were well conceived or not, their purpose was clear—to make compensatory adjustments. As abuses arose out of the changed relationships of economic power or as shifts in the demand for the factors of production caused hardship for particular groups or communities, or played havoc with their settled expectations, governments intervened to redress these situations. Out of these interventions came the mixed economy, mainly motored by private enterprise but regulated, controlled, and often licensed by governments.

Once this process got well started, the abuses and hardships called to the attention of governments multiplied rapidly, at least some of them actually the result of earlier interventions by government. At first, there was much caution about these interventions, thought to be exceptional. As long as there was an influential public which held that the government that governed least governed best, there had to be special justification for such interventions. The abuses and hardships had to be genuine and dangerous, generating serious conflict, and threatening public order if not mended.

However, growing familiarity with the process made it clear to many groups that governments, in addition to caring for their prime functions of maintaining public order and general security and warding off external threats, could be used to do many things that private enterprise and cooperative initiative either fumbled or found difficult. Enough electoral opinion was mobilized to press governments into a wide range of service functions. It ceased to be necessary to have these new functions certified as guards against risks to public order or general security. Their number increases every year as groups that used to resist these developments decide instead to get in and try to get something out of the trough for themselves.

What else is to be expected when so many groups, including powerful private economic organizations, are so highly visible there? Of course, many of the economic organizations can show that governments have moved extensively into what used to be their private domain of operation. They can often show that, to maintain their productivity, they have to negotiate with governments for permission to do this or that. However, in the complexities of the mixed economy, it has become so hard to distinguish self-serving ventures from activities which serve a public interest that the demonstration has little restraining effect.

Here we have at least one of the main roots of the frightening inflation which moves to new heights—the rise of governmental expenditures and budgetary deficits at a constantly accelerating pace. More and more groups no longer waste time taking their troubles to the Lord in prayer: they seek at once to lay the burden of them on governments. The fact that sometimes their troubles arise from their being far out on the limb of interdependence and in danger of being sawed off (a twentieth-century addition to the category of "acts of God") does not alter the financial consequences of government succour. And governments have set so many precedents for coming to the rescue that they can find little ground of principle for refusing the next demands. Government expenditures keep rising to new highs.

As the waves of inflation, from whatever causes, go on mounting, they become a quite independent cause of demoralizing hardship, which threatens to swamp numerous sections of the population and launches new sets of rescue operations by governments. The clamor for lifeboats diverts attention from measures that might be taken to save the ship.

More generally, the captain and the crew of the ship of state have become so preoccupied with plugging leaks, battening hatches, manning the pumps, tinkering with the machinery, and supplying services for the comfort and convenience of the passengers that considerations bearing on the purpose of the voyage, its destination, and the seamanship required to get there, have slipped from the central place they should have in navigation. The passengers have been diverted in much the same way.

More correctly, and to drop the metaphor, the public which political parties early in the century used to be able to mobilize around competing conceptions of the public interest (sometimes aided by sleight of hand) has been fragmented into a number of publics, each clustered around, and concerned with, some particular adjustment, correction, rescue, or repair. Pluralistic tendencies, always lurking in democratic politics, are no longer furtive: they have been legitimated and intensified. They flower luxuriantly.

A slogan of early twentieth-century constitutional democracy, never fully honored but widely believed in, was "equal rights for all and special privileges for none." It was directed against existing and irksome forms of privilege. Today, it has lost its stirring appeal. The stronger push now is rather towards universalizing privilege (or as I shall call it, special status) through the actions of government.

Most of these status-creating activities of governments are costly, either in direct subventions to—or exemptions for—private persons or groups or in the size of the bureaucracy needed to administer and enforce them. A common feature is that they advantage some persons and groups—or reduce their disadvantages—and shift burdens to others, including the taxpayers, and rouse supporters and objectors, whose concern with matters of particular status leads them to put on these particulars an inordinate share of their attention to public issues.

To justify fully the status-creating activities of governments, it must be possible to show that they are supportive of the public interest. Some of these activities can readily be shown to be of this order. For example, laws providing for unemployment compensation create a kind of status. To put the matter at the lowest level, mass unemployment without the cushion of this status would be a clear peril to public order. Other instances would require longer chains of reasoning to show their relationship to the public interest, reasoning which would carry less conviction. In still others, the relationship would be tenuous in the extreme in any definition of the public interest that would be widely acceptable.

The fact is that nearly all instances of special status require a chain of reasoning to link them to the public interest, a chain whose cogency depends on a considerable knowledge and understanding of the complex socioeconomic structure. So, for the exercise of clarifying the political consequences of the proliferation of special status, the central difficulty is not so much the defining of the public interest and demonstrating what it covers. It is rather the knowledge and understanding called for and the length of the chain of reasoning required to establish the linkage.

The government activities under discussion can be seriously divisive because the burden of demonstrating the linkage is too great, partly because demonstrations always arouse counterdemonstrations.

In the result, the issues are likely to be confused rather than clarified. Anyway, it will continue to be much easier for persons to understand and line up for or against particular and immediate interests than to see the linkage—or nonlinkage—with the public interest. As governments continue to enlarge their status-creating activities, it becomes ever harder for issues bearing directly on the public interest (whether arising out of these particular activities or from other sources) to get to the center of the stage, and to be given top priority when they do.

Most of the time, public discussion does not dramatize community, a shared vision of what brings men together, but presents issues that divide them. Such of the public as does not share in special status is tempted to think of governments as "lords of misrule" and is angered by the scramble for status, which often seems to use dubious means. Confidence and trust in government progressively decline. A sense of helplessness and isolation enhances alienation.

There is other evidence of the fading of a vivid sense of the public interest. Disturbed by the confusion of counsel on what governments should do, by the growing apathy, rebelliousness, and violence, many voices wail over the loss of any clear conception of national purpose. They plead for the articulation of overall national goals and purposes to restore coherence and steadfastness. (The plea is more often put in the plural than in the singular.) So far, no one has raised a banner that the thoughtful will flock to.

The last time constitutional democracy had a common purpose was during World War II. Its effects were magical, resulting in the creation of a war machine more efficient than the Axis powers, and without their coercion. No doubt a unifying sense of purpose works wonders, and the lack of it breeds most of the troubles that now afflict constitutional democracy. But by what magic is the hodgepodge of expedients which is now the most striking feature of public policy to be shown to be the expression of unifying collective purpose? Is it really within the reach of political systems that are held together, in great part, as someone has said, "by compromise, ambiguity and contradiction?" This is particularly questionable when the prospect indicates more rather than less collectivization of the economy, making politics still more of a battleground for contending interests.

To conjure up the magic of common purpose would require a massive turnaround of the politicoeconomic systems, and some tempering of the ideologies that support them. It would probably require some dismantling of big organizations, both political and economic, some decentralization of power, bringing institutions back to something closer to the human scale where men could feel assured that they were sharers rather than pawns. Because there is great difficulty in seeing how to reconcile low profile institutions with high productivity, such action would almost certainly require a lowering of material expectations. So it would embark us on a distasteful journey that almost no one wants to make. More than that, only a passionate, unswerving, and widely held common determination would provide the sustained drive needed for this turnaround.

That determination would certainly have to be backed by renewed allegiance to some of the main elements of "the public philosophy" which Walter Lippmann expounded so clearly and urged so eloquently twenty years ago. "The public philosophy," well enough summed up as the traditions of civility, lies at the heart of Western constitutionalism. It was well articulated in venerable theory and significantly honored in practice by constitutional regimes before they were democratized. But full adherence to it has a price which democracies in the twentieth century have declined to pay in full. Indeed, it seems likely that the price is higher than a democracy can pay when so much that deeply concerns its members has to be settled in the public domain: we are not civilized enough to be restrained by the traditions of civility in respect of so many of our conflicting interests. And Lippman had no strategy for its restoration beyond saying that it would require the passionate conviction of intellectuals and philosophers. What signs are there of a great mass conversion?

Of course, there has been tension between constitutionalism and democracy in the twentieth century, the tension between individual liberty and socioeconomic equality. In North America as long as important residues of the earlier democratic outlook lingered, the tension was little noted. Individual liberty and social equality were thought to be two faces of the same coin: if you had individual liberty, you also had rough economic and social equality. And the unifying national purpose scarcely needed to be articulated. It was implicit in the widespread belief that individual liberty and equality before the law gave to all the potential for realizing their full capacities. As the century wore on, this belief crumpled in collision with too many hard facts: it was seen that liberty and equality weren't always wholly compatible; to have more of one, you often had to be satisfied with less of the other. Fruitful tension aimed at reconciling them is one thing: incompatibility is another.

In these last decades, democracy has persistently strengthened its equalitarian impulse, encroaching on liberty in reaching for equality. This trend needs no underlining. How far the common sense of common men, left to itself, would push this trend is perhaps open to question. However, it is clear that, for many members of the intellectual community, equality has become a surrogate for religion. Under their leadership, the universal yearning for justice finds its main concrete expression today in demands for rapid advance towards equality in material terms.

The demands are pressed, of course, as the necessary basis for realizing the brotherhood of man and for sharing together in a restored and vital community. For this prerequisite to be realized under constitutional-democratic forms, the means to be used are clear enough. Governments would be compelled to move further on two fronts. First, they would have to assume a still larger direction of the economy. Second, they would have to redistribute a larger portion of the national income on some equalizing formula, struggled over and hammered out in the political arena. Insofar as successful, the result would be further increments of special status for particular groups, created by governments.

We come back once more to the status-creating activities of governments. The much longed for unifying national purpose has to base itself firmly on perceived common interest. But the common interest is obscured, if not diluted, by the multitude of particular and diverse policies the governments pursue. So, predictably, the search for national purpose gives way to a search for national goals.

For example, the Science Council of Canada, trying to work towards the framing of major programs in scientific research, identified a number of national goals which "appeared to contain the main aspirations of most Canadians." The goals selected—and capitalized—are laudable aspirations, but they strain for inconsistent things. The goals of National (economic) Prosperity and Health will fight one another on the environmental pollution front and elsewhere. The goal of Freedom, Security, and Unity is not internally self-consistent: new increments of security will rouse the objection in many quarters that they are at the expense of freedom. The goal of National Prosperity specifically calls for a high rate of economic growth and full employment along with reasonable price stability. Does experience suggest that these can be effectively pursued at the same time? These are the staples of governmental policy, but even if uneasily reconciled by compromise they do not add up to a unifying national purpose. This conflict is inevitably inimicable to the public interest.

Other evidence from more than one constitutional democracy testifies, perhaps not quite unequivocally, to the fading of the common interest. Reports come in, always puzzling and frequent enough to be alarming, about bystanders who are unwilling to help the victims of hooligans. This is not in the tradition of staunchness for the law and spontaneous reaction against violence toward others. Rather it is reminiscent of the distant past when the wretched poor crowded to watch public executions.

How explain it: is it just physical fear? It can scarcely be the rarity of the spectacle: it is on the television every day. Or is it that the bystanders don't identify with the victim, don't realize any more that the breaching of public order is an attack on themselves? Is it that inflation of the laws with endless regulations has sadly depreciated the currency? So many of the laws of the past generation either buttress the new order of special status or appear silly or incomprehensible to the ordinary citizen. Are we back with Mr. Bumble: "if the law does that . . . the law is a ass"? When the ordinary citizen thinks about the law, does he think of the older law which shields his physical safety and personal possessions? Or does he think of the welter of twentieth-century laws that confer special status, or can be bent to that purpose?

When the English colonists came to North America, they brought with them the tradition, and what they knew of the corpus, of the common law. They never wanted to live under any other law. Even in their struggles against George III they clung to it because it was their law, in rough correspondence with the community sense of right. How deeply committed are their descendants to the many laws of today? How well do these latter fit with any widespread community sense of right? Which of these latter laws would American migrants to another planet want to take with them?

At an earlier time before the proliferation of special status, the community sense of right, based largely on custom, generated a consciousness of common interest, including standards of some importance for judging the actions of politicians and public figures, and proposals for legislation. The talk about common interest here may be taken as a lament about the decline of that consciousness, or at any rate its obscuring by other concerns. Lament or not, the harkening back does not envision a restoring of that lively sense of common interest or its reincarnation in some modified form. It belongs to a past that is gone.

The complexity of the socioeconomic structure, the wide diversity of interests, the inability to rely heavily on the market to regulate economic activity, and the consequent need for governments to preside over social change, prevent such a restoring. Even reducing the size of institutions to something nearer to the human scale would not make it possible. Governments would still have to reconcile a great diversity of interests. There is no prospect of regulating government activities, the great bulk of which would be backed by an active sense of common interest, by means of the community sense of right. We have to live with "compromise, ambiguity and contradiction" which no elaboration of national goals and purposes will overcome.

The repeated references to the obscuring or diluting of the common interest were only for the purpose of sharpening contrasts, to emphasize a support which constitutional democracy tends to take for granted and which is unreliable. Also it was to underline the dangers of proliferating special status because of the frailty of that support. Special status as defined here is divisive even when sophisticated analysis can bring it within a fair definition of the public interest. The cohesiveness of constitutional democracy is under continuous threat.

Apart from the obvious minimum requirements for internal public order and for security against external threats, perhaps only rarely at any time has constitutional democracy achieved unity in substantive government action. Perhaps it came closest to unity on such issues in the days of laissez faire and reliance on the free market—not on what government should be doing, but on what it should not be doing. Even those days were not free of status and privilege but the thicket was not nearly so dense or extensive. It is its present scale that is so threatening.

Perhaps constitutional democracy has always found its cohesiveness mainly in agreement on procedures, on the methods to be used in exploring and composing sharp differences on issues of substance in the public arena. Due process of law, in its widest sense, is a major contribution of constitutionalism to democracy. The handling of the impeachment proceedings, and matters ancillary to it, in 1973–4 in the United States showed steadfast loyalty to due process at both legislative and judicial levels and near-unanimity in support of the procedures on the part of the public. Commitment to procedures is to be cherished and nourished even though that alone is not a substitute for substance.

There can be little doubt that the party systems are markedly affected by the divisiveness of the issues in the public domain. These systems transmit to legislatures and executives the urges that are dominant in the polity. The greater the number of groups or sections which have special stakes in the outcome of public policy, the harder it becomes to contain the diversity by compromises within one or other of two parties. One might expect multiple-party systems to develop.

In the United States, the requirements for electing a president severely limit tendencies towards a multiple-party system. In countries with parliamentary systems, such limitations do not operate. On the national scene in Canada, there have been for some time third and fourth parties. In Britain, the recent resurgence of the Liberal Party has given it a significant share of the popular vote and some seats in Parliament. In both countries in these last years, elections have occasionally failed to produce over-all majorities for one single party in Parliament. It would be interesting to explore how far the divisiveness of issues contributed to these results. But there is not yet enough evidence to show whether minority governments are more than temporary aberrations.

The continuously enlarging scope of government action in the last forty years, quite apart from its specific content, has been an important cause of mistrust and apathy. It is not merely the interrelationships of programs and the ever-widening circles of their consequences. These are beyond the grasp of most of the electorate, but that is not a new phenomenon within the last generation; it has been true for a longer time. It is, in addition, the crowding in of commonsense impressions of the cumbrousness of central governments, and of suspicions that they are becoming nearly unmanageable.

These impressions and suspicions are not illusions: they have substance. Members of legislatures do get a grip on sectors of government activity of special interest to themselves, their constituencies, and their regions, but not, of course, on the scheme of things entire. Not even presidents, prime ministers, and cabinets, with the aid of their many advisers, really comprehend the whole range. And even if they did, it would still be an immense task to force all these activities into the mold of an overriding general purpose, and harder still to get them to respond to major shifts in the direction of general policy.

All bureaucracies have their inflexibilities, and their biases for stability and a quiet life and against innovations that threaten to rock the boat seriously. The bureaucracies of central governments are now so large, and have, for the best of reasons, so many tenured positions, that they become vested interests within governments. Also, for the best of reasons, measures are required to ensure financial accountability for the expenditure of public money. There are regulations designed to keep government activities within the law that mark out the boundary between public power and private right. There is the caution enforced on bureaucrats by political considerations to ensure that all their clients in a given category, or subcategory, are given equal treatment. For these reasons, government bureaucracies have their own brand of inflexibility, and their own elephantine gait. In short, the requirements of constitutionalism for keeping government servant rather than master mean that big government cannot be an efficient operator of large, complex, interlocked programs.

One further important point supporting this conclusion may be made. If there is caution, delay, and diluting compromise over turnabout innovations, movement against obsolete and obsolescent programs is glacial in its pace. Here bureaucratic deliberateness is compounded by political pressures. The clients of such programs lobby against their dismantling. They are much more alert than the general public, which would profit from such dismantling.

The commonsense impressions and suspicions adverse to big government which have just been underscored therefore do rest on weighty evidence. Also, more reflective students of government, better apprised of what is going on, and more fully aware of the secular trend towards bigger and bigger government, are becoming apprehensive about the possibility of combining efficiency in government with constitutional controls. The fear is that massive central governments will become unmanageable on both scores, that they will not only elude the controls but also fail in efficiency through sheer size and complexity.

Fear of unmanageability is not restricted to the conduct of big central governments. Much more widely apprehended is the plight of government in very large cities. Although the malaise has rather different causes there, it is even more serious in an immediate way. The crisis in city government is thrust on our attention every day. It is not necessary to rehearse it here.

The gross size of the great cities is, to a degree, both cause and consequence of the great rise in productivity. The tribulations of the cities now threaten the system they shared in creating. The cities are the main seats of the apathy, boredom, and alienation, the mindless violence and aimless rebellion. No matter what steps are taken, or not taken, to ensure the manageability of central governments, continued disintegration of the great cities could inflict mortal wounds on constitutional democracy.

If, as is argued here, institutions have been growing beyond the human scale and thus forming one of the main threats to constitutional democracy, it is hard to know how to improve the situation. Pragmatic trial-and-error tinkering is not to be dismissed out of hand: the Anglo-American world in particular has made many of its solid achievements this way. It may be possible to mediate effectively between men's private troubles and the massive politicoeconomic institutions. Many expedients could be tried: restoring the supremacy of law by reducing the great accumulation of administrative discretions in the hands of governments, enlarging the categories of fundamental freedoms and ensuring greater vigilance by the courts in protection of civil rights, reforming the structure, operation, and financing of political parties, designing measures to make governmental bureaucracies more sensitive to the range of men's private troubles and more responsive to political leadership, and further computerizing of the data that must be handled in making political decisions.

However, doubts about the effectiveness of such expedients keep crowding in. The gains to be expected do not seem commensurate with the troubles. They resemble too much the attempts to curb inflation by price and wage controls. They are like efforts to control the flow of water in the garden hose by sitting on the sprinkler instead of turning off the tap.

Better calculated for getting to the roots of the matter are two other proposals. (Whether having got there, they would achieve what is needed is another matter.) First, decentralizing many government operations by transferring them from the national government to state, provincial, and local governments, thus reducing congestion at the center and bringing programs closer to the people affected.

Transfers to local governments may indeed serve these purposes. But so far decentralization within federal structures appears to make state and provincial operations bigger without getting zero-growth at the center, let alone making it smaller. It might, of course, slow down growth at the center. Again, in relation to federal structures, it is not clear that such proposals take enough account of the requirements of the national politicoeconomic systems for single centers of decision on many matters.

Second, there are the demands strongly pressed just now for opening up large organizations, both public and private, for much greater participation at all levels of decision by those who will be directly affected.

As already noted, the case for participation on the floor of the work place is irresistible when the work force is both literate and alert to the world around it. But taken over-all, decisions on the floor of the work place are only a part of the decisions that shape people's lives, and they are a part of lesser importance. There has not yet been enough experience of sharing in decisions at the higher levels of big organizations to tell us much. Such evidence as there is of sharing at any level suggests that it provides forums for only a few, and that interest and concern are difficult to sustain. As Oscar Wilde said of proposals for guild socialism in Britain early in the century, "The trouble with democratic socialism is that there wouldn't be any free evenings." Nevertheless, for those who stay with it, the experience of sharing has values not to be shrugged off.

Also, the demands for participatory democracy assume too readily that the managed, in their participation, would speak with a united voice in dealing with the presumption of the managers. They are more likely to speak with many voices, delaying responses to urgent questions, and making accommodations to diverse interests more imperative than the steering of a firm coherent policy. Such consequences would not necessarily be deplorable if that were all that was involved. But the main case for bigness rests on its contribution to productivity. That contribution requires a considerable measure of predictability in the decisions of the organizations that are strategically placed in relation to production. Predictability would be considerably reduced if many interests, through their representatives, had to put their imprimatur on what was to be done.

This raises the central dilemma of trying to deal with bigness, whether by decentralization or through wholesale participation of those affected. How does one reconcile low profile institutions, or a lowered profile of institutions, with high productivity? The high stretch of expectations which shows no sign of subsiding sets a warning signal against moves that are more likely to lessen than to increase productivity. On the other hand, the continuing erosion of the legitimacy of the present dispensations, unless checked, poses threats of disruption that will also lessen productivity.

So perhaps the real trouble is spiritual, an obsession with material things. One hastens to add, however, that this is a reproach which the comfortable ought to feel uncomfortable in making. If the disease is indeed of this order, selecting and applying measures for its cure will be no less difficult, and also beyond political therapy. At this point, it is time to say that considerably greater confidence in diagnosis must precede prescription.

Samuel H. Barnes • The Dark Side of Pluralism: Italian Democracy and the Limits of Political Engineering

Pluralism is a wonderful concept. It seems to go along with a number of other concepts that political scientists consider "good," such as democracy, constitutionalism, freedom, independence, and—in the contemporary idiom—everyone doing his own thing. It is a Protean concept, and like such concepts it can be operationalized in many ways. These operational meanings are not necessarily contradictory; and as they share a number of common features, it is possible to identify some of the basic components of pluralism. These fundamental ingredients include, above everything else, the existence of relatively autonomous and voluntary institutions, associations, organizations, and groups between the individual and the state. Moreover, it is widely accepted that these intermediate bodies are legitimate and indeed essential to the functioning of constitutional democracies. Pluralism assumes the legitimacy of social conflict but posits that multiple memberships in voluntary groups and associations result in crosscutting cleavages that mute conflict and promote consensus. Pluralism is the opposite of a monolithic political system in which individuals are authoritatively mobilized into structures that tie them directly into the state power system.

Also implicit in pluralism is the assumption that individuals and groups compete freely in the political market place and that the outcome of the policy process is the result of the parallelogram of forces involved in politics. Elections are at the very least a way of keeping score. That is, elections permit the weighing of the political strengths of various groups and, in a rough and imprecise manner, the relating of mass opinions to the policy outputs of polities.

In recent years critics have pointed out some unarticulated and generally unexamined consequences of the functioning of pluralistic systems.[1] Some critics allege that pluralism is a facade behind which the dominant elites manipulate the political process. They point out that advantages and disadvantages are not randomly distributed in the free play of political competition, and that as a result some groups

1. The general literature on pluralism and its critics is voluminous and will not be discussed here.

are systematically excluded from effective participation in the political process while others compete at a grave disadvantage. Patterns of access to decision makers, resources required to mount effective campaigns, and the skills required to compete effectively in a complex political market place are all cited as limitations on the ability of a pluralistic system to meet the needs of all its citizens. These critics point out that the weak, the poor, and the socially marginal are unable to take advantage of the claimed possibilities of pluralism for the furtherance of their interests.

In this essay I will examine other unanticipated consequences of pluralism: these are that an effectively mobilized pluralistic political system may be so highly fragmented and immobile that dominant elites lack incentives to provide effective government for coping with societal problems, that the interests of the rulers and the interests of the society may be mutually incompatible, and that there may be no simple institutional remedy for this state of affairs in the short run.[2]

This essay is about Italy rather than pluralism. My concern is with understanding the reason for what the conventional wisdom labels the ineffectiveness of the Italian government. But a great deal can be learned about pluralism in the course of talking about Italy. For it is my contention that the lack of effectiveness of the Italian governmental system can be attributed to the extreme pluralism of the society, the existence of high electoral mobilization, and the importance of institutions that intervene between the citizen and the governing authorities.

In the pages that follow I will briefly outline the institutional structure of constitutional democracy in Italy and discuss the bases of the present structure of political conflict and of the dominant position of the Christian Democratic party. Then I will examine the reasons it is so difficult for the system to be more responsive to demands from its constituents and from its physical and international environment. I will conclude with a review of a debate concerning the changes needed to alter these patterns.

2. I begin with most of the assumptions articulated by Giovanni Sartori in "European Political Parties: The Case of Polarized Pluralism," in Joseph LaPalombara and Myron Weiner, eds., *Political Parties and Political Development* (Princeton: Princeton University Press, 1966), pp. 137–76; but my analysis of the consequences differs from Sartori's. That is, I am less pessimistic than he is concerning the possible future role of the Italian Communist Party.

Democracy in Italy

The institutional structure of the Italian government is a familiar one.[3] It is a parliamentary system with a two-chamber legislature. The lower chamber, the Chamber of Deputies, is more important politically than the Senate though they formally are equal in power. The president of the republic, the head of state, is elected by a joint session of the legislature, augmented by representatives of regional bodies. The president has somewhat more power than the head of state in, for example, Great Britain or West Germany; but he lacks the powers of the president of the French Fifth Republic. The president appoints the president of the Council of Ministers (prime minister) and he in turn names his cabinet. Each new prime minister and cabinet must receive a vote of confidence in both houses within ten days. There is also a constitutional court in Italy that has rendered several important controversial decisions; without acquiring the prestige of the U.S. Supreme Court, it nevertheless has played an innovative role in the system.

Discussions of the problems of Italian democracy sometimes begin and end with the problem of a stable government. Up to a point this is quite proper, but the problem of governmental stability must be traced back further—to the electoral bases of the party system and the evolution of the Italian electorate. Since no party has a majority of seats in the legislature, each government must be a coalition or a one-party government supported by other parties. Yet the Christian Democratic party (DC) is so large and so well located in spatial terms that no coalition is feasible without it. As a consequence, every prime minister since 1946 has been a Christian Democrat and that party has held a majority of the cabinet positions, including most of the important positions. The location of the Christian Democratic party near the center of the spectrum of Italian parties represented in parliament is a crucial feature of the system. As a result, Italy is a dominant party system, and any examination of the sources of instability of the system must take into account the nature of the internal political process within the dominant party. That discussion in

3. For an introduction to the structure of the Italian political system see Raphael Zariski, *Italy: The Politics of Uneven Development* (Hinsdale, Ill.: The Dryden Press, 1972); Dante Germino and Stefano Passigli, *The Government and Politics of Contemporary Italy* (New York: Harper and Row, 1968); John C. Adams and Paolo Barile, *The Government of Republican Italy* (Boston: Houghton Mifflin, 1966); or Norman Kogan, *The Government of Italy* (New York: Crowell, 1966).

turn must begin with an understanding of the relationship between the Christian Democratic party and other parties of the system.

Parties and Elections. Italian parties are conventionally viewed as stretching from the Communist party on the left to the neofascist Italian Social Movement (MSI) on the right, and it has been demonstrated that Italians view politics in terms of spatial models.[4] This habit is probably acquired at the same time that the attachment to a particular political party is learned. That is, the complexity of the party system encourages left-right thinking about politics in order to simplify information gathering and processing.

Of course there are far more dimensions to Italian politics than can be captured by a single left-right scale.[5] But for an overwhelming majority of the electorate, these dimensions coincide rather well with the overall left-right dimension. Furthermore, the other dimensions that are of considerable importance in Italian politics have relatively high saliency for only a few people. For example, the Christian Democrats generally are not as conservative on the socioeconomic dimension as the parties to the right of them—the Liberals and Neofascists. But since these parties received a maximum of 15.7 percent of the vote (in 1953), overall measures of association between left and right on socioeconomic matters correlate strongly with the left-right dimension. And the same is true of the clerical–anti-clerical dimension, as the Liberals, who are conventionally viewed as being on the right, are much less clerical than the Christian Democrats. Since there are few Liberal supporters, an overall relationship between left and right and clericalism is extremely strong. Similar dynamics hold on

4. See Samuel H. Barnes, "Left, Right, and the Italian Voter," *Comparative Political Studies* 4 (July 1971): 157–75. See also: Giacomo Sani, "A Test of the Least Distance Model of Voting Choice: Italy, 1972," *Comparative Political Studies*, forthcoming; and G. Sani and Phillip Miller, "Multiple Cleavages and the Left-Right Continuum," forthcoming.

5. On the dimensionality of Italian politics see Samuel H. Barnes and Roy Pierce, "Public Opinion and Political Preferences in France and Italy," *Midwest Journal of Political Science* 15 (November 1971): 643–62; Giacomo Sani, "Determinants of Party Preference in Italy: Toward the Integration of Complementary Models," *American Journal of Political Science* 18 (May 1974): 315–29; Gabriel Almond and Sidney Verba, *The Civic Culture* (Princeton: Princeton University Press, 1963); Mattei Dogan, "Comportement politique et condition social en Italie," *Revue française de sociologie* 7 (1966): 700–734; and Vittorio Capecchi et al., *Il comportamento elettorale in Italia* (Bologna: Il Mulino, 1968). This work and others of the Istituto Carlo Cattaneo project on participation in Italy are summarized in Giorgio Galli and Alfonso Prandi, *Patterns of Political Participation in Italy* (New Haven: Yale University Press, 1970).

the foreign policy dimension: of all Italian parties the Christian Democrats are perhaps the most closely tied to the Western alliance and especially to friendship with the United States, but the parties to the right of the DC share these preferences in foreign policy.

Because the left-right dimension is the most important one in the formation of governmental coalitions, I will henceforth speak of the left-right dimension as if it were the only one dividing Italian parties. But it must be acknowledged that reality is much more complex, that this is merely a method of simplifying analytical problems. The Communists and Neofascists are conventionally viewed as the two extreme parties, and the Liberals are conventionally placed to the right of the Christian Democrats and to the left of the MSI. The Monarchist party declined throughout most of the postwar period and finally merged with the MSI in 1972. Only the space between the Christian Democrats and the Communists must now be accounted for. This space has been occupied by the very small Republican party (PRI), which is a non-Marxist, secular, technocratic, modernizing party, and a number of socialist parties.

During the period since World War II Italian socialists have been torn between their desire to bring about substantial changes in Italian society and its economy, on the one hand, and their devotion to parliamentary democracy, on the other.[6] As a result, they have wavered between supporting an alliance with the Communist party (PCI) in order to bring about the former and joining with the center parties in the protection of the latter. In 1948 the Socialists ran a joint campaign and electoral list with the Communists, with the latter having emerged with more seats.[7] One group of socialists had refused to go along with this unity-of-action pact and formed the Social Democratic party (PSDI). Since that time the PSDI has been available for coalitions within the Christian Democratic party. But the larger socialist party, the PSI, remained outside the governmental

---

6. On the internal divisions of the PSI see Samuel H. Barnes, *Party Democracy: Politics in an Italian Socialist Federation* (New Haven: Yale University Press, 1967); Franco Cazzola, *Il partito come organizzazione—studio di un caso: il PSI* (Roma: Edizioni del Tritone, 1970); Cazzola, *Carisma e democrazia nel socialismo italiano* (Rome: Istituto Luigi Sturzo, 1967); and Raphael Zariski, "The Italian Socialist Party: a Case Study in Factional Conflict," *American Political Science Review* 56 (June 1962): 372–90.

7. Two good reviews of postwar Italian politics are Norman Kogan, *A Political History of Postwar Italy* (New York: Praeger, 1966); and Giuseppe Mammarella, *Italy After Fascism* (Notre Dame: University of Notre Dame Press, 1966).

coalition until the 1956 Hungarian uprising, the destalinization campaign in the Soviet Union, and the general evolution of the Italian system caused it to move gradually toward cooperation.

Table 1. Votes (in %) and Seats in Chamber of Deputies won in Italian Elections 1946–1972

	1946	1948	1953	1958	1963	1968	1972
Votes (%)							
Communists (PCI)	19		22.6	22.7	25.3	26.9	27.2
Social Proletarians (PSIUP)	— >	31	—	—	—	4.5	1.9
Socialists (PSI)	20.7		12.7	14.2	13.8	> 14.5	9.6
Social Democrats (PSDI)	—	7.1	4.5	4.5	6.1		5.1
Republicans (PRI)	.4	2.5	1.6	1.4	1.4	2	2.9
Christian Democrats (DC)	35.2	48.5	40	42.4	38.3	39.1	38.8
Liberals (PLI)	6.8	3.8	3	3.5	7	5.8	3.9
Qualunquists	5.3						
Monarchists	2.8	2.8	6.8	4.8	1.7	1.3	> 8.7
Neo-Fascists (MSI)	—	2	5.9	4.8	5.1	4.5	
Others	5.8	2.3	2.9	1.7	1.3	1.4	1.9
Seats (House)							
Communists (PCI)	104		143	140	166	171	179
Social Proletarians (PSIUP)	— >	183	—	—	—	23	—
Socialists (PSI)	115		75	84	87	> 91	61
Social Democrats (PSDI)	—	33	19	22	33		29
Republicans (PRI)	23	9	5	6	6	9	15
Christian Democrats (DC)	207	305	262	273	260	265	267
Liberals (PLI)	41	19	14	17	39	31	20
Qualunquists	30	—	—	—	—	—	—
Monarchists	—	14	40	25	8	6	> 56
Neo-Fascists (MSI)	—	6	29	15	27	24	
Others	35	5	3	5	4	10	3
Electoral Turnout—							
% voting of those eligible	89.1%	92.2%	93.8%	93.8%	92.9%	93%	93.1%

Source: 1946–68, Zariski, *Italy*, pp. 156–57; 1972, Alberto Spreafico, "Le elezioni politiche italiane del 7 Maggio 1972," *Rivista italiana di scienza politica*, vol. 3 (December 1972), 525–68.

Coalition Formation. As Table I indicates, the arithmetic of Italian elections and parliamentary seats made it more and more difficult to form a majority coalition. Of course, the Christian Democrats remained the cornerstone of any coalition. But to form a government with the MSI was unthinkable, and to include both the Liberals and the Social Democrats in the government became more and more difficult in the 1950s. There were a number of *monocolore* (one party) governments in which the Christian Democrats controlled all cabinet positions and were supported on crucial votes by members of some other parties. But these were fragile governments at the mercy of negative votes even from snipers within the Christian Democratic party itself, due to secrecy on important legislative votes.

For many years, the dependence of the Christian Democratic party on the church made an alliance with the left unthinkable. But in the 1960s the party acquired increasing organizational independence from the civic committees of Catholic Action, which had been a major vehicle of clerical influence under Pope Pius XII; and under Pope John XXIII the church began to assume a less intransigent stance vis-à-vis the left and also began to restrict somewhat its direct involvement in Italian politics. These developments in the DC and the PSI led to the "opening to the left" in Italian politics, under which the Christian Democrats governed first with the programmatic abstention of the PSI and then with its actual participation in the cabinet.

The tension lingered between the PSI's commitment to reform and its defense of the constitutional order. When the PSI entered the center-left cabinet in 1964 its left wing broke away and formed the Italian Socialist Party of Proletarian Unity (PSIUP), a party that remained in close alliance with the PCI. The PSIUP was unable to elect a single deputy in 1972 and voted to dissolve, with most of its leaders entering the PCI. The PSI and PSDI finally merged in 1966—at least at the top—but great tension was generated by a fierce struggle over the orientations and leadership of the merged party. The merger could not be pushed to completion and the party split again in 1969, with the two parties eventually reassuming their previous names.[8]

Since it is highly unlikely that any party will secure a majority, the necessity of a coalition government is taken for granted; and, since the concept of a left-right continuum is so deeply rooted in Italian political thinking, it is to be discounted that a government coalition comprised of the left and the right can be formed.[9] This means that the center Christian Democratic party will always be in whatever coalition is formed.[10] It is very difficult though not inconceivable for the Christian Democratic party to collaborate with the Liberals and

8. A review of the period of socialist unity and of the reasons for its failure is Felice Rizzi's, "Dall'unificazione alla scissione socialista (1966–69)," *Rivista italiana di scienza politica* 3 (August 1973): 407–24.

9. Robert Axelrod analyzes coalition formation in Italy in *Conflict of Interest* (Chicago: Markham, 1970), pp. 165–87.

10. The DC as a "dominant party" is analyzed in Alan Arian and Samuel H. Barnes, "The Dominant Party System: a Neglected Model of Democratic Stability," forthcoming in *Journal of Politics*.

at the same time obtain sufficient support from the PSI to have a majority in parliament. The opening to the left was an attempt to secure a stable basis for a coalition government that would have agreement upon a progressive program and that could begin to attack the accumulated problems of modernization in Italy.

A fundamental complication is that the Christian Democrats, PSI, and PSDI are not monolithic blocs. Each party is divided into factions based upon policies, ideologies, personal ambitions, and socioeconomic groupings.[11] Thus the Christian Democratic party is an uneasy alliance of notables with a clientelistic following, organization-based career party officials, business-oriented conservatives, clerically-oriented conservatives, agricultural and rural groups, left ideologues, and trade unionists. In a sense, the Christian Democratic party contains within itself a substantial segment of the left-right continuum. As it moves along one direction of the left-right continuum, groups and individuals at the other end feel increasingly threatened. The party could hardly function were it not for the perception of the need for unity by the church and especially the real rewards that the party is able to hand out as a result of its hold on power. But the major price it has to pay is incoherence of direction and fragmentation.

Each ministry tends to pursue the personal and group-related goals of the minister rather than a coordinated national policy. Thus in the opening to the left, the great enthusiasm generated at the prospect of a unified and progressive government was soon replaced by the realization that the hopes of reform were giving way to the inclusion of the socialists in the patronage system. The importance of the new patronage and clientelistic ties that came with public office led to an intense struggle for personal advantage within the socialist party. When some of the former PSDI leaders saw that they might do poorly in that competition they led a schism in the unified party and the reconstitution of the old PSDI.

A decade of socialist support of and sometimes participation in the governing coalition led to a number of substantial reforms, including the nationalization of electric energy, the implementation of the regional structure called for by the constitution, and restructuring of

11. There is an extensive literature on Italian factions. For an introduction see Raphael Zariski, *Italy*, and "Intra-Party Conflict in a Dominant Party: The Experience of Italian Christian Democracy," *Journal of Politics* 27 (February 1965): 19–34; and Franco Cazzola, "Partiti, correnti, e voto di preferenza," *Rivista italiana di scienza politica* 2 (December 1972): 569–88.

governmental involvement in the economic system. But it also led to the extension of patronage politics to parties that had formerly been in opposition. The number of factions in the governing parties continued to be large, and public policy emerged from these factional disputes.

The Bases of Stability and Instability

The Italian situation just described is hardly the ideal type of pluralist system envisaged by the conventional wisdom. Yet it is my contention that it is the strongly pluralistic nature of Italian society combined with the high levels of electoral mobilization and institutionalization of political support that are responsible for this seeming instability. Proponents of pluralism generally point to the support for the system generated by citizens having the possibility of participating in the making of decisions that affect them. Critics of pluralism emphasize its imperfect nature. Italy in many respects combines the worst of both worlds. It is highly pluralistic but it is the intermediate institutions rather than the political system that receive the loyalties of the citizenry.[12] And the high levels of mobilization and institutionalization eliminate the flexibility in electoral politics that makes change not only possible but rewarding for political entrepreneurs.

Institutionalized Tradition. Students of Italian politics emphasize the existence of different subcultures, the importance of ideological differences, and the critical role of the social networks in which people find themselves.[13] These social networks are in part subcultures and they also involve ideological differences, so the various explanations of the bases of pluralism in Italy are not mutually incompatible. Most Italians are born into a political tradition that has an ideological expression, that receives support from some social groups

12. To my knowledge only one scholar has raised the question of the compatibility of "loyalties to subcultural groups and to the state": Hans Daalder, "The Consociational Democracy Theme," *World Politics* 26 (July 1974): 611. It is fundamental—but currently unanswerable—for the Italian political system.

13. See Samuel H. Barnes, "Italy: Religion and Class in Electoral Behavior," in Richard Rose, ed., *Electoral Behavior: A Comparative Handbook* (New York: Free Press, 1974), pp. 171–225. The theme of institutionalized tradition is developed in Samuel H. Barnes, *Representation in Italy: Political Traditions and Electoral Choice*, forthcoming. See also Giacomo Sani, "Canali di informazione e atteggiamenti politici," *Rivista italiana di scienza politica*, vol. 4 (July 1974).

more than others, that involves citizens in interaction with others sharing the same social network, and that limits political access largely to contacts with others within the political tradition.

The criticism that those of low political resources are not able to compete in a pluralistic system is in part met in Italy by the importance of institutions such as the Communist party and the Catholic church and their affiliated organizations, both of which are able to provide channels of influence or at least of communications to the very weakest and most marginal of individuals. The dominant institutions of Italian society, including the political parties and the church, are largely bureaucratic. There is a strong tendency to consider bureaucratic position as a form of property to be exploited in a clientelistic fashion for personal gain.[14] Italian institutions are more clientelistic in their functioning than is generally expected in bureaucratic organizations. Without developing measuring instruments and securing comparable data from several countries it is of course impossible to be very precise about this point, but Italy is probably more ascriptive and clientelistic in the distribution of rewards than the other advanced industrial societies with which it is frequently compared. Because of these numerous bureaucratic institutions—and the state machinery would have to be listed as one of the most important of the institutional actors in the political system—Italian society and polity are both hierarchically organized. One makes a career or one exercises influence by carefully cultivating ties with those above and below one in the hierarchy so that the hierarchies themselves are simultaneously modern bureaucracies and patron-client networks. In emphasizing ideological and cultural themes, it is easy to ignore the ubiquity of these face-to-face ties throughout Italian society. For most individuals political power is simply a means of rewarding one's friends and punishing one's enemies. Thus, as

14. On traditional clientelism in Italy a good place to begin is with Luigi Graziano, "Patron-Client Relationships in Southern Italy," *European Journal of Political Research*, 1 (April 1973): 3–34 and the works cited therein; and Sidney Tarrow, *Peasant Communism in Southern Italy* (New Haven: Yale University Press, 1967), pp. 40–95. On the importance of the phenomenon within the political parties see Alan Zuckerman, "On the Institutionalization of Political Clienteles: Party Factions and Cabinet Coalitions in Italy," a paper prepared for delivery at the 1973 Annual Meeting of the American Political Science Association, Jung Hotel, New Orleans, Louisiana, September 4–8. Zuckerman points out that while a class approach leads to individuals identifying their interests as being similar to those of others with a similar status, clientelism encourages conflict with others at the same level in the stratification system and cooperation with those occupying higher and lower positions. This difference has immense implications for political mobilization.

LaPalombara pointed out, the pattern of interest group activity in Italy falls short of that expected in a truly pluralistic society.[15] While it is true that the governmental bureaucracy treats with people of all socioeconomic conditions, the government determines which of the many claimants will be granted access. And it is usually those who share what LaPalombara calls a parentela or political kinship relationship. Thus the Communist party and its spokesmen—who represent more than a quarter of the Italian electorate—are generally disbarred from direct or continuing interactions with most of the decision-making apparatus. That is why the opening to the left and the inclusion of the Socialists were such important events. Yet it is also understandable why the Socialists should have quickly become a part of the patronage system, for there were rewards and no immediate drawbacks: one of the weaknesses of the Italian system is that it has no effective means of electoral rewards and punishment.[16] The electoral arrangements do not effectively do either; for, as Table I has shown, there is very little change from one election to another.

The Policy Process and the Status Quo. In fact in Italy there is virtually no relationship between the electoral game and the policy-making game. The former merely determines what the strength of the forces in parliament will be. It is true that over a long period of time the slight weakening of the Christian Democratic party caused it to admit the PSI to the circle of governors. But policy emerges from the political process within the governing parties, from the struggle of factions and personalities for position and influence. It is hard to relate electoral inputs to policy outputs.

It has been widely demonstrated that the Italian party system reflects deep divisions within the Italian electorate. It is not necessary to go into the data here, but the differences between Communists and Christian Democrats are very great on most of the major themes of politics, including socioeconomic questions, clericalism and the role of the church in politics, the orientation of Italy in international affairs, and many other questions.[17] And these differences exist at the

15. Joseph LaPalombara, *Interest Groups in Italian Politics* (Princeton: Princeton University Press, 1964).
16. This point has been made by many observers, especially Giorgio Galli in *Il bipartitismo imperfetto* (Bologna: Mulino, 1966); and *Il difficile governo* (Bologna: Mulino 1972).
17. See especially Barnes, "Left, Right and the Italian Voter," and Barnes and Pierce, "Public Opinion and Political Preferences."

mass level as well as the elite level. In fact, on a number of issues Christian Democratic elites are more moderate than Christian Democratic mass publics. This is in striking contrast to findings for the United States, which indicate that the Democratic and Republican rank and file are much more similar to one another than the Democratic rank and file are to the Democratic elite and the Republican rank and file are to the Republican elite.[18] In other words, in Italy party differences reflect differences in subcultures, ideologies, beliefs, policy preferences, and attitudes.

I strongly reject the view that politics is simply a reflection of social forces.[19] It is a sociological illusion that politics is a dependent variable, and that the motive force of change in society is to be found only in the line-up of social forces. Politics, politicians, and policies all make a difference. Applying these assumptions to the analysis of Italian politics, I do not conclude that social conflict in Italy makes change impossible. But present Italian policy makers are reluctant to alter the status quo more than the minimum necessary in order to remain in power. There are two principal reasons why this is so, and each merits separate analysis. The first is the nature of the groups that support the DC; the second is the nature of the policy process within the DC itself.

The groups that support the Christian Democratic government are not likely to benefit as much from change as other groups in society. This is not to deny that benefits might accrue to all Italians by a more effective utilization of resources. Nor is it to suggest that many groups that support the Christian Democratic party are not likely to benefit from a general redistribution of wealth and power. But among the most visible and powerful supporters of the Christian Democrats are groups that benefit most from the status quo. The Christian Democrats are the establishment and are relatively satisfied with things as they are. They are by and large intelligent people who are knowledgeable about the major trends in industrial society, and it must seem obvious to them that evolutionary trends are not working to their advantage.

18. Herbert McClosky, "Consensus and Ideology in American Politics," *American Political Science Review* 58 (June 1964): 361–79.
19. On this point I agree strongly with Giovanni Sartori's views in "From the Sociology of Politics to Political Sociology," in S. M. Lipset, ed., *Politics and the Social Sciences* (New York: Oxford University Press, 1969), pp. 65–100; and Sartori, "European Political Parties: The Case of Polarized Pluralism," p. 166; Herbert J. Spiro, ed., *Africa: the Primacy of Politics* (New York: Random House, 1966), p. 152.

The most obvious example is what change entails for the Catholic church. The church can hope to benefit very little from change. A major complaint brought by students of development against the elites of Italy is their failure to bring about a thorough secularization of politics. Given the close ties between the present political elites within the Christian Democratic party and the church, it would be extremely surprising if the DC should lead a movement toward secularization.[20] Indeed, it is perhaps surprising that it has accommodated as well as it has to the secular trends of industrial society. As previously mentioned, on some issues it is clear that the elites are more accommodating than the mass publics of the Christian Democratic party. And it seems to be a characteristic of dominant parties that they rely heavily upon the support of groups that do not demand too much of them, thereby simplifying their problems of choice, especially concerning redistribution.

The economic elites who support the Christian Democratic party likewise have little to gain by a governmental policy of modernization. While the evidence is by no means unambiguous, the more dynamic and modern Italian economic forces seem to support the secular parties of left and right such as the Liberals, Republicans, Social Democrats, and to some extent even the Socialists rather than the Christian Democrats. It is obvious, of course, that these economic elites must accommodate to the Christian Democratic regime. They have often done this successfully, but accommodation is different from enthusiastic support. The Christian Democrats are more likely to be supported by enterprises dependent upon government patronage, and by the less modern economic sectors. Thus while the Christian Democratic party may be heavily supported by conservatives it is by no means the favorite party of the dynamic entrepreneurial class in Italy.

There are factions within the Christian Democratic party that favor thorough modernization. One of the most important of these is the labor-oriented faction, which had had close ties to the Christian Democratic oriented trade union, the CISL. But this is very much a minority faction, and in recent years the realization of that fact has propelled Christian Democratic unionists into increasing cooperation

20. On the Church in Italian politics see A. C. Jemolo, *Church and State in Italy: 1850–1950* (Oxford: Blackwell, 1960); Alfonso Prandi, *Chiesa e politica* (Bologna: Il Mulino, 1968); Gianfranco Poggi, *Catholic Action in Italy: The Sociology of a Sponsored Organization* (Stanford: Stanford University Press, 1967); Carlo Falconi, *La chiesa e le organizzazioni cattoliche in Italia (1945–1955)* (Turin: Einaudi, 1956).

on economic matters with their Marxist counterparts in other unions.

If we turn to the Christian Democratic political elites themselves rather than to their supporters, we still find few reasons to expect rapid change. Lacking a majority and searching for marginal electoral advantages vis-á-vis other parties, the party must court particular groups and individuals. Moreover, individual leaders must compete with other leaders for influence in the party and for preference votes in elections. Hence the party depends heavily upon patronage and clientelistic networks.[21] The resources of government are used to secure votes, not by means of a favorable public reaction to intelligent policies effectively administered but rather by specific benefits obtained by particular individuals as a result of particular governmental activities. Thus the cost-benefit calculus is based as much on individuals as upon socioeconomic categories and broad policies. Each minister operates his ministry as a personal fiefdom that is to be used to further his own strength within the party and that of his faction, and, of course, the strength of the Christian Democratic party within the electorate as a whole. Governmental largesse is available only to Christian Democrats in good standing and to those recommended by them. The hierarchy of the church, stretching from the village priest into the Vatican itself, is deeply involved in this highly personalized clientelistic network. Governmental services are provided in return for votes or monetary payoffs or often both. Public expenditures—whether new industrial plants, road construction, or new educational programs—are dispensed utilizing criteria that are much more heavily political than would likely be the case in other advanced industrial democracies. None of this of course is unique to Italy. What is different is the degree to which these criteria permeate decision making at all levels and the absence of control over the system, the inability to punish those who step over the limits of tolerable activities.

The opening to the left was expected to be a prelude to an opening up of the Christian Democratic dominated system and a conversion to universalistic criteria, to a more scientific and rational approach to the problems facing the country. Instead, it has largely meant that some particular Socialist leaders have been given a slice of what had previously been a Christian Democratic (and to a lesser extent Social

21. These ties are investigated in Zuckerman, "Institutionalization of Political Clienteles."

Democratic and Republican) preserve. The opening to the left broadened the bases of groups participating in the system; it did not alter the system itself. But it has at the same time greatly complicated decision making, for it has widened the range of interests that must be accommodated. Since policy making emerges from the interplay of personal and factional interests within the ruling coalition as well as from the demands and needs of supporting groups, it is difficult for the system to act decisively.

As long as it is simply a question of redistributing material and other goods within Italy, the inadequacies of the Italian system are more tolerable. But there are many decisions that governments must make that they do not control. The economic problems stemming from the increase in the price of oil are a good example of the kind of problem that must be confronted and dealt with rationally, but which the Italian system simply cannot easily digest. There are of course many other problems of this nature and they seem to be increasing because of the increasing importance of international balance of payments questions, questions that are in part more important because of increasing prosperity within Italy. Every leader within the party must interpret all actions in terms of how they affect his particular interests. Everyone must make this rather crude form of calculation if he is to remain a viable political force. The increasing importance of international questions and the difficulty of forecasting consequences make it appear to be safer to stick with the status quo; it is easier for political leaders to stay with the present situation than to risk venturing into the unknown. The fragmentation of the parties is paralleled by fragmentation throughout the bureaucratic mechanism and a fragmentation of decision making. There are many veto groups and blockage points within the system. It is very easy to do nothing and very difficult to accomplish anything.

The Italian political system lacks flexibility because it is a pluralistic system that is extremely highly mobilized. It shares with other pluralistic systems the existence of alternatives and the independence of intermediary organizations and associations between the individual and the state. But with a very high electoral turnout there is almost no change from one election to another. In most pluralistic systems there exists a reserve of floating voters who can be mobilized for particular elections when certain issues become sufficiently salient. And even if there is minimal switching from one party to another, the surge of voters into and out of the electorate makes possible a genuine shift. This is true even in political systems that rely upon proportional representation and multimember districts, even though the shifts are seemingly accentuated by single member districts.

In the Italian political system there are mechanisms for involving, at least at the level of voting, almost everyone in the society. The switch voters tend to be those who are most highly involved and knowledgeable, especially those from minor secular parties such as the Liberals, Republicans, Social Democrats and Socialists, who are apt to be amenable to the logic of an electoral campaign. The two largest parties, the Christian Democratic and Communist parties, and the MSI as well, mobilize individuals who are least likely to be swayed by the arguments of a particular campaign.[22] Consequently, changes in the fortunes of these two parties tend to reflect the evolution of Italian society and differential birth and death rates rather than the impact of particular electoral campaigns. In a society in which almost everyone is mobilized, a policy of minimal change and maximum exploitation of incremental and marginal differences seems to be the policy best calculated to lead to continued political success for the elites of the dominant parties.

Political Engineering

If we assume that a political system is more than a simple reflection of its social and economic environment, then politics itself must make an independent impact. And if politics makes a difference, we must face the classic question, "What is to be done?" What can be done in the way of changing political structures, legal norms, and behavioral patterns in order to alter the functioning of the system? Political engineering is engaged in to facilitate the achievement of desired ends, and of course, the problem always remains of specifying these desired ends.[23] There are undoubtedly as many desired end states for Italian politics as there are ideological positions, and perhaps far more than that. However, our concern is very modest and hence easy to specify. We want to know what are the most likely

22. Barnes and Giacomo Sani, "Partisan Change and the Italian Voter: Some Clues from the 1972 Election," paper prepared for delivery at the International Political Science Association Congress, Montreal, August, 1973.

23. On the concept of political engineering see Giovanni Sartori, "Political Development and Political Engineering," in *Public Policy*, vol. 17 (Cambridge: Cambridge University Press, 1968), pp. 261 ff.

possible changes in the short run rather than what is most desirable in the long run. Thus this discussion will be limited to proposals for change that are seriously considered by observers of the Italian political scene.

Predicting the future of a political system is a rash, unscientific, and probably futile undertaking. There are many variables involved, and some of them either do not yet exist or have not yet been identified, though their importance may seem obvious in retrospect. Furthermore, the interdependence of political systems means that Italian political evolution is greatly affected by events outside of Italy itself. Consequently, I am not predicting the political future of Italy. I am examining some proposals for change and am evaluating their likelihood of being implemented based upon previous Italian political experience.

As my criteria for evaluating what needs to be changed, I posit a modest set of goals. I will look at proposals for change that promise to bring about greater coherence in the determination of policy and greater effectiveness in its execution. Without attempting to specify what specific substantive changes should be facilitated by alterations in the structure, I would suggest that any changes should make it easier for the government to settle upon a coherent set of policies and to provide the government with an increased capacity for carrying out its policies.[24] I will briefly review several of the proposals being seriously considered in Italy, starting with those that would incorporate the largest number of changes.

The Authoritarian Solution. This solution has few advocates among students of Italian politics. I begin with it because it has been too widely discussed to be discounted. And there have been enough unexplained incidents involving the Italian army, police, and intelligence services, as well as hints of high governmental involvement in dubious intrigues, to make this a plausible solution. The extreme pluralism and high levels of mobilization of Italian society of which we have already spoken make any authoritarian solution less likely. But an authoritarian solution could be either of the right or the left. An authoritarian communist "take over" seems highly unlikely in

24. Joseph LaPalombara refers to the "crisis of government capacity": "Penetration: A Crisis of Government Capacity," in Leonard Binder et al., *Crises and Sequences in Political Development* (Princeton: Princeton University Press, 1971), pp. 205–32.

contemporary Italy. The anticommunism of the army and of the police render this an unlikely scenario. However, authoritarianism of a clerical, military, and bureaucratic nature would encounter far less institutional opposition than would that of the left.

In both cases it would be easier to take power than to exercise it. With over a quarter of the population giving its loyalty to a communist party and an additional one-sixth supporting other groups of the left, it would be extremely difficult to rule over the determined opposition of such a large minority. And it would be even more difficult for the left to rule against such institutions as the church and the state bureaucracy, not to mention the army, police, and other specialists in coercion.

The example of other authoritarian solutions in the Mediterranean, such as Spain, Portugal, Greece, and even Gaullist France, may appeal to many segments of Italian society. But time seems to be against these regimes, as the events of the 1970s in France, Portugal, Greece, and even Spain would seem to indicate. Furthermore, the Italian party that has most strongly advocated "strong" solutions to the country's problems—the MSI—is a very small party and almost certainly would not be the chief benefactor of an authoritarian solution.

Authoritarian restructuring of the political system would indeed be political engineering on the grand scale. However, since such restructuring would likely be carried out by the same forces that dominate the present political system, there is little reason to believe that an Italian authoritarian regime would function effectively. The authoritarianism most likely for Italy would probably, like the fascism of Mussolini, be a facade behind which traditional forces continued business as usual. It seems easier to make the trains run on time than to deliver the mail quickly. A strong state might reduce labor slowdowns and rationalize some practices, with a seemingly rapid improvement in public services as a result. But the efforts would probably be short-lived, unless drastic alterations were made in the structure and functioning of the government. And the most likely candidates for authoritarian rule are unlikely to do this.

Moreover, while not without blemishes, the record of the present republic on personal and civil liberties is quite good, and after the fascist experience these things are highly valued in Italy. Although an authoritarian solution always lurks in the background, I do not consider it to be the most likely for Italy.

Consociational Democracy. Many highly pluralist political systems have evolved patterns of mutual accommodation that have come to be labelled consociational democracy in the literature of political science.[25] This is a pattern under which elites mobilize masses within particular subcultures or social categories, accept the rules of the game, and bargain among themselves to protect their own subcultures and to further those mutual goals upon which they are able to secure agreement. Examples of consociational democracies include the Netherlands (though almost certainly more so in the past than at present), Austria, and Switzerland. It is often pointed out that the protagonists in these systems have at times in the past been extremely bitter enemies, and that it was the overriding need for national survival combined with the inability of any single segment or subculture to dominate the others that led to the growth of consociational democracy.

At first glance it is somewhat strange to think of Italy as a potential consociational democracy. However, as Pasquino points out, the German socialists of the nineteenth century were quite alienated, yet eventually they sought accommodation with the system. The Italian Communists might as easily follow the same path, so the possibility of Italy's evolving in the consociational direction cannot be rejected out of hand.[26] The PCI has been increasingly cooperative, and it has deeply involved itself in the political system at many levels and in many ways.[27] Furthermore, Communist party leaders are among the strongest defenders of republican institutions.

25. This literature is now quite extensive. For an excellent review see Daalder, "Consociational Democracy." The first full-length statement in English is Arend Lijphart's, *The Politics of Accommodation: Pluralism and Democracy in the Netherlands* (Berkeley: University of California Press, 1968). The theme was developed simultaneously by Gerhard Lehmbruch, *Proporzdemokratie: Politisches System und Politische Kultur in der Schweiz und in Oesterreich* (Tubingen: Mohr, 1967).

26. Gianfranco Pasquino, "Il sistema politico italiano tra neo-transformismo e democrazia consociativa," *Il Mulino* 22 (July–August 1973): pp. 549–66. The evolution of the SPD is analyzed in Guenther Roth, *The Social Democrats in Imperial Germany* (Totowa, N.J.: The Bedminster Press, 1963). For a somewhat similar analysis of Weimar Germany see Sartori, "European Political Parties: The Case of Polarized Pluralism," pp. 165–66.

27. On the PCI and its growing institutionalization in Italy see Giacomo Sani, "Mass Level Response to Party Strategy: The Italian Electorate and the Communist Party," in Donald L. M. Blackmer and Sidney Tarrow, eds., *Communism in Italy and France* (Princeton: Princeton University Press, 1974). "La strategia del PCI e l'elettorato italiano," *Rivista italiana di scienza politica* 3 (December 1973): 551–79; Sidney Tarrow, "Political Dualism and Italian Communism," *American Political Science Review* 61 (March 1967): 39–53; Franco Cazzola, "Consenso e opposizione nel parlamento

The fear is widely felt and sometimes articulated that the PCI in power would not adhere to the Republican constitution. However, it is the nature of consociational democracies that no single political force has a monopoly of power. It is not expected that the PCI would be in a majority position; consequently it would continue to favor the democratic republic. On the other hand, none of the existing consociational democracies has or has had a large Communist party. Moreover, while the clerical forces in Italy may not be in a majority, they have the mentality of the counterreformation as well as of a dominant elite and it is not certain that they could adjust easily to the genuine sharing of power that is involved in consociational democracy. If present trends continue, if there are no dramatic events to alter the evolution of the system, the consociational solution may be the most likely one for the long run. The trouble is that it is impossible to specify what the long run is. The PCI wants to enter the government now; most of the DC is opposed. The grand coalition, the "historic compromise," seems, at the moment of writing, an unlikely outcome. Moreover, many observers predict that this experiment would result in an authoritarian solution of left or right. The future remains open.

A Coalition of Left Parties. Closely related to the consociational democracy solution, which would involve a coalition of most of the parties and especially the large ones, is the possibility of a coalition of left parties. This is not presently a possibility, for all of the left parties together, from the PCI to the PRI, receive less than 46 percent of the vote. Moreover, opposition to the PCI is a major tenet of the PSDI, so even the present votes of the left are not available for a left parliamentary majority. But increase in votes for left parties might make a reform-oriented coalition irresistible if the PCI continues to develop in a direction that is nonthreatening to parliamentary democracy. A left coalition would be especially appealing if the DC were to fail to accommodate to a leftward shift in the electorate. Moreover, in that case a split in the DC would become more likely, as its left wing might despair of the future of that party and opt for

italiano: Il ruolo del PCI dalla I alla IV legislatura," *Rivista italiana di scienza politica* 2 (April 1972): 71–96; Robert Evans, *Coexistence: Communism and Its Practice in Bologna, 1945–1965* (Notre Dame: University of Notre Dame Press, 1967); and Donald L. M. Blackmer, *Unity in Diversity: Italian Communism and the World* (Cambridge: MIT Press, 1968). For a negative view of these trends see Domenico Fisichella, "L'alternativa rischiosa: considerazioni sul'difficile governo," *Rivista italiana di scienza politica* 2 (December, 1972): 589–613.

extensive reforms carried out on a pragmatic basis by a left coalition. But this coalition would be even more frightening to traditional groups than the consociational one, and hence would be more likely to generate a preemptive authoritarian response from the right.

A New National Electoral Law. Manipulation of electoral laws is an obvious form of political engineering. Few alterations can have the dramatic impact of a change in the method of elections. In particular, the shift from proportional representation (PR) to single member districts and vice versa is likely to produce substantial alteration in the distribution of seats in the legislature. The debate over PR has a long history. Hermens attributed many of the evils of the twentieth century to it and argued that single member district systems could have prevented the rise of National Socialism and Fascism.[28] Duverger has also posited a relationship between single-member districts and two-party systems.[29] Rae has dispassionately examined the consequences of electoral laws.[30] Many critics have pointed out the inadequacies of assuming a simple relationship between electoral systems and party systems. Many single-member district systems and seemingly two-party systems, including the British, Canadian, and American, have at various times had several political parties. And while the single-member district system may reduce the competition within a particular district to two sides, it does not and cannot assure that it is the same two parties that compete in all districts. Furthermore, there are many polities in which the existence of only two parties would put an intolerable burden on the system; many people think that this is the case with Italy, as a two-party system would almost certainly pit Christian Democrats against Communists. Few think that these two would function as Labourites and Conservatives in Britain or Republicans and Democrats in the United States. Would either give up power graciously to the other?

There are good reasons why so few people advocate changing the

28. F. A. Hermens, *Europe Between Democracy and Anarchy* (Notre Dame: University of Notre Dame Press, 1951); and *The Representative Republic* (Notre Dame: University of Notre Dame Press, 1958).

29. Maurice Duverger, *Political Parties* (London: Methuen, 1954). Criticisms of Duverger include Georges Lavau, *Partis politiques et réalitée sociales* (Paris: Colin, 1953); and Aaron Wildavsky, "A Methodological Critique of Duverger's *Political Parties*," reprinted in Harry Eckstein and David Apter, ed., *Comparative Politics* (New York: Free Press, 1963), pp. 368–750.

30. Douglas Rae, *The Political Consequences of Electoral Laws* (New Haven: Yale University Press, 1967).

Italian electoral system.[31] The main one stems from the equation of democracy with proportional representation in Italy and the historical reasons for this belief. The Fascists achieved a majority in the Chamber of Deputies in 1924 by providing that the party winning a plurality of at least 25 percent of popular votes would get two-thirds of the seats. When the Christian Democrats in 1953 pushed through the adoption of a revised electoral law that provided that a party or group of allied parties getting over 50 percent of the popular vote for the Chamber would get 65 percent of the seats, the Communist and other parties outside the coalition launched a vigorous campaign accusing the Christian Democrats of copying the "swindle" law of the Fascists. The center coalition of the DC, PSDI, and PLI received 49.85 percent of the votes—thus just under the required majority—and the previous electoral law was quietly restored.

The consequences of the single-member district system would depend on how the constituencies were drawn. Most alternatives would benefit the Christian Democrats. But while the PCI would continue to be heavily represented, because of its concentrated strength in the Red Belt of Central Italy and other areas, the small parties could be virtually eliminated in most versions of the single-member district system. But everything would depend on the particular plan adopted.

Apart from these pragmatic considerations, there are other reasons why a major change in the electoral law is unlikely. Regardless of its consequences, the system of proportional representation receives widespread support in Italy. It may be one of the few principles upon which there is substantial consensus. The democratic republic and the present electoral law seem to go together in the popular mind, hence electoral reform does not seem a viable alternative. As a result, what in theory seems to be a reasonable solution to the problem of a majority is simply not politically feasible.

Alter Party Electoral Law. In an earlier section of the essay we discussed the important role that factions play in the governing parties. Cazzola has noted that voters engaged in electoral engineering in the 1972 election by eliminating two parties, the PSIUP and the Manifesto,[32] and all of the minor parties that ran—with the exception of

31. An exception among academics is Fisichella, who favors single-member districts with a second ballot runoff, "L'alternativa rischiosa," p. 613.

32. Manifesto was led by several Communists who bolted the PCI and formed a separate bloc in the Chamber. Despite a vigorous campaign, Manifesto failed to obtain any seats in the 1972 election. See Samuel H. Barnes and Giacomo Sani, "The

the regional parties.[33] However, Cazzola also notes that there were "24 more or less official" factions within the seven major parties following the 1972 election and that in 1968 there had been eight parties with the same number of factions and in 1963 eight parties with a total of eight factions.[34] In other words, reducing the number of parties may not greatly facilitate decision making as long as the parties are themselves fragmented.

Factional strength within the parties is measured essentially in two ways. One is by the number of preference votes that factional leaders receive in the general election. Italian voters choose a party and may, depending upon the size of the constituency, list three or four particular names on the ballot. The number of seats a party gets depends upon the number of votes it gets, but the election of particular individuals on the list is determined by the number of preference votes each candidate receives. Hence a candidate has little chance of being elected unless he has an organization behind him or wide visibility within the electorate. These preference votes in turn are indicative of the strength that the particular individual has in the electorate, and consequently of the strengths of the factions with which they are associated. A second way in which factions are measured is in the voting for representation on internal party organs. Although the details differ from party to party, various forms of proportional representation assure representation on the party's central committee to most factions roughly proportional to their following within the party organization.

A debate in the *Rivista italiana di scienza politica* has indicated the general scope of the arguments over the internal electoral laws of the parties. The debate was set off by an article by Sartori that blamed the existence of a large number of factions on the use of proportional representation elections to the major organs of the parties.[35] Arguing that the normal politician feels it is "better to be a general of a small faction than a lieutenant of a large faction," Sartori hypothesizes that factions proliferate as long as there are positions to colonize, on the condition that the division of positions and spoils

New Politics and the Old Parties in Italy," forthcoming; and Alberto Spreafico, "Le elezioni politiche italiane del 7 Maggio 1972," *Rivista italiana di scienza politica* 2 (December 1972): 525–68.

33. Franco Cazzola, "Partiti, correnti, e voto di preferenza," *Rivista italiana di scienza politica* 2 (December 1972): p. 569.

34. Ibid., p. 570.

35. Giovanni Sartori, "Proporzionalismo, frazionismo, e crisi dei partiti," *Rivista italiana di scienza politica*, 1 (December 1971): 629–55.

is by faction.[36] While Sartori accepts that factions can be of principle as well as of opportunity, he believes that the proliferation of factions in Italian parties results largely from the desire for spoils. He proposes changes in intraparty elections to reduce the number of factions.

Passigli argues that proportional representation is the result rather than the cause of factions.[37] He says that many factions do reflect genuine ideological differences though he believes that ideologically based factions are declining in favor of clientelistic factions based upon the struggle for power. Furthermore, Passigli contends that the absence of governmental alternatives to the center coalition causes politicians to respond in terms of internal party requirements. "Change in an unchangeable coalition more and more assumes the characteristics of a change in factions, in which the clientelistic struggle for power and genuine ideological ferment are in various ways interrelated, even with a progressive decline of the latter and growing strength of the former."[38]

In a similar vein Lombardo argues that the lack of alternatives to the center-left coalition takes any genuine political content out of the factional struggle and reduces it to a competition over the spoils of office.[39] And Pasquino concludes that the introduction of PR in the parties merely exacerbates a previously existing condition.[40] He writes that "the slowness of the decision process of our political system and the compromised laws that often emerge from it derive substantially from the need of the party with a relative majority to conciliate all the interests that it must deal with internally" and that "if it makes it a party of factions, it also makes it a representative party whose social ramifications stand in the way of all movement."[41]

Few observers would challenge the statement that the leaders of the center-left coalition parties benefit from the factional system. As these parties are themselves coalitions of competing forces held together by spoils and tradition, it seems unlikely to expect dramatic

36. Ibid. Sartori distinguishes between "correnti" (currents of opinion), "fazioni" (factions), and "frazioni" (fractions), but these different usages are not relevant to our discussion.

37. Stefano Passigli, "Proporzionalismo, frazionismo, e crisi dei partiti: quid prior?" *Rivista italiana di scienza politica* 2 (April 1972): 125–38.

38. Ibid., p. 132.

39. Antonio Lombardo, "Dal proporzionalismo intrapartitico al fazionismo eterodiretto," *Rivista italiana di scienza politica* 2 (August 1972): 369–81.

40. Gianfranco Pasquino, "Le radici del frazionismo e il voto di preferenza," *Rivista italiana di scienza politica* 2 (August 1972): 353–68.

41. Ibid., p. 363.

changes in their behavior if such changes are not required for survival.

More of the Same. Political survival is undoubtedly the key phrase in this entire discussion. The present Italian constitutional system may not generate extreme and vocal support from the citizenry; indeed, precisely the opposite is true. But it is the system that divides Italians least. No other system is likely to receive anywhere near as much support. Political leaders will certainly continue to exploit the system in every way that they can. They are interested in survival. Leaders from all of the major parties have up until the present time always drawn back from steps that would be totally destructive.

Italy suffers in its public image from being among the poorest and least developed of the rich and advanced countries, rather than the richest and most progressive of the developing countries. The achievements of the republic are often overlooked. Italy often functions poorly, but it functions.

Crisis itself has a role in the functioning of the system, for it is only through crisis that the political elites are able to generate agreement on important programs.[42] Crisis is itself part of the decision-making process. Things that can be postponed will be postponed. When decisions must be made, they are generally made—or at least they have been up until the present.

All Italian elites are concerned with their own survival. Most are equally concerned with the survival of their party and the traditions that it represents. For most of them, that survival is linked to the survival of the present republic; so even if their primary loyalties may be to the intermediate structures rather than to the constitutional order itself, most elites would have little to gain from dramatic changes in the structure of the political system. Those in a position to make changes are the ones who benefit most from the present system. They are likely to favor only those minimum changes that will preserve it. Crises demonstrate to them that certain changes are necessary. Others are likely to be postponed.

Italian elites have been reasonably successful in dealing with domestic conflict, but there are aspects of politics that are outside of

---

42. Joseph LaPalombara pointed out in 1958 the importance of crisis for decision making: "Political Party Systems and Crisis Governments: French and Italian Contrasts," *Midwest Journal of Political Science* 2 (May 1958): 117–42.

their control, such as those stemming from international balance of payments difficulties. The resulting crises are the ones most likely to generate substantial internal change, for they are thrust upon the country in a manner that makes it impossible to ignore them. They will likely be confronted reluctantly and seemingly half-heartedly.

As long as the Christian Democrats and Communists continue to support the constitutional order it is likely to survive. What impact economic crises could have on their determination to do so cannot be predicted. Nor can the eventual impact of continued violence be anticipated. The electoral stability of the past two decades may erode as the patience of the Italian public wears thin. It is difficult to foresee who would benefit from electoral changes. And it is difficult to see who could bring them about, given the high levels of electoral mobilization and the near absence of a floating vote. While the present era must some day end, the current elites have demonstrated remarkable staying power.

Shortly after the war I heard Paul Tillich express the opinion that the dividing line separating eastern Germany under Russian control from the western sectors was a frontier cutting right through the German mind. At that time I was unable to agree with the eminent theologian and I still think he was mistaken. There was no such thing as an internal frontier in postwar Germany. Risking a generalization in a field in which all general judgments are perilous, one might rather maintain that the Germans at that time were prostrate, stunned by their own misery and horrified by the misdeeds of their former rulers. But they were united not only in consternation and despair, but also by the firm resolve to rebuild their shattered country not as a Fourth Reich but as a free and peaceful country. Their memory, it is true, was not stocked with historical experiences of liberty triumphant like that of their British or American contemporaries. But the privation of freedom inflicted upon them by National-Socialist rule had impressed upon their minds a fresh idea of its supreme value. Their scope of action was sadly limited. Yet they were allowed to express what they felt, to say what they thought. Enjoying the privilege of unhampered communication, long denied them by dictatorial censorship, they felt restored to the community of Western civilization.

Though compelled to repudiate their own immediate past, both history and tradition were still with them—they still knew themselves to be sons of the occidental world and heirs to its spiritual treasures. In the dark but not hopeless years that followed its defeat, Germany, morally and intellectually considered, was more one than it had been for a long time. The partition forced upon it by the victorious powers had no basis whatsoever in its internal structure, its past history, or its present mood. The victors, quite understandably, dreaded the idea of a Germany recovered to its former strength. Fear, coupled with a lack of farsighted wisdom, gave birth to the idea of a partitioning which was to reflect a divided world.

The division of Germany by the Potsdam Agreement was a surgical operation designed to produce two innocuous rump states. But even a rump state must live. Can a polity, artificially set up by foreign powers with no regard for the desires, fears, and hopes of its citizens ever become a living body politic, a state animated and unified by that spontaneous internal life which we associate with the idea of nationhood? This question lies at the bottom of the political life of the Federal Republic. For almost twenty years it could seem a merely academic problem, irrelevant to the actualities of day-to-day life. Today this is no longer true. Once again the silenced question presses for an answer. An otherwise solid political fabric, bursting with vitality and risen, by its own amazingly successful efforts, to the rank of one of the leading powers of the world, finds itself confronted with no lesser question than that of its own identity.

Many years ago, listening to the news report of a Viennese radio station, I was struck by the frequency and unaffected insouciance with which the reporter referred to Austria as "our country." I do not think I ever heard a German reporter calling the Federal Republic by that familiar name. Do we have a country which we can call ours with the careless complacency of bygone days under the German empire or the German republic? About the same time I discussed the word *fatherland* with a number of German boys and girls between fifteen and twenty. They did not care for that high-sounding term and bluntly refused to acknowledge the Federal Republic as their fatherland. Urged on by further questioning they finally showed some willingness to award this title to Bavaria. These were straws in the wind, and in recent years we paid too little attention to them. "*Was ist des Deutschen Vaterland?*"—this refrain of a popular song, once intuned with patriotic assurance, voicing a rhetorical rather than a real question, had taken on mocking overtones. The question has turned out to be a crucial one.

Eastern Germany, or rather that part of it which was to become the territory of the German Democratic Republic, was never put to the test of our searching query. The eastern tribes, the Prussians and Pomeranians, the Saxons and the Silesians, were not allowed to voice their opinion, let alone to choose their political status. Under Hitler they had learned to bow to the harsh commands of a totalitarian state, and enthusiastic affirmation of national greatness had been a duty incumbent on every *Volksgenosse* and jealously watched over by the secret police. Now, after the downfall of the Third Reich, the change they had to undergo seemed drastic and yet, in a sense, it was but slight. The new uniform held in readiness for them by their Russian masters was that of a satellite state and they slipped into it without visible effort. Released by one totalitarian state they found themselves in another one. Again there were the ample trappings of democracy and nothing of its substance. Again there were flags, brass bands, goose-stepping soldiers, the vociferous demonstrations of an officially ordered enthusiasm. The creed, it is true, was the exact antithesis of everything they had been expected to believe heretofore. But there was the same kind of sham grandeur and doctrinaire rigidity, a similar set of standard phrases, quickly grasped and easily remembered, eminently fit for setting highlights on official addresses and for being echoed by emotionalized crowds. Certainly this state, though not quite a state, did not lack an end and a purpose. Every child had to know about it. What a glorious thing for the little boy to play the Thalmann-pioneer, to feel like a budding folk-soldier, *Volkssoldat*, to learn about the wonders of Moscow, of the Kremlin especially and its Spaskij tower, the finest tower in the world, with the big red star on top, or to march through the streets chanting lustily "*Venceremos . . . venceremos*"—the battle song of the Chilean revolutionaries. No doubt about the dominant purpose in all phases of life—in the home and in public gatherings, in education and literature, in industrial and artistic production—and this purpose was a threefold one: wholehearted devotion to the victorious struggle of the working class for emancipation, unflinching dedication to the absolute and saving truth embodied in Marxism-Leninism, restless participation in the destruction of the capitalist system of exploitation and its criminal proponents. For the majority of Germans of all classes this was a novel truth indeed. Yet it showed a certain affinity to a native tradition and the new rulers made the most of it. In 1920 Oswald Spengler, historian and journalist, a Nietzschean admirer of violence and a German nationalist, published a book entitled *Preussentum und Sozialismus* driving home the idea of an unacknowledged kinship tying together the apparently hostile partners. On this basis, the author prophesied the marriage of Prussianism and Socialism to be accomplished in an heroic age that would put an end to the dishonesties of bourgeois morality. Meanwhile this crazy dream seemed to have come true, though in a most unheroic way. At any rate, the rump state called the German Democratic Republic became a living thing to the extent that life can be nurtured and tolerated by a totalitarian government. Thus our particular problem, the problem of prefabricated statehood, really concerns only the other half of Germany, the Federal Republic.

During the first two decades of the life of the new republic searching questions were silenced by its amazing success. The whole country hummed with reconstructive activities and very soon the expenses covering the urgently needed expansion and improvement of the road system by far exceeded the costs of rebuilding ruined houses, villages, and towns. The rapidity of the rise from helpless misery to the position of one of the leading industrial powers and purveyors of exportable goods was breath-taking, and so was the increase of consumer goods enjoyed in various degrees by all classes. Almost overnight, a society ridden by deprivation had been turned into a luxuriant society. Nowadays western Germany ranks with France and England as one of the foremost members of the North Atlantic Treaty Organization and as a representative of that European "third power" which tries to win a foothold between the two giant powers, the United States of America and Soviet Russia. Certainly the Federal Republic owes this success not solely to the indefatigable industry and ingenuity of its citizens. It was favored by circumstances. With remarkable flexibility America had shaken off the illusions of wartime and re-education days and had come to look upon Germany as a friend and ally. Thanks to the Marshall Plan, it was enabled to put its feet on the road toward wealth. So the Federal Republic became the chief beneficiary of the cold war. The disaster which had rent the German Reich into two fragments, artificially alienated from each other by ideological barriers, now carried a compensation: the solidarity of the Western world, in conjunction with the open market of a largely pacified global society, provided a fairly solid economic and political basis on which the new republic was able to thrive. Did the Atlantic world supply also a moral basis?

No body politic can live and grow without a purpose firmly rooted in the minds of its citizens. Generally this purpose is the gift of tradition handed down from generation to generation along with fundamental political institutions. Certainly the Federal Republic, though deprived of the benefits of a continuous tradition, did not lack a dominant purpose justifying its existence in the eyes both of its citizens and the contemporary world. Asked about the nature of this purpose, one might venture the reply that itself, the existence of a sovereign German state, was also its purpose, conceived at the moment of the annihilation of the Reich and all its institutions. Implied in the very existence of this new polity there was a collective self-affirmation in the face of total destruction. When, with the approval of the victorious Allies, it came into being in 1949, it was the mere shadow of a real state, but also the vessel of a fervent hope. The great desire which animated the new state was to attain to full-grown reality, to cast off the stupor of defeat, to restore order, to give bread and work to its citizens, to rebuild and develop its homes, towns, factories, to recover wealth and strength. Of course the same desire is alive in all peoples and all commonwealths. But for the Germans of those postwar years it reached that desperate intensity which is born at the brink of destruction. There was no need for the government to appeal to the citizens for cooperation. Industry became a popular passion. The generation which had lived through the suffering and privations of the war, climaxed by the destruction of the German cities in the air raids of 1944 and 1945—this same generation put forth the enormous effort required for the rebuilding of their shattered lives. Nothing succeeds like success. Problems which at first seemed insoluble were not only solved, but their solution contributed to an unexpected triumph. The vindictive dismantling of industrial plants after the cessation of hostilities seemed to deal a mortal blow to production. In fact, it freed it from the fetters of antiquated machinery. Similarly the problem of refugees from the eastern provinces: what was to be done with all those uprooted people from Pomerania and Mecklenburg, from Brandenburg and Silesia, from eastern and western Prussia? Eventually these fugitives proved the hardest working of all, setting the pace for the great reconstructive achievement. In short there was no failure of inspiration in the young republic. It was propelled by a mighty impulse. The philosophy which directed this effort and bestowed meaning on it might be summed up in the word *reconstruction*. At the beginning of the sixties the reconstruction was well-nigh completed. This moment of saturation coincided with a change of climate in international life. People all over the world came to feel that the postwar era had come to an end. A change of language and of tactics had occurred: the cold war was discredited and detente became the generally accepted watchword. For the Federal Republic the purpose of its existence, assumed to be clear, effective, and unquestionable, turned out to be an open question. The attempts at an answer revealed the disturbing fact that the unanimity which so far had prevailed amidst the strife of opinions and parties was no longer to be counted upon. The split that opened reached down to the foundations. Was the partition, which had been externally imposed, on the point of becoming an internal division?

Reconstruction was the purpose of political life in the early republic. But there was a dynamic and, at the same time, illusory element in its reconstructive political purpose. A consummate reconstruction was unthinkable without re-union. Adenauer's policy was conceived as basically a German policy, not merely the policy of the western republic. The idea of a Germany reunited in freedom—with freedom ranking above unity—was, and still is, anchored in the basic law. It defined the Federal Republic of Germany as a democratic and social polity, but also as a merely vicarious state: it had to vanish from the earth with the attainment of its supreme political goal. In point of fact, this was strictly speaking no political goal at all, but rather a deeply cherished though ineffectual hope. The non-recognition of the DDR was a refrainment from action rather than a political act. Otherwise no steps were to be conceived that might even remotely suggest a progress toward the proclaimed goal. The dreamlike quality of the idea of re-union, obvious from the start, turned still paler as time went on, while it continued to infect German political thought with an element of self-contradiction. The political partnership in the global community of nations demanded recognition of the status quo which, thanks to Soviet propaganda, had taken on the appearance of some sort of sanctity: it alone, maintained as it was by the "balance of terror," seemed to protect mankind against the threat of total destruction by a third world war fought with atomic weapons. Yet precisely this status quo implied the denial of the right of the Germans to unite. Nothing, absolutely nothing, was done or could be done toward giving substance to an idea which, though naturally dear to the Germans, was at variance with an established global order. Direct political action serving the purpose of re-union was out of the question, a moral and intellectual preparation for it hardly imaginable. At any rate, it was not forthcoming, and it would have been unreasonable indeed to expect schools to educate their pupils in view of their future citizenship in a country no longer or not yet in existence. So the youngsters had to put up with what existed—the Federal Republic of Germany. They accepted it—they had no choice. But they did not succeed in loving it and calling it fatherland. Even talking about "our country" sounded odd in their ears—and who could blame them? Shortly after the war, someone suggested to Richarda Huch the idea of producing a German counterpart to Selma Lagerlof's *Nils Holgersson's Voyage with the Wild Geese*—a collection of folk tales from all German regions and provinces, reaching from East Prussia down to Suebia, from Silesia to the Rhineland, a literary document of a Germany peacefully united by its imaginative creativity in a world of myths. But Richarda Huch died and there was nobody to take up the project. Literature, it is true, turned more and more to policy. But the standard by which the progressive intellectuals measured political reality—the reality of the Federal Republic and of the occidental world in its entirety—was furnished by an eschatological vision rather than by political experience, and a keen imaginative interest in the drama of revolution was the link, tying this type of thought to the actual drama of history. No help was to be expected from this quarter. On the whole, the surrender of literature to political radicalism as typified by Magnus Enzensberger's periodical *Kursbuch* resulted in sterility.

We return to our question: did the integration of western Germany into the community of the occidental nations help the Germans to develop a political philosophy adequate to the predicament of their actual status and opening a prospect for future generations? Frenchmen, Englishmen, and Americans, according to the solemn proclamations of their leaders, had fought the Second World War in defense of freedom against National Socialist totalitarianism. From the victorious crusaders for the cause of liberty one might have expected a great effort toward crowning the hard-won military victory by a moral victory—by the conversion of their former enemy to their own inspiring creed. Letting the loser participate once more in the cultural and political heirloom of the Occident—this would have been an act of generosity as well as of self-affirmative prudence. In point of fact, there were some high-ranking Americans in the Military Government, men like John McCloy and George N. Shuster, who were fully responsive to the demands of the hour. In addition the numerous visitors from and to the United States, encouraged and assisted by governmental grants, did much in furthering a moral and intellectual rapprochement. But the great effort which might have been hoped for did not and could not occur. The reintegration of western Germany into the Western world failed to become a political inspiration to the Germans carrying their plans and hopes beyond the somewhat barren purpose of restoration and giving nourishment to the starved political imagination of the young generation. There is more than one reason to account for this failure.

In the first place the cessation of hostilities in April, 1945, did not really mark the end of the war. The great conflagration was extinguished but the fire continued to smoulder, breaking forth again and again at various times in various places, first in Korea, then in Vietnam, then on American soil under the form of civil strife initiated by the Civil Rights movement, and further disturbances loomed up in the East. Waves of strikes disrupted economic and political life in Italy and in England. Social peace was in jeopardy throughout the world which dared to call itself free and the operation of parliamentary rule was severely hampered by the aspirations of labor unions even in the country where the venerable mother of parliament resided. A universal crisis of democracy seemed to be afoot. Evidently, this was not the hour for the Western democrat to teach lessons in the democratic way of life to the newcomer from central Europe. In fact this newcomer, refusing to let himself be dragged into the spreading turbulence, set a model by maintaining a useful though limited consensus of labor and government. For two decades the Federal Republic might pride itself on making up for its lack of democratic tradition by a newly acquired spirit of conciliatory patience and political tolerance. The three important parties—the alliance of two Christian Union parties, the Social Democrats and the Free Democrats—disagreed on a number of issues. But their disagreements were largely concerned with nuances of attitude and differences of procedure rather than principles. The area of concord was larger than that of dissent.

Western Germany was a field for missionary action in the service of the democratic faith—this was out of the question for still another reason. Deeds preached more effectively than words, and the deeds which counted were, from the German point of view, in the first place those fateful decisions reached by Stalin, Roosevelt, and Churchill at Yalta and Teheran and confirmed by the Potsdam Agreement, all of them bearing the stamp of Stalin's ruthless will to power. Cynically disregarding the basic law of international policy they ran counter to democratic philosophy and tradition. It became obvious that, in the last analysis Soviet Russia alone had won the war—a Russia prepared to make the most of her victory. And the Nuremberg Court was conceived in the same spirit. The victors, Americans and Russians side by side, sat in judgment over the defeated enemy—a travesty of justice. Democracy, sheltered by tradition, survived in its old abodes, but certainly not in the role of the victor. Its shield was tarnished, its self-assurance shaken, its radiance gone. The Atlantic world which received into its fold a Germany cut in half and yet revived, was itself a patient rather than a nurse. Se we need not be surprised by the fact that the political disease, which the western powers contracted in the sixties and which signalized the termination of the postwar era, speedily infected the Federal Republic and wrought ravages in some respects worse than elsewhere. Here it produced a poisoned political atmosphere, a new tenseness and a novel division of minds. As yet its consequences cannot be safely gauged. They may be grave, eventually giving a new direction to German policy. But it may also be true that the shock of novelty tempts us into exaggerating its significance. Instead of prognosticating we try to see things as they are— in balance, with the main questions left open, the outcome uncertain.

Not long ago, throughout the postwar period, the prevalent attitude of people in the Federal Republic had been one of acceptance slightly tinged with resignation—acceptance of the republic as a viable method for solving the most pressing of our political problems, acceptance of our alliances as a reasonable safeguard against war, acceptance also of the social and economic conditions granting a high standard of living to all classes and keeping the difference of wealth within the bounds of social justice. In short, there was an almost general consent on the chief issues of political life, and favored by this popular mood the two major parties, the Christian Union parties and the Social Democrats, were able to form a coalition government, leaving the opposition to a small minority, the Free Liberals (FDP). This happened in 1966. But in subsequent years the mood changed, and this change is still in progress. There was a shift from acceptance to nonacceptance or even to rejection, from acquiescence to critical irritation, from the desire to keep things going as before to the impatient insistence on turning over a new leaf. The turn came by leaps and bounds. People, that is to say some people and a good many of them, changed their minds overnight. The abruptness of conversion was painfully reminiscent of the multitudes that had flocked around the swastika in the years of Hitler's rise to power. Into the temperate climate of opinion, in which alone the democratic dialogue can achieve agreement, a whiff of radicalism blew and threatened to grow into a gale.

The transformation was by no means universal. A cleavage of opinion opened and families, friendships, schools, and political parties broke up under the impact of dissent. On the one hand there were those who called themselves "progressives," the vessels of the new pioneering spirit, ardent lovers of a future perfect society and impatient with the shortcomings of bourgeois culture, an active minority under the leadership of intellectuals and composed largely of young people of all classes, but especially of the sons and daughters of wealthy and educated parents. The majority opposed to this movement, its doctrines and tendencies is not to be described by the term conservative, let alone reactionary, nor by any other predicate indicative of a uniform conviction. The very word *opposition* is unfit to denote their attitude. They are simply nonparticipants, perplexed and disturbed spectators, vacillating between sympathetic astonishment and angry disapproval, endowed, for one reason or the other, with immunity from ideological infection. Literature is almost entirely on the "progressive" side, and the few spokesmen of the silent resistance find it hard to gain a hearing. Meanwhile the cleft, though not identical with the traditional party strife, has become so marked that mutual understanding and conciliatory debate are rendered difficult if not hopeless. People speak two different languages and one may wonder whether Germany is fated to suffer another division, this time a self-inflicted one, a breakup of that fundamental consensus, without which the body politic is doomed to ailment. The question of purpose, long kept in abeyance by the pressing problems of day-by-day policy, began to stare politicians in the face.

The first signal of impending change came soon after the formation of a "big coalition government" in 1966 with the appearance of an "extraparliamentary opposition" (APO). A vociferous group of intellectuals and radical politicians, not content with voicing a just dissatisfaction over the weakness of the parliamentary opposition, rejected the principle of parliamentary opposition, rejected the principle of parliamentary government as such, which to them was nothing but a tool of capitalist oppression. But the voice of this group was soon drowned by the noise and hubbub of a mightier and even more vocal movement, starting in the Free University of Berlin in 1967 and reaching a first climax in 1968: the New Left, an international rebellion of youth without precedent in ancient or modern history. Its origins were in England and America, especially in the University of California at Berkeley, where it learned its first lessons from the Civil Rights movement, and it was carried across the ocean by self-appointed messengers, in the first place by three assistants of the Free University, who had held scholarships in American universities. By now the movement has ebbed. Only rivulets of the powerful stream are left. But its success surpassed all expectations—a largely posthumous success. Far worse than the disruption of academic life and work by violent demonstrations in the early years of the upheaval was the destructive university legislation worked out by submissive parliaments and now being carried into execution: a lamentable mixture of outright revolutionary ideas with muddled conceptions of reform. And this legislation, decided upon under the pressure of a current of public opinion, is indirectly an outcome of the rebellion. For this is the real triumph of the youthful rebels: their revolutionary ideas, couched in a vocabulary puzzling in its mysterious novelty, rousing by the high promises it carried and, at the same time, inspiring confidence by its borrowings from democratic speech, have, thanks to sympathetic mass media, percolated down to the more sophisticated of the "men in the street," among them the representatives of the various Länder parliaments and of the Bundestag. Measured by its own standards the movement was a failure. The impassioned adolescents marched and shouted and demonstrated, arranged sit-ins and go-ins, stormed presidential offices, engaged in endless debates, sang *Wacht auf, Verdammte dieser Erde*, hurled eggs at lecturing professors and erected barricades. But the revolution, which they heralded, did not occur. When darkness fell after a day's hot revolutionary work everyone returned home for supper. What started as a revolutionary drama turned out to be a mere psychodrama. Yet in a sense this failure was a successful one. It succeeded in creating a new political atmosphere, it modified political thought and language to such an extent that one may speak of the emergence of a newfangled idiom. Eventually the shift in public opinion had a profound effect on the life of the political parties and thereby on the functioning of government and the processes of political decision. All parties were affected, but the strongest party, the Social Democrats, more than the others. The cleft in opinion threatened to disrupt party unity by a radicalization of the left wing.

The paradox of the "successful failure" applies to the fate of the New Left as a movement as well as to its doctrinal message. It is the attempt at a revival of Marx as the greatest political philosopher of the modern age, or even of all times. In him, so the leaders of the movement proclaim, the inspiring purpose of political action and the solution of the riddle of our time is to be found. However, there is an absurdity in the endeavor to raise Marx to the position of a supreme authority. Nothing could be more foreign to Marx himself, to the letter as well as to the spirit of his work, than his enthronement by neo-Marxism. Marxism as conceived by Marx stems from three different sources, each contributing an element of the Marxian synthesis. There is, in the first place, the eschatological vision which generally sustains socialist faith. Man is good, and once he has freed himself from the fetters history has forged for him, especially from the curse of private property, his essential goodness will flower into the perfect society, an earthly paradise. As a writer, Marx is content with brief hints at this ultimate consummation. Yet its anticipation is the cornerstone of his theoretical edifice. In the second place, Marx, following in the footsteps of Adam Smith and David Ricardo, developed an analysis of socioeconomic life in the capitalist era. This research resulted in *Das Kapital*, a fragmentary work of unsurpassed grandeur. These two heterogeneous elements are welded into an imposing doctrinal unity by a third element—by dialectic, that is to say by the Hegelian logic, onesidedly interpreted as the basis of a philosophy of history. The greatness and above all the effectiveness of Marx depended on this third ingredient. As a philosopher of history, he rose to the rank of a tribune of the people and the prophet of socialist revolution. For his visionary interpretation of world history bestowed upon the proletariat the role of the subject of the final revolution and the savior of mankind.

This historical vision, however, the chief source of Marxist inspiration, is also the cause of the caducity of Marxism. Marx regarded himself as a man of science whose theory, fruit of painstaking labor, was to stand the test of experience. Moreover, he felt he had demonstrated with scientific exactness the necessity of a development which inevitably would result in world revolution, in the destruction of capitalist society, the abolition of private property, the dictatorship of the proletariat and subsequently in the withering away of the state and the establishment of the true Society of Man, liberated from the triple curse of property, rulership, and labor. But here metaphysical fantasy slipped into the place of sound reasoning and the product was not philosophy but an ideology. Marxist thought, based as it is on an interpretation of history, is essentially prognosis. But real history was soon found out not to move along the path prescribed to it by the economist philosopher: it gave the lie to all his predictions. His idea of historical dialectics inexorably forging ahead like a giant mechanism blinded him to the self-corrective power of parliamentary democracy. In his time his error was a highly effective one: it provided the struggling class of working men with a mighty, though two-edged, weapon. But the attempt to revive his doctrine as a message of salvation for our time is nothing less than an absurdity. And precisely this absurdity was embraced by the New Left.

In order to adapt the obsolete doctrine to modern conditions the Neo-Marxists, by an act of grand simplification, had to do away with the antiquated rationality of the doctrinal system. Mao and the philosophizing guerilla fighters of North Africa and Central America had pointed out the direction. The road from indignation to action was shortened: the terrestrial paradise had to be torn down from heaven by violence. Millenarianism, in the original teaching of Marx hidden under the garb of science and logic, showed its true face.

The dismissal of reason in favor of irrational eschatology did not, however, imply sheer emotionalism. In a somewhat amateurish way the rebels restated Marx's searching critique of modern capitalism, substituting contemporary fictions for the realities which Marx had been dealing with but which were no longer there. It was difficult to resuscitate the language of class struggle in the absence of an impoverished, exploited and rebellious class. So they replaced the nonexistent proletarian by themselves, the allegedly repressed students, by the inmates of prisons and lunacy asylums and by the peoples of underdeveloped countries. Moreover, they undergirded their critique of the social-economic system by a withering condemnation of present-day culture, its history and all its works. The critical tools were provided by the members of the Frankfurt School of Critical Sociology who in turn borrowed arguments from Nietzsche, Freud, and Heidegger. Max Horkheimer, the founder of that school, asserted that philosophy as produced by the oppressive aristocratic society of ancient Greece could not possibly be true—away with traditional philosophy! The judgment passed upon Christianity by Marx and Nietzsche was remembered and approved also by an increasing number of theologians both Protestant and Catholic. In their minds, Christian eschatology and Marxist eschatology flowed together. "The eschatological future of the kingdom of God is mutually bound up (*wechselseiting verbunden*) with the future of the free man in a free world"—so wrote Jürgen Moltmann, Professor of Evangelical Theology at the University of Tübingen![1] God-is-dead theologians preached revolutionary violence as the timely materialization of Christian charity.

1. *Christentum als Religion der Freiheit* in: *Schöpfertum und Freiheit in einer humanen Gesellschaft*, Marienbader Protokolle, 1969, p. 153.

Modern society is repressive from top to bottom and unworthy of man—this global indictment is firmly rooted in the progressive mind. It goes without saying that anyone animated by this conviction cannot possibly be interested in introducing this or that improvement, in reforming this or that institution: everything has to be turned upside down. And every meaningful activity, political, educational, or cultural, must be guided by the principle of emancipation. Implied by this notion is—to put it pointedly and in the Marxist idiom—the petit bourgeois anarchist's concept of freedom.

"Progressiveness" has grown into a powerful movement. But the majority of the thousands and thousands who in one way or another participate in it or are influenced by it are far from being Marxists or Neo-Marxists. Most of them have only a dim idea of Communist doctrine and might reject it if they knew more about it. The fact, however, is that the ideological brew can be swallowed in small doses and in various forms of dilution. The receptacles in which the drink is passing round from hand to hand or rather from mouth to mouth are words. Words hardly ever used before or entirely new ones attain prominence in political discourse and everyday speech, and they all serve the same purpose of which the speakers themselves are generally unaware. They instill particles of the ideological faith and recommend attitudes and actions in conformity with it. The wholly adapted and truly modern person, the embodiment of the "progressive man," requires a language of his own: the Neo-Marxist propagandist puts the appropriate words into his mouth. There is a long list of which a few samples may suffice. Pride of place belongs, of course, to "emancipation" and "emancipatory." Also science and scholarship have to be emancipatory in order to be worth our while. Implied is the repressiveness of all our institutions which, in view of their present status, are referred to as "the establishment." The overtones of this word express the contemptuous superiority of the speaker who, to his dismay, finds himself not in a fascist but in a "fascistoid" society. The inherent repressiveness of its structure is also suggested by the term *system* which invariably associates with the word *overcoming*. "Overcoming the system," *Systemüberwindung*, is almost synonymous with emancipation. It is particularly convenient for the Young Socialists, Jusos, at the left wing of the Social Democratic Party. It may, but need not mean, revolution—it admits of a harmless interpretation as meaning "system-overcoming reforms," *systemüberwindende Reformen*. Of course, you cannot feel at home under the regime of "repressive tolerance" as adopted by the Western fascistoid democracies—you must suffer the fate of "alienation," taking comfort, however, by looking around upon this present world of ours. Then your ideological guide will inform you in an offhand way (for him, all that goes without saying) that you are living in the years of "late capitalism," *Spätkapitalismus*, a word which leaves you in no doubt as to the approaching demise of the "establishment" or "the system." Meanwhile, it is incumbent upon you to speed up the coming of the New Society by furthering all acts of "democratization" in the service of the emergent "participatory democracy" in which, at long last, everybody will have a vote on everything which, even though remotely, is of concern to him.

The intrusion of words loaded with ideological significance produces a mental fog which blurs the outlines of reality. Soviet Russia ceases to be the Russia of Lenin, Stalin, and Breshnev, and the policy of détente deteriorates into a unilateral attempt at fraternization with Communism. The university ceases to be a school but appears as a miniature body politic composed of three or four groups (professors, assistants, students, personnel) propelled by divergent group interests. Reform ceases to be an activity directed toward the better functioning of a factory, a firm, or an institution. Instead it comes to be regarded as a move towards a more democratic distribution of authority. The main issue is no longer "how does it work?" but "who controls it?" It would be difficult for any statesman to steer the ship of a parliamentary democracy through that dense a mist of agitated confusion, and in fact the havoc wrought is considerable. The university had to bear the brunt of the day and it came down as a first victim. It will take not years but decades to repair the damage done to it and to the entire educational system. In this field the urgently needed reform can only begin after the ideological haze has been blown away. But the immediate danger to the Federal Republic lies elsewhere. The philosophy of the New Left has pushed its way into the Bundestag, represented there by the left wing of the Social Democrats, and its representation in the party organization is even stronger than in the parliaments. The Young Socialists, Jusos, working in close association with the Young Liberals, Judos, are, in body or else in spirit, identical with the students who started the university upheavals in 1968. Evidently their principles are at variance with the declared program of the Social Democratic party. But for tactical reasons they move cautiously and dissimulate their revolutionary intent. Though growing in number and influence they are still far from controlling the party. Should they ever attain to leadership they certainly would set an end both to the democratic order of the Federal Republic and to her Western alliances. So there is reason for concern though not for alarm.

Still we are puzzled as to the lessons to be drawn from the events we have surveyed. Shall we conclude that the uproar among the young people of almost all nations was nothing but tomfoolery, a giant prank practiced by irresponsible youngsters upon the generation of their parents? There may be an element of truth in crude statements of this sort and we may even add the suspicion that symptoms of insanity are characteristic of the movement and its leaders. But these remarks do not really answer our question. There are, I believe, good reasons for the indignant protest, and by paying some attention to them we may learn through it, though not from it. We have no right to shrug our shoulders and pass along as though nothing had happened. We must take the young rebels seriously, though the obsolete ideas they dote on are not worth being taken seriously. Wisdom is not to be expected from youth: "Woe to the city whose prince is a child." But alive in them, unknown to themselves, is an element of wisdom which the older people, in their pride of adult reasonableness, are too ready to lull into sleep. There must be something in our lives, also in our political life, which is worthy and able to enlist not only our approval but our wholehearted and enthusiastic adherence. No body politic can live without such a regnant purpose. Undoubtedly the modern democratic state is informed by a purpose of this nature: the maintenance of freedom in the modern industrial mass society—of a freedom which implies fulfilment for everyone here on earth and in the life hereafter—is purpose enough. But the people of the Occident may have been on the point of consigning it to oblivion or even to disrespect. And this may have been particularly true of the country which could least afford to indulge in the luxury of democratic lightheartedness—the Federal Republic of Germany— the rump state artificially put together out of the remnants of the former Reich. So the young people, pampered by the ease of life amidst a newly acquired wealth, felt that much was offered but not the essential thing: the purpose for which they could live or, if this should be ordained, to die. So the riches granted by a high living standard meant spiritual starvation to them. For this is youth's elementary wisdom: not to be able to live without something to live for. Since the affirmation they unconsciously yearned for was withheld, they fell in love with a grand negation. Not the youth is in the dock. Their rejection of our world is a judgment, though we trust not a final one, on ourselves.

Francis Canavan, s.j. • The Prospects for a United Ireland

Ireland in recent years has been illuminated on American television screens by the rocket's red glare and bombs bursting, not in the air to be sure, but in the corner pub and outside the local station of the Royal Ulster Constabulary. Yet democracy is a working system in the greater part of Ireland and, leaving aside for the moment the intractable problem of the North, the prospects for constitutional government in Ireland are good. Appearances to the contrary, violence is not the ordinary method of Irish politics.

It is true that Irish independence from Great Britain was won by force in the prototype of twentieth-century guerrilla wars. It was immediately followed, in 1922–23, by a bitter civil war between those who accepted and those who rejected the Anglo-Irish Treaty. This was the document that established an Irish Free State having dominion status within the British Empire and including twenty-six of Ireland's thirty-two counties. Unyielding devotion to an idealized thirty-two-county republic, to be wrested from the British oppressor by physical force, persists to this day in the IRA, the illegal Irish Republican Army. There is and has long been a small but significant part of the Irish people who believe that the freedom and unity of Ireland can be achieved only by force, and that force can accomplish everything they dream of. Violence, then, is certainly part of the Irish political tradition.

But in southern Ireland the more important fact is that the bulk of the anti-Treaty forces, defeated in the Civil War, entered constitutional politics in 1926 under the name of Fianna Fail. Led by Eamon de Valera, they became the country's normal governing party, and proceeded to dismantle the Treaty settlement with Britain and to gain by constitutional means most of what they had fought for—except, of course, the missing six counties of Northern Ireland. (Ironically, it was left to their pro-Treaty opponents, now organized as the Fine Gael party, to make the formal change of the state's name to the Republic of Ireland in 1949.) Party politics in the republic today assume, and do not contest, the legitimacy of the constitutional regime. Political murder is at present unhappily a daily fact of life in the

North, but a rare occurrence in the republic, where the level of even nonpolitical crimes of violence is low among European countries. The overwhelming majority of the republic's people, despite a sentimental reluctance to condemn the IRA, take constitutional democracy for granted. Elections take place regularly and peacefully; governments succeed each other in orderly fashion. Only Fianna Fail has ever won a majority of seats in the national parliament, Dail Eireann. But Fine Gael is occasionally able to form a government in coalition with the small but enduring Labour party, and such a coalition is, in fact, in power at the moment of writing. The proportional representation scheme used in elections tends to encourage, and in past decades produced, a multiplicity of parties. But, as Maurice Manning puts it, Irish political life since 1957 has "settled into being a three-party system made up of one dominant 'majority-bent' party, one stable large minority party (with majority aspirations) and one stable small minority party."

He immediately adds: "It is not certain how long this pattern will continue and it is quite possible that one of the repercussions of the Northern crisis will be a return to the fragmentation and multi-partyism of earlier years."[1] It is hard, however, to foresee any other crisis which would produce this effect, much less threaten the stability of the state. Ireland is a steadily modernizing country and will face problems—e.g., the end of an era of economic growth—that, as in any other modern Western state, may put severe strains on her political and constitutional system. But there is no perceptible reason to believe that her system is less able to cope with them than that of other Western democracies.

If the Northern crisis should result, as one day it may, in a united Ireland including all of the island's thirty-two counties, Irish politics would of course undergo a notable, but not a radical change. A new constitution would probably be necessary and is already being advocated by certain individuals. But it would still be the constitution of a parliamentary democracy. The Irish nationalists who founded the Free State inherited a liberal tradition that emphasized popular representation from their former allies in the Westminister Parliament, the Liberal party. The Protestants of Northern Ireland inherited a Tory tradition that emphasized governmental decision-making power. But one may assume that a Northern Protestant minority in

1. *Irish Political Parties: An Introduction* (Dublin: Gill & Macmillan, 1972), p. 113.

an Irish republic would find new merit in the liberal tradition and in a stress on representing all the people.

To assuage the fears of Northern Protestants, the guarantees of fundamental rights that exist in the present constitution[2] would probably be made more specific and rigid. The Irish Supreme Court in recent years has begun to exercise its power of judicial review more vigorously and to claim the function of finding specific and enforceable rights in such general constitutional phrases as "the personal rights of the citizen" (Art. 40, sect. 3, 1) and "inalienable and imprescriptible rights [of the family], antecedent and superior to all positive law" (Art. 41, sect. 1). This process would surely continue and grow stronger in a united Ireland.

Ireland, once united, might evolve into a biconfessional state on the model, say, of Lebanon, with political parties based on religious denominations. But this is unlikely; for one thing, the very coming into existence of the new state would probably be contingent on the lessening of religious tensions in the North. It is more likely that socioeconomic issues, formerly subordinated in the North to sectarian and constitutional issues, would come to the fore and provide the ordinary stuff of politics. One might anticipate, for example, a stronger Labour party drawing on both the Catholic and the Protestant working classes.

Roman Catholics are about 95 percent of the population in the Irish Republic as it now exists, and would be roughly 75 percent in a united Ireland. Northern Protestants fear that they would become a helpless minority in such a situation. But a full quarter of the population includes too many votes for the politicians to ignore in an open democratic society, particularly in one that uses proportional representation in its elections. The Protestant vote in an all-Ireland republic would necessarily be an influential one.

Indeed, one wonders whether Irish Catholics or Irish nationalists—who are often the same people, of course—have thought through what achieving the goal of a united Ireland would entail. A political society covering the whole island would be a pluralist and more secular society. The acids of modernity are at work in Ireland in any case, and the era of mass Catholicism—or mass Christianity, for that matter—is coming to an end. The unification of the country would hasten the process. It would also force a redefinition of the meaning of being

2. On these, see J. M. Kelly, *Fundamental Rights in the Irish Law and Constitution*, 2d ed., (Dublin: Allen Figgis & Co., 1967).

Irish. Whatever it would mean, it could no longer include the insistence on the Gaelic culture, the Irish language, the Fenian political tradition and the celebration of the heroes of the 1916 Easter uprising which have formed so large a part of Irish nationalism until now.

But will there ever be a united Ireland? That depends on the outcome of the crisis in the North, and that outcome is, as they say in these parts, dicey. This paper is being written in Dublin in the spring of 1974. It must now address itself to a situation so fluid that even the best-informed Irishmen hesitate to make predictions about it. Moreover, events will outrun anything said here before it gets into print. But some comments, offered with much less confidence than their tone perhaps suggests, may be ventured.

First, the Northern Protestants regard themselves as a people apart —British, yet neither English nor Scottish nor Welsh—and would regard incorporation into the republic as a loss of communal identity. Historically, they have always been a distinct ethnic and religious group, beleaguered settlers among feared and despised natives. The North of Ireland happens to have been the last part of the country to be conquered by the English, in the closing years of the reign of Queen Elizabeth. Her successor, the Scottish king who became James I of England, sought to consolidate the conquest by the Plantation of Ulster in the early years of the seventeenth century. British Protestant colonists, many of them Scottish Presbyterians, were brought in to settle on confiscated lands. Naturally, the "planters" took the best land and either drove the native Irish Catholics out of the province or shoved them aside into Ulster's hills and bogs. To this day, a map of the distribution of land by quality coincides closely with a map of the distribution of population by religion.

Ireland had often before managed to absorb her conquerors, making them, in the medieval phrase, more Irish than the Irish themselves. But, the Reformation having intervened, the religious division prevented intermarriage and the gradual blurring of differences. Two antagonistic communities persisted side by side, with their ethnic, cultural, historical, and economic differences summed up in and expressed through their religious identifications.

When home rule for Ireland was proposed in the British Parliament in the late nineteenth century, the Ulster Protestants reacted violently against it with the slogan, "Home Rule is Rome Rule." They still point to the Irish Republic's strict laws on divorce and contraception as evidence of the Catholic domination that they will not accept. But it is hard to believe that the Battle of the Boyne was fought in 1690 to defend divorce, or that the Northern Protestants who imported guns from Germany in 1912 and threatened to fight the British army if the Home Rule Act were implemented meant to man the barricades for contraception. In fact, the Irish Supreme Court has recently declared a significant part of the republic's anticontraceptive law unconstitutional,[3] but this has evoked no sign from the Protestants of the North that they find the republic more palatable as a result.

Their fear of domination by the Catholic Church and their antipathy to everything summed up in the word *Rome* are genuine to the point of being passionate. For them, civil and religious liberty depend precisely on Ireland not being unified. But what they reject is not this or that article of faith or morals, but a whole socioreligious complex. What they affirm is their own more individualistic culture. "No Pope Here" expresses their attitude very well, but it is no more a carefully refined proposition in theology than was "Algérie Française."

Northern Irish Protestants have been able to conceive only of utter subordination or unquestionable supremacy as the political alternatives open to them: they must either rule or be ruled. It was to guarantee their supremacy that the six northeastern counties of Ireland were partitioned off and, by another of history's ironies, were given home rule within the United Kingdom under the British Parliament's Government of Ireland Act of 1920. Thus was born what Ulster Protestants frequently and proudly refer to as their country: Northern Ireland.

Unfortunately for them, they are not alone in it. Only east of the River Bann, in Counties Antrim and Down, do Protestants constitute a large majority of the population. In two other counties, Tyrone and Fermanagh, Catholics are the majority, and they form at least a third of the population of Northern Ireland as a whole. What is more, the Catholics have a higher birthrate than the Protestants.[4] Consequently, as a recent book puts it, "The Protestants in the Northern Ireland state have always been an embattled community, fearing

3. *McGee* v. *Attorney General*, decided 19 December 1973. See *Irish Law Times*, vol. CIX, nos. 5652, 5653.

4. In the 1961 census Catholics were 34.9 percent of the population of Northern Ireland, but 40.2 percent of those were under age twenty-five. Rose, Richard, *Governing without Consensus* (London: Faber & Faber, 1971), p. 366.

absorption by the Republic on the outside, and wary of the birth-rate of the Catholics on the inside."[5]

Could the Catholic minority in Northern Ireland have been won over to at least a passive loyalty to the state by a policy of scrupulous fairness, including full admission to a share in political power? Possibly so. One Northern Irish Catholic remarked to this writer twenty years ago: "All we want is British law and justice, for British justice is the best in the world." There are still those who say the same today. But then again, possibly not. The Northern Catholics were by and large Irish nationalists, and did not look on Northern Ireland as being in any sense their state. At any rate, the experiment of treating them as equals was never tried. Given the reasons why Northern Ireland was set up in the first place, it would probably be unrealistic to think that it could have been tried.

As Barritt and Carter said more than ten years ago: "One great issue has so far dominated all others in Northern Ireland politics, the issue of whether or not the State should exist at all. . . . The division is between those who support the constitution and those who wish to change it; and, to the loyal supporters of the constitution, the second group is not Her Majesty's Opposition, an alternative government, but a gathering of those who are intent on treason against Her Majesty by robbing her of part of her rightful dominions."[6]

The Northern Ireland regime was a formal democracy on the British model, electing members to the House of Commons of the Northern Ireland Parliament at Stormont from single-member constituencies. The Unionist party, dedicated to preserving the union with Great Britain, always had a majority and always formed the government. Since the minority were regarded as a standing threat to the state, the Royal Ulster Constabulary was used, not as an ordinary police force, but as a national security force, and was backed up with an armed Protestant militia, the B-Specials. The party also saw to it that very few Catholics were employed by the government.

The sentiment on which Unionist hegemony was built was succinctly expressed by a Unionist M.P., Nat Minford, shortly after the IRA began a quixotic and unsuccessful campaign to end the par-

5. Martin Dillon and Denis Lehane, *Political Murder in Northern Ireland* (Harmondsworth: Penguin Books, 1973), p. 264.
6. Denis P. Barritt and Charles F. Carter, *The Northern Ireland Problem* (London: Oxford University Press, 1962), p. 35.

tition of Ireland by force in December 1956. "We Protestants," he said, "are running this country, and are going to run it. We want to live in a country where peace will prevail. If we find that these attacks are going to continue, then we Protestants ourselves will have to determine what the future will be."[7]

The same sentiment prevailed at the local level where, with the help of gerrymandering, the Unionists were also in control. The public jobs which were theirs to dispense, they granted with few exceptions to loyal Unionists, who were always Protestants. Private business, largely Protestant owned, followed similar policies. Access to public housing was not limited to Protestants, but was heavily biased in their favour. An American journalist, writing in the *New Yorker* a few years ago, summed it up with the remark that the issue in Ulster was not religion but religious politics: whether Catholics or Protestants would get the jobs, the housing, and political power.[8] Behind the religious politics lay the aim of encouraging Catholics to emigrate, lest, with their higher birthrate, they should become the majority.

One further element of the situation needs mention: the Orange Order. "Behind the [Unionist] party, and giving it something of the character of a mass movement stands the Orange Order," wrote Barritt and Carter. They described this unofficial but politically powerful body as "a mixture of the religious and the secular, the social and the political; at its best, it is an effective way of maintaining a warm and united spirit among 'Protestant brethren' from all social classes."[9] The Orange Order, however, is not always seen at its best, and particularly not in the numerous parades that it holds every spring and summer.

The following is a description of one of the more provocative and, as it turned out, more disastrous parades, given by a group of British journalists who write under the collective name of the Insight Team.

The Apprentice Boys' Parade around the old city walls of Derry each 12 August is a matter of solid Protestant citizens celebrating their continued enjoyment of something which they hold to be

7. Quoted by Tim Pat Coogan, *The I.R.A.* (London: Fontana Books, 1971), p. 389. Mr. Minford, by what alchemy this writer does not know, later became the Speaker of a Northern Ireland Assembly established on the premise that Protestants and Catholics ought to share power.

8. I quote from memory and with apologies to the journalist, Jane Kramer, if I have got her name or her words wrong.

9. Barritt and Carter, *Northern Ireland*, p. 46.

required for their survival: political hegemony over their Catholic fellow-citizens. On 12 August 1969 the parade took its normal form: 15,000 men in dark suits, sashes and bowler hats (the Orange "uniform") marching along the walls which enclose the old Protestant town and look down upon the impoverished Catholic Bogside. They were accompanied by bands and banners, and they sang, "The Boyne," and other blood-curdling anti-Catholic songs. As they went, various members of the parade threw pennies down into the Bogside—an area of about one in four male unemployment.

As the journalists go on to remark, that day's parade was no more provocative than those of other years, and it was not an idle exercise. "The point of the Apprentice Boys' parade is that it is an annual political experiment of the most empirical kind. If the Catholics take the insult lying down, all is well. If they do not, then it is necessary to make them lie down." [10] The Catholics did not take that particular parade lying down, and it developed that they could not be made to lie down. They responded on this occasion with the Bogside riots, from which followed in due course the total alienation of the Catholics from the Royal Ulster Constabulary, the introduction of the British army to restore order, the rise of the Provisional IRA and, ultimately, the downfall of the Unionist regime.

Yet through the bloodstained months that followed August 1969, the Orange Order insisted again and again on holding its parades, near or even through Catholic districts. The Unionist government at Stormont refused to prevent it from doing so, even though at several crucial points in the steadily worsening situation, it was precisely the parades that pushed Ulster deeper into the maelstrom of violence. The mounting disorder finally determined the British government to relieve the Stormont government of its powers and to institute direct rule from Westminster in March 1972.

According to the Insight Team of reporters, Stormont brought about its own demise through what they call "a fatal error by the ruling Protestants. It was to mistake the Civil Rights movement of the sixties for an attack on the State of Ulster itself." The demands that this Catholic movement was making were "moderate by any sensible standards." They could have been granted because "by the

---

10. The *Sunday Times* Insight Team, *Ulster* (Harmondsworth: Penguin Books, 1972), pp. 114–15.

mid-1960s Ulster was secure" and "the IRA no longer posed a violent threat: the Catholics of Ulster had discarded them." In the opinion of these British journalists, "the time was now ripe to begin dismantling the apparatus of total Protestant supremacy."[11] But the regime met the Civil Rights movement with police hostility, conniving at Orange rioting and grudging reforms that were too little and too late.

It was in this atmosphere that the Bogside exploded in wrath in August 1969, and Ulster began its descent into the maelstrom. Not until then did the Provisional IRA break off from the now Marxist-dominated "Official" IRA which refused to resort to force until the conditions were ripe for a socialist revolution. Not until mid-1970 did the Provisionals have enough men and arms to go into action. It was February 1971 before they "declared war" on the British army and for the first time killed a British soldier. It may well be true, as many Irishmen believe, that it was the Provisionals who brought down Stormont. But the root causes of Stormont's downfall long antedated the Provisional IRA.

Reform, undertaken in time, presumably would have saved Stormont and the Unionist regime. So another journalist, Henry Kelly, seems to believe when he says, "Stormont came to an end through a combination of elements some of which it could have controlled with more careful tactics . . . most of which it could have avoided through more generous attitudes years beforehand."[12] But, from the Unionist point of view, reform would have been a radical step to take. Despite the Insight Team's remarks about the reception that the Civil Rights movement should have received, they point out that "there was an essential philosophical contradiction about the notion of reform. Dismantle the apparatus of Protestant supremacy, and you have destroyed Northern Ireland's only justification for being a State on its own. It might just as well not exist. That, in the end, although neither side may have formulated it in so many words, is why reform was halfheartedly proffered and mistrustfully received. It made no sense."[13]

The Unionist regime died because it aroused the active hostility of too large a part of its population. Yet Northern Ireland remains, with its problem of two antagonistic communities condemned to live

11. Ibid., pp. 27–28.
12. Henry Kelly, *How Stormont Fell* (Dublin: Gill & Macmillan, 1972), p. 141.
13. Insight Team, *Ulster*, p. 307.

together. Professor Richard Rose, in a book on Northern Ireland whose title, *Governing without Consensus*, reveals its thesis, concludes bleakly that "a clear and final solution to the Northern Ireland problem" is not to be looked for: "In the foreseeable future, no solution is immediately practicable." Yet he knows that Northern Ireland must be governed somehow. What he means, then, is that no possible course of action "is likely to create a fully legitimate regime." [14] That is to say that Northern Ireland may not expect to have a regime that enjoys a high degree of diffuse support among its subjects and a high degree of compliance with its basic laws. [15] In the light of the present situation, that is to put it mildly.

The British government's next attempted solution to the Northern Ireland problem was summed up in two words: "power sharing" and "Sunningdale." It had the support of all major political parties in Great Britain and in the Irish Republic, but it failed and in its failure revealed with harsh clarity why no clear and final solution is immediately practicable.

First, then, "power sharing." In 1973 the British Parliament enacted a Northern Ireland Assembly Act and a Northern Ireland Constitution Act. The latter affirmed that Northern Ireland would remain a part of the United Kingdom until a majority of its citizens, by vote, should declare their wish to leave it. [16] In the meantime, the acts abolished the former Northern Ireland Parliament and created a single-chamber Northern Ireland Assembly with seventy-eight seats to be filled by proportional representation. The British secretary of state for Northern Ireland would appoint from among its members (though he could also go outside it) a Northern Ireland Executive, composed of a chief executive and the heads of the Northern Ireland departments. The principle of the new regime, and the key to the whole scheme, would be power sharing among all parties willing to take part—in effect, among moderate Protestants and Catholics.

In the election to the Assembly, a majority of seats was won by the pro-Assembly Unionists, led by the old Parliament's last prime minister, Brian Faulkner; by the largely Catholic SDLP (Social Democratic and Labour party); and by the small, mainly middle-class Protestant, Alliance party. These parties furnished the members of

14. Ibid., p. 21.
15. Ibid., pp. 28, 32.
16. A "border poll," taken in 1973, showed a strong majority in favor of Northern Ireland's remaining in the United Kingdom; under the Constitution Act, no further vote on the matter could be taken until 1983.

the Executive, which took office on 1 January 1974, with Mr. Faulkner as chief executive. The Loyalists, as the Unionists opposed to power sharing became known, tried to disrupt the early meetings of the Assembly, but the new regime succeeded in coming into existence at Stormont and in functioning for some months.

The other part of the formula was worked out in December 1973, at a meeting in Sunningdale outside London. There the British and Irish governments, together with the parties involved in the Northern Ireland Executive, acknowledged that they had different views on the desirability of a united Ireland but agreed unanimously that Northern Ireland would become part of it only by the consent of a majority of its people. In the meantime, a council of Ireland would be set up (but in fact never came into being). It would comprise a consultative assembly, composed of equal numbers from Dail Eireann and the Northern Ireland Assembly, and a council of ministers, composed of equal numbers from the Irish government and the Northern Executive. The council of ministers, in addition to consultative and harmonizing functions, was to have certain executive powers in the whole of Ireland, but these would be exercised only by the unanimous agreement of the council's members. What these powers would be was left to be defined in detail, but clearly they would not at first have been great. Initially at least, the council of Ireland would have been but a dipping of the toes in the water of national unity.

James Callaghan, M.P., now Britain's prime minister, was, as home secretary in the previous Labour government, closely involved in Northern Ireland's affairs, about which he wrote a book, *A House Divided*. In it he commented on the newly legislated power-sharing regime:

> Much depends upon the order of political priorities of the two communities. Peace and progress does not mean that it will be necessary for the Catholic community to put aside the reunification of Ireland as their ultimate objective. What is required from them is that they should cease to regard reunification as the first priority to which everything else takes second place. If the minority were to decide to make economic reconstruction, jobs and housing their first priority for the mid-term future, then a political partnership with the majority would make sense. Conversely, the Protestants do not need to give up their conception of a separate Northern Ireland. In the mid-term

future all that is required of them is that they should be willing to share political power with the minority in order to achieve the very necessary economic and other improvements in the life of the people. It is not too much to expect.[17]

It may not have been too much to expect but, as events proved, it was more than could be realized. The Northern Irish Catholics with whom this writer spoke in late 1973 and early 1974 were all convinced that the new Assembly and Executive "won't work" because they did not believe that the Protestants were genuinely willing to share power. The Loyalists, who claim to represent the majority, not only of Protestants but of the whole population of the province, certainly are not so willing. In their television appearances, Loyalist leaders have repeatedly made it plain that they reject "Sunningdale" as an attempt to force Northern Ireland into the republic and "power-sharing" as a travesty of democracy. The only authentically British version of democracy, they say, is majority rule, and the policy of the British government was depriving the majority in Northern Ireland of its democratic right to rule.

The protests of Loyalist political leaders were unavailing. The British government had determined on the power-sharing formula and would not budge from it. But in May 1974 a group of Loyalist workers, organized as the UWC (Ulster Workers Council), took matters into their own hands and called a general strike aimed at forcing the British government to abandon the Sunningdale agreement and to call new elections to the Northern Ireland Assembly which, they were confident, would this time return a Loyalist majority opposed to power sharing. The government took no effective action against the strike and, as the province slid into economic paralysis, the Loyalist politicians rallied to the UWC. On May 28 Brian Faulkner and his pro-Assembly Unionists resigned from the Northern Ireland Executive. A Stormont regime had fallen for the second time, and probably for the last time under British rule.

It may be, as some commentators hold, that the Sunningdale proposal of a council of Ireland, which so deeply alarmed Northern Protestants, was a mistake and that without it power sharing would have worked. By the time this paper appears in print, a sounder estimate of the feasibility of power sharing will be possible. The British government has suspended the Northern Ireland Assembly for four

17. James Callaghan, *A House Divided* (London: Collins, 1973), p. 181.

months and will use the interval to see if a power-sharing system of government can be established on a basis that the Loyalists will accept. But the Loyalists, as this is written, are convinced that they have found the weapon that can bend the British government to their will: the control of Northern Ireland's key industries by Loyalist workers. Listening to Loyalist politicians on television, one gets the impression that these are men for whom the old Orange slogan, "Not an Inch—No Surrender," still passes for a policy. They believe that they can exact the repeal of the Constitution Act of 1973 and an end to power sharing as the price of averting a return to industrial chaos. If the government's effort to save power sharing fails, it is hard to imagine what course the government can then choose that will be compatible with continued British rule in Northern Ireland.

It would be possible, of course, to abolish Northern Ireland as a distinct political entity and to incorporate the province fully into the unitary state of the United Kingdom. But this is not a move that the British government is likely to make. Under direct British rule, Northern Ireland's Catholics would probably have their civil rights better guaranteed (British Catholics have no serious complaints about discrimination against them), and a majority of them would probably accept it as a short-term remedy for their situation. But as a permanent solution they would reject integration into the United Kingdom on nationalistic grounds. The Loyalists, for the most part, would reject it for the opposite reason: they fear that the British government would make a deal over their heads with the Irish Republic and cede Northern Ireland to a united Ireland. The Irish government, committed to the reunification of the island as a national goal, would have to object to integration. Nor does the British government want it: for all the major parties in Britain, Ireland has become a problem of which they would gladly be rid, though not yet a responsibility which they are ready to shed.

Incorporation of the North into the unitary state of the Irish Republic, against the wishes of the Protestant population, is not feasible and is not in fact being suggested. Desmond Boal, a former Unionist leader, has proposed an "amalgamated" Ireland, in which Northern Ireland and the other provinces of Ireland would enjoy regional autonomy under a federal government in Dublin. He was seconded by the political wing of the Provisional IRA, which saw in the proposal a resemblance to its own plan for a federal Ireland, but no one else supported his suggestion. This solution might become attractive to Northern Protestants if, but only if, Great Britain announced her intention of withdrawing altogether from Ireland and left them on their own. But they would probably first make an attempt to go it alone as an independent State of Ulster.

Three Loyalist parties, factions of the old and now fragmented Unionist party, met in the spring of 1974, before the UWC strike, and came up with their solution: a federal united kingdom. This meant a regional government in Northern Ireland protected by legal guarantees against "interference" by the Westminister Parliament. Support was to be sought from the nationalist parties now growing in strength in Scotland and Wales. These parties want independence for their countries but, the Loyalists hoped, might be willing to endorse their view of federalism. But, since the Loyalists insist that power sharing in Northern Ireland is intolerable to them, a federal Britain is only another way of saying, "give us back Stormont as it originally was." This the British government is unwilling to do, and could hardly do if it wanted, because it would only ensure a repetition of the disorders of the years since 1968.

There is a growing feeling of Ulster nationalism among the Loyalists, and mutterings are heard about an independent state of Ulster. They would not choose independence so long as they had hopes of remaining in the United Kingdom on their own terms. But Great Britain cannot grant their terms and will have to accept their disassociation from the United Kingdom if they insist intransigently on them. A peaceful and stable Northern Ireland is the only one that it is any longer in the British interest to keep. But it is questionable whether an independent and politically isolated Protestant state in Northern Ireland would be viable.

The Provisional IRA is as opposed as are the Loyalists to power sharing in Northern Ireland because it means keeping the province in the United Kingdom. Its policy is based on the traditional assumption that the remedy for Ireland's wrongs is to get the British out. The means of accomplishing this is the classical IRA strategy of making the country ungovernable by attacks on the British army and the police, interference with the functioning of the civil authorities and—a late twentieth-century innovation—bombing town centers. The object is to force the British government to declare its intention to relinquish Northern Ireland politically and to withdraw its army within a stated period of time. This hope is not entirely unfounded. Leading members of the now-governing Labour party in Britain have sent up trial balloons warning that the troops may be withdrawn, and British public sentiment is swinging in that direction.

In the interval between the declaration of intention and the departure of the British troops, according to the Provisionals, Catholics and Protestants would work out their differences on the basis of their common Irish nationality, and a new Irish republic would arise to replace the essentially illegitimate regimes now existing in both parts of the island. If not, then the IRA is prepared to take on the well-armed Protestant paramilitary organizations—such as the Ulster Defence Association, the Ulster Volunteer Force and the Ulster Freedom Fighters—and establish the new Ireland after its victory. This smacks of political romanticism, but romanticism is the IRA's besetting vice.

The Protestant extremists might join with the IRA to force the British out, but not in order to establish a united Ireland on any terms. Their present objective is a political settlement worked out "among Ulstermen," without the interference of the London and Dublin governments. Catholics, they say, would of course take part in the settlement, but it is understood that they would do so as a minority coming to terms with the majority. The dilemma of the present moment is that power sharing has not worked; it could only work if both sides were willing to live with deep and unresolved political differences; but nothing else will work. Whatever may be the situation when these words appear in print, this underlying dilemma will remain.

In this situation, civil war is an undeniable possibility. On a minor scale, it has been going on for the past few years, with Protestant gunmen prowling the streets and roads of Northern Ireland hunting for victims and the Provisional IRA pursuing its calculated campaign of violence.[18] Retaliatory bombing has now begun against Dublin and other towns in the republic. The prospects for democracy and constitutional government in Northern Ireland, one must confess, are at present dim.

Yet constitutional democracy has a future there if only because there is no viable alternative to it. These words are written before it is known what Great Britain intends finally to do or can do about

18. Two *Belfast Telegraph* reporters, Dillon and Lehane, in *Political Murder in Northern Ireland*, conclude that Protestants have been responsible for the bulk of civilian assassinations, the Provisionals for more bombing and killing of soldiers.

Northern Ireland.[19] But she is now in a position only to support a regime which is recognized as a constitutional democracy by both parts of the population and by the Irish government. The Irish Republic, for its part, has neither the will nor the means to take over the North by force. Within Northern Ireland, there is no longer the possibility of maintaining a coercive regime by which one community would simply dominate the other. If it is tried in an independent six-county Ulster, the result will be civil war, and at that point the Irish Republic would have to intervene.

It may take the bloodbath of a civil war before all parties concerned come to understand the realities of their situation. It may even take a second partition of Ireland, resulting for a time in a Protestant state, much reduced in size, trying to go it alone. Since "Ireland has been said to be a country in which the impossible always happens and the inevitable never occurs,"[20] there may be a drawing back from the brink before it is too late. But, one way or another, a regime based on political and religious equality is the only one under which the people of Northern Ireland can live with each other, whether in the United Kingdom or, as now seems ultimately more probable, in a united Ireland. There is really no other way out of the impasse.

19. Since this paper was first written, the British government has determined to make one more try at power sharing. A 78-member constitutional convention is to be elected by proportional representation to frame a new constitution for Northern Ireland, subject to approval by the British Parliament. The one condition that the British lay down is that the constitution must include provisions for power sharing. But, as the *New York Times* reported on 11 November 1974 (and all other observers agree), "Most Protestants and Catholics give the convention very little hope of success because a majority of the delegates are expected to be hard-line Protestants against any significant sharing of power with the Catholics." If the convention fails, says the *Times*, "many have come to the conclusion that Britain has run out of ideas and plans nothing more than indefinite direct rule from London." (As we go to press, the convention has failed, and the *Times'* prediction has come true.)

20. R. F. V. Heuston, *Essays in Constitutional Law* (London: Stevens & Sons, 1961), p. 28.

Howard A. Scarrow • Participation Through
Decentralization: The Case of Britain

Can democracy, or at least stable democracy, survive in Britain?
Merely to raise the question may be to invite glances of incredulity.
For Americans in general, and for American political scientists in particular, Britain has traditionally been regarded as the quintessence of
democratic stability, the system against which other nations' per-
formances have been measured. In 1974, nevertheless, the future of
stable democracy in Britain was being questioned. Doubts were being
raised most dramatically by journalists as they reported the formation of vigilante groups, wondered out loud whether labor union
leaders had begun to run the country, and recalled that never in
history had a democracy been able to survive the 20 percent rate of
inflation which some economists were predicting would be reached
in Britain in 1975. Even the staid *Economist* suggested that perhaps
the end of parliamentary government in Britain was in sight.

While such warnings were mainly speculative and were in response
to an immediate economic crisis, there was hard evidence that, at
the very least, the political landscape in Britain had begun to change.
Especially noteworthy was the decline in support for both the Conservative and Labour parties, a decline which could be charted back
to the 1950s.[1] Erstwhile supporters of the major parties were either
switching allegiance to the Liberals and to the nationalist parties of
Scotland, Wales, and Northern Ireland, or else they chose to remain
home on election day, and thus vote for no party at all. The consequences of these shifts in voter loyalties became apparent in the
general election of February 1974, when for the first time since 1929
no party was able to win a parliamentary majority.

One interpretation of these shifts in voting behavior has stressed
the decline in the salience of social class. According to this argument,
voters are decreasingly prone to view the two major parties as vehicles of the class struggle; they cannot be persuaded that it makes
much difference which party controls the government at West-

1. See Ivor Crewe, "Do Butler and Stokes Really Explain Political Change in
Britain?", *European Journal of Political Research*, 2 (1974): 47–92.

minster.[2] Another interpretation of changed voting behavior is much more sweeping in its implications. This interpretation holds that British society has entered a new stage of development, a postindustrial stage, where different interests, concerns, and values are emerging. In addition to the decline of class loyalties, one of the major components of this new outlook is said to be the desire for increased political participation. In his survey of attitudes in Britain and in five other European countries, Inglehart found that political participation (along with freedom of speech) assumed more importance in the value hierarchy of youth than it did in that of older generations, and he argued that European societies could thus be seen as abandoning the older "acquisitive" values in favor of "postbourgeois" values.[3] About the same time Jo Grimond, then leader of the British Liberal party, advanced a related thesis: in his view, a major division in Britain has become the division between the government and the governed; what people are looking for, he argued, is an increase in their participation in the many government decisions affecting their lives.[4]

One dimension of political participation, namely the decentralization of government authority, is the concern of this paper. To what extent can it be said that Britons want a devolution of authority from London to smaller, grass roots units of government? The question is important not only in relation to interpreting political change, but also because the Scottish and Welsh nationalist movements have thrust the question into the political arena. In addition, since 1957 no less than five official commissions of inquiry have been appointed and have reported on Britain's system of local and proposed regional government; each has had to consider the question which has been posed. Finally, Britons' attitude toward local participation is central to an issue which has confounded students of British local government, viz., which of two competing models of subnational govern-

2. See, for example, David Butler and Donald Stokes, *Political Change in Britain* (New York, 1969), pp. 115–22.

3. Ronald Inglehart, "The Silent Revolution in Europe: Intergenerational Change in Post-Industrial Societies," *American Political Science Review*, 65 (1971): 9910–1015.

4. A good statement of his views will be found in "Community Politics," *Government and Opposition*, 7 (1972): 135–44. Seemingly confirming Grimond's analysis was the increase during the 1960s in the number and activities of citizen groups such as tenant's associations, neighborhood councils, amenity societies, and consumer groups.

ment should guide thinking on the subject. Comparison of those two models provides a convenient focus for the discussion which follows.

The question of participating through decentralization may be clarified by distinguishing between two models of subnational government. According to one model, which we may label "home rule," subnational government combines three conditions: (1) local jurisdictions enjoy policy-making autonomy within certain defined policy areas; (2) these policy areas relate to matters which local citizens feel should be left to local self-determination; and (3) local elections are the ultimate sanction to insure such self-determination, and they bestow legitimacy on the decision makers. In the United States the term *home rule*, like the term *states' rights*, has become an emotional rallying cry precisely because it encompasses these dimensions of meaning.

There is another model of subnational government, however, which we may label the "administrative model." According to this conception, subnational government is not a question of home rule; rather it is a question of the best way for central governmental services to be administered. Subnational government is not an end in itself; rather it is a means by which national governmental policy is executed. One method of execution is for the central government to take complete charge, but for practical reasons, using a network of field offices; in Britain social security benefit payments are administered in this fashion. Another method is for the central government to appoint appropriate local citizens to administer a particular service in their area; the British hospital service has been administered in this manner. Finally, that board (or council) may be made an elective body, and to it may be entrusted the administration of more than one service.

The administrative service model of subnational government envisages this last alternative. It differs from the home rule model in important ways. Whereas under each of the three administrative options there may indeed be a question of how much autonomy should be bestowed upon the area field office, the appointed board, or the elected board, the question of autonomy is to be answered not in terms of rights or demands for local self-determination, but rather answered pragmatically, in terms of certain practical goals: (1) the quality and cost of services (roughly summed up by the term *efficiency*); (2) the possible desirability of nationally uniform standards of services; (3) flexibility, i.e., administration which can take account of local conditions and habits, and hence can be responsive to local needs and wants; and (4) possible psychological benefits which may be derived by citizens who are able to participate in local elections and deal with locally elected administrators. Of these four goals, only the last two—flexibility and psychological benefits—clearly mandate the option of more, rather than less, local autonomy, and only the goal of possible psychological benefits cannot be realized through officials appointed by the central government.

The problem for the student of British local government has been that it has never been clear which model, home rule or administrative service, British local government is intended to approximate. In the literature terms like *local autonomy, local decision making,* and *government by the people* are usually left undefined, thus allowing the reader, particularly the American reader, to envisage the model of home rule. Yet these terms will be found used side-by-side with discussions of the provision of services, thereby suggesting more the administrative service perspective. Some writers have explicitly argued for the latter perspective. Professor J. A. G. Griffith, for example, has asserted that the "primary purpose of local government today is to provide services as efficient as they can be. . . ." and accordingly he sees no particular merit in having elected persons rather than appointed persons in charge of administering these services.[5] "Local authorities' principal *raison d'être* is to provide services. It is true that they also enrich our democracy by increasing political participation and awareness, but their success or failure is primarily judged by the quality and efficiency of the services they provide."[6]

Viewpoints such as these are by no means uniformly shared. J. P. Mackintosh, for example, has argued that the question of comprehensive schools and public housing rents, questions which have aroused considerable controversy in Britain, "are precisely the sort of issues" which local citizens wish to settle for themselves rather than have the central government decide.[7] The argument clearly suggests the home rule model.

Three opinion surveys carried out for official commissions of inquiry have done much to clarify British attitudes toward local participation. One was administered in 1965 for the Committee on Local

5. See his evidence presented to the Royal Commission on Local Government in Greater London, *Minutes of Evidence*, pp. 747–48.
6. Bleddyn Davies, *Social Needs and Resources in Local Services* (London, 1968), p. 289.
7. J. P. Mackintosh, *The Devolution of Power* (Harmondsworth, 1968), p. 47.

138 • *Howard A. Scarrow*

Government Management (covering England and Wales); one was administered in 1967 for the Commission on English Local Government (covering England only); and one was administered in 1970 for the Commission on the Constitution (covering England, Scotland, and Wales).[8] Although only the last of the three surveys was specifically focused on decentralization and participation, all three provided important evidence on the subject. That evidence strongly points to the conclusion that it is the administrative service model, not the home rule model, which dominates British thinking on subnational government.[9]

Lack of Concern. First it may be noted that the first two surveys failed to include a question asking respondents to state their attitude toward local self-determination. Rather, respondents were asked about services. Thus instead of being asked whether they thought a local community should be able to determine for itself questions of schools, rents, or land use, respondents were asked whether they thought such services to be "quite well run." The findings showed that respondents evaluated locally run services as being no better or worse than services administered by the central departments or statutory boards; but attitudes toward local legitimacy versus central legitimacy remained unexplored. In other words, both questionnaires were conceived in an administrative perspective—a fact that tells as much about entrenched perceptions of local government in Britain as do any of the results reported in the studies.

The 1967 survey did ask respondents for their opinions regarding the size of local government units—whether they wished to see the boundaries of the units in which they lived expanded, contracted, or kept the same. Since feelings of self-determination are normally thought to be associated with demands for a devolution of authority towards smaller units, a stated preference for smaller units could

8. Ministry of Housing and Local Government, Committee on the Management of Local Government, *Management of Local Government,* vol. 3, *The Local Government Elector* (London, HMSO, 1967); Royal Commission on Local Government in England, *Research Studies 6: Community Attitudes Survey: England* (London, HMSO, 1969); Commission on the Constitution *Research Papers 7: Devolution and Other Aspects of Government: An Attitudes Survey* (London, HMSO, 1973). The first and third surveys were conducted by the government Social Survey Division; the second survey was conducted for the division by Research Services, Ltd.

9. The minority report of the 1970 Commission on the Constitution argued the opposite, viz., that the attitude survey done for the Commission demonstrated the high value which Britons placed upon local participation. See Commission on the Constitution, *Minority Report* (London, HMSO, 1973).

possibly be interpreted as expressing this sentiment. In fact, however, the responses were precisely the opposite: only 23 percent expressed preference for change, 18 percent in favor of expansion and only 5 percent in favor of contraction. The pattern held for units of all sizes, from the largest cities to the smallest districts. Respondents were also asked how strongly they felt about the matter (very strongly, quite strongly, just a little); only 48 percent of the respondents felt at least "quite strongly" about their stated preference, whether for change or for keeping the status quo.[10]

Regional Sentiment. When finally, in 1970, respondents were asked to give their views on local self-determination, the question was put in terms of a hypothetical regional government; hence the replies given are not as valuable as they would have been if they were given in terms of existing units of local government. Nevertheless, the replies are strongly suggestive of the relative absence of home rule sentiment at the mass level.

The respondents were asked to choose one of five responses in answer to the question: "For running the region[11] as a whole, which of these five alternatives would you prefer?" The alternatives and the proportion of respondents are shown in Table 1.

It will be seen that the first of these scalar statements was an option for no change at all; the second and third statements were variations of "keep things pretty much the same, with the exception of . . ." the fourth and fifth were options or variations of introducing a new system of regional government. Perhaps the most striking result of the survey is the failure of Welsh and Scottish respondents to show themselves greatly different from their English compatriots. Nine of the ten English regions recorded a higher percentage than did Wales of respondents choosing the fifth, most extreme option. And while Scotland did record the highest percentage choosing this option, the level was only marginally higher than some regions in England. Also of interest is the fact that the survey found very little variation in responses among different age groups; in particular, the youngest respondents showed no tendency to opt for the most extreme degree of change.

10. See *Community Attitudes Survey: England*, p. 128.
11. In addition to Scotland and Wales, the ten English regions covered by the survey generally conformed with the standard statistical regions: North, Yorkshire, North West, West Midland, East Midland, East Anglia, South East, Greater London, South, South West.

Table 1. Preference for Devolution

	Total	South*	South West*	Scotland	Wales
(1) Leave things as they are at present	13	11	20	6	15
(2) Keep things much the same as they are now but make sure that the needs of the region are better understood by the government	24	23	28	19	27
(3) Keep the present system but allow more decisions to be made in the region	24	20	20	26	21
(4) Have a new system of governing the region so that as many decisions as possible are made in the area	21	25	17	24	23
(5) Let the region take over complete responsibility for running things in the region	16	21	12	23	13
(6) Don't know	2	0	2	1	0

Question: "For running the region as a whole, which of these five alternatives would you prefer?" *Devolution and Other Aspects of Government: An Attitudes Survey,* p. 62.

*Results were not reported for England as a whole; for brevity, only two English regions are shown in this table, ones which recorded the highest and lowest devolution sentiment among the ten English regions.

Additional interpretation of the results depends largely upon how one perceives option number three. The authors of the survey chose to group together the third, fourth, and fifth options and label them as options in favor of some form of devolution of authority from the central government. Accordingly, 61 percent of the respondents were coded as being in favor of devolution. However, since the third option in the series begins with the phrase *keep the present system,* an argument could be made for grouping together options one, two, and three, in which case the proportion of respondents choosing to keep the present system is also 61 percent. Fortunately, other parts of the survey help clarify these responses.

Answers to three other questions demonstrate that whatever sentiment may exist for a devolution of authority to the regions, that sentiment is relatively weak in intensity and, more important, it does not appear to reflect a desire for regional self-determination per se. In one question respondents were asked whether or not they thought that each region should be able to "set its own standards" for services or whether instead standards "should be the same in every part of Britain." It would be expected that those who chose devolution options one and two would come down on the side of uniformity, and they did so (56 percent, 56 percent). But majorities of those who chose options three and four also wanted uniformity (57 percent,

52 percent). Even among those who chose the most extreme devolution option, a full 44 percent wanted uniformity.[12] This pattern of response hardly suggests a deeply felt commitment to regional or local home rule.

Responses to another question point to the same conclusion. When asked whether they would still opt for some form of regional devolution if it meant that the region would suffer financially, rather than 61 percent chosing devolution, only 10 percent did so.[13]

Finally, in another question respondents were asked to register their degree of agreement, on a five-point scale, with "a number of suggestions (which) have been made by people in different parts of Britain for improving things in their own regions." Only two of the six stated suggestions could be interpreted as pointing to the creation of new regional decision-making bodies: "To have more decisions made here . . ." and "To have more ordinary people running things." The other four suggestions implied working within the present system. Although the two types of statements were intermixed in the order of presentation to the respondents, each of the four "present system" statements elicited a higher degree of agreement than the two statements suggestive of devolution.[14]

Administrative Perspective. Perhaps the most revealing parts of the various surveys are those which show the respondent's general perspective toward local or proposed regional government. The evidence clearly shows that the perspective is more in accord with the administrative service model than with the home rule model.

The 1970 survey included four questions which bear on this point. First, before they were asked about their choice among the five devolution statements for "running the region as a whole," respondents were asked to assign one of the same five choices to five specific services; two (police and schools) were the responsibility of local government; two (health, gas and electricity) were the responsibility of area administrative boards; and one (building main roads) was the

---

12. *Devolution and Other Aspects of Government: An Attitudes Survey,* p. 104.
13. Ibid., p. 98.
14. The proportion giving a score of 5, strongest agreement, to the two devolution statements was 46 percent and 19 percent. The other four statements were: "For the government to take more trouble to understand the region's special needs" (57 percent); "To allow each Member of Parliament to have more influence over what the government does in the region" (50 percent); "To make it easier for people in the regions to explain their special problems to the government" (49 percent); "To make sure that M.P.'s have stronger regional ties" (47 percent). See ibid., p. 22.

responsibility of the central government. The choice for the devolution options (3, 4, and 5) increased directly in proportion with the amount of dissatisfaction which (in a previous question) had been expressed regarding these services, with main roads and schools receiving the highest devolution scores as well as the highest dissatisfaction ratings. This pattern strongly suggests that any desire for a devolution of authority is rooted in pragmatic, efficiency considerations.[15] This conclusion is reinforced by the fact that in the case of schools, a preference for shifting authority to a proposed regional government represents more, rather than less, concentration of authority.

A similar question asked respondents to express degrees of agreement with three statements of possible outcomes if, in fact, "the regions had more say in running their own affairs." One of the statements pointed to increased administrative efficiency, one statement pointed to increased ability of government to provide for people's needs, and one suggested that "the ordinary man could have more say in what is done in the region." Although all three statements elicited agreement, strongest agreement was registered for the first two statements, ones which suggested an administrative rather than participatory outcome.[16]

A noteworthy aspect of the responses to the "increased efficiency" and "people's needs" statements is the widespread agreement which they elicited. Even those respondents who wanted no devolution whatsoever (devolution option number one) agreed by a 50 percent to 34 percent margin that with devolution "things would be run more efficiently" and by a 58 percent–28 percent margin that "the needs of the people would be looked after much better." Agreement with the statements steadily increased among those choosing the second, third, fourth, and fifth devolution options, respectively. Again, therefore, the evidence strongly suggests the pragmatic, administrative basis for most of whatever devolution sentiment exists.

The perception of local or regional government as a question of administration is suggested further by the responses to a type of

15. Ibid., p. 100.
16. The three statements, and the proportion of "agree strongly" and "agree a little" responses, were: "If the Region had more say in running its own affairs, (1) things would be run more efficiently in the region" (34 percent, 42 percent); (2) "The needs of the people in the region would be looked after much better (40 percent, 41 percent); (3) "The ordinary man could have more say in deciding what is done in the region" (32 percent, 44 percent). See ibid., p. 7.

question included in the 1965, 1967, and 1970 surveys. The question was designed to compare citizen perception of locally elected councillors with perception of the permanent officials who serve local government. Respondents were asked whom they would contact if they wished to "find out more about" local governmental services (1965) or if they "wanted to make an enquiry or complaint about" any of the local government services (1967). The replies were heavily weighted in favor of the permanent officials, 70 percent to 9 percent (1965) and 67 percent to 12 percent (1967).[17] The 1970 survey question was worded somewhat differently: respondents were asked which of three types of people they would like to see "mainly responsible for making decisions" in the region in the event the region "had more say in running its own affairs." The choices presented, in order, were "civil servants" (undoubtedly interpreted as referring to central government officials), "people elected by those who live in . . . [the region]," or "people appointed because of their special expertise [qualifications]." Only the second of these alternatives is compatible with the "home rule" model; yet no more respondents (48 percent) chose that alternative than chose the other two (three percent civil servants, 45 percent appointed experts). Even among those who had chosen the most "extreme" devolution option (number five), only a bare majority (52 percent) chose elected representatives to run their preferred regional governments.[18] Also of interest is the fact that the authors of the survey, in their commentary, refer to the three choices as referring to "three types of administration."[19]

It should be noted, finally, that both the 1967 and 1970 surveys revealed that those of higher social-economic status tended to choose the "administrator" response, whereas those of lower status tended to choose the "elected representative" response. Indeed, the authors of the 1967 survey themselves revealed their perceptions of the "correct" answer when they spoke of persons who would approach the appointed official as those who would go to "the top."[20]

A final clue to citizen perception of local government is provided by the answers given in 1970 to the open-ended question regarding what groups respondents thought would benefit from a devolution

17. *The Local Government Elector*, p. 36; *Community Attitudes Survey: England*, p. 98.
18. *Devolution and Other Aspects of Government: An Attitudes Survey*, p. 86.
19. Ibid.
20. *Community Attitudes Survey: England*, p. 100.

of authority to the regions. Mentioned most often (among the minority believing there would be any difference at all) were the elderly, infirm, and disabled (29 percent). School children and young people were next most frequently mentioned (12 percent). Also frequently mentioned were the poor, homeless, and unemployed (10 percent).[21] Such groups are precisely those who are the recipients of local government services; yet, they are hardly those whose political influence would increase with more regional self-determination. The image of local government as the provider of services to these and other relatively low-status groups is confirmed by the replies to another question posed in the 1970 survey: asked whether they thought (national) civil servants or local government officials were "better at understanding the needs of the elderly," "small businesses like shopkeepers," and "the ordinary man," respondents chose local officials by about a three-to-one margin in each case.[22]

The Central-Local Distinction. There is strong evidence that Britons draw no sharp distinction between central and local government. As already indicated, they tend to rate the services provided by the two levels more or less the same, and at least a third of the electorate are unaware which services are provided at the two levels.[23] However, perhaps the most persuasive evidence concerning citizen failure to draw a sharp distinction between central and local, or regional government was provided by responses to questions asked in 1967 and 1970 concerning members of Parliament. The 1967 survey found that to make an enquiry or lodge a complaint concerning a local service a citizen would turn to his member of Parliament more readily than he would turn to his elected local councillor.[24] The 1970 survey found a similar high regard for the M.P.; 60 percent agreed with the statement that "Most M.P.'s are on the side of the man in the street and are always willing to listen to his views."[25]

More significant was the pattern of responses given to the question already described, asking the respondent's reaction to various suggestions for improving things in his region. The two suggestions which would utilize the services of M.P.'s received more agreement than did either of the two suggestions, identified above, which pointed

21. *Devolution and Other Aspects of Government: An Attitudes Survey*, p. 93.
22. Ibid., p. 34.
23. Ibid., p. 9; See also *Community Attitudes Survey: England*, pp. 83–85.
24. *Community Attitudes Survey: England*, pp. 102–4.
25. *Devolution and Other Aspects of Government: An Attitudes Survey*, p. 20.

to the creation of new regional decision-making authorities.[26] Clearly, then, it would seem possible to satisfy desires for regional betterment through the existing mechanisms of central government.

Conclusion. Samuel Beer has pointed out that there exist in the British political culture two conflicting conceptions of authority: the participatory conception, whereby the people are supposed to govern; and the nonparticipatory conception, whereby the people are governed by governors who make decisions according to their interpretation of the national interest.[27] The two models of local government which have been considered in this paper, home rule and administrative service, may be seen as corresponding, at least approximately, to these concepts; the one clearly emphasizes government *by* the people, the other focuses much more on government *for* the people. If the analogy is correct, then the evidence presented in the paper may be interpreted as confirming the existence in the British culture of both conceptions of authority but, as expressed in attitudes toward local government, of the relatively greater strength of the one than the other.

To return to the question of political change, posed at the beginning of this paper, there is no evidence from the surveys considered to suggest that a concern with political participation is replacing a more traditional concern, broadly summed up in the phrase "effective government." Quality of services provided, not the means of providing them, would appear to be the overriding standard by which government arrangements are evaluated. As the 1970 survey demonstrated, such an emphasis is by no means incompatible with a desire for a devolution of decision-making authority, and hence that question may well continue to confront governments during the 1970s and perhaps beyond. However, the challenge would seem better described as one of means rather than ends, of delivery of services rather than satisfying an emerging substantive demand for a new, more legitimate level of government.

26. See footnote 14 above for the wording of the questions and the proportions expressing strongest agreement.
27. "The British Political System" in Samuel H. Beer et al., *Patterns of Government* (New York, 1973) pp. 139–41.

J. Harris Proctor • Communal Representation in the Republic of Malawi

The national assembly provided for by the republican constitution of Malawi which came into effect on July 6, 1966, two years after the attainment of independence, contained a rather remarkable feature. Seated across the aisle from fifty elected Africans who were constitutionally required to be members of the Malawi Congress Party (MCP) were five Europeans who belonged to no party and who had been appointed by the President, Dr. H. Kamuzu Banda. They were led by the man who had been Banda's principal antagonist in the pre-independence struggle. These white legislators participated actively in the work of the House until November 1, 1973, when they withdrew in compliance with a resolution passed by the party's annual convention. An analysis of this experiment in communal representation illuminates the meaning of constitutionalism and democracy in a new state whose leaders have been seeking to build political unity and to accelerate economic growth amidst the tensions of a multi-racial society.

The development of parliamentary government in Malawi (previously known as Nyasaland) has been complicated by the presence of a European community which was a tiny minority numerically but played a major role in the economy and in the bureaucracy. The 1966 census reported that there were 4,020,724 Africans and 7,395 Europeans; but the latter controlled the overwhelming bulk of commerce and industry, and owned or managed the tea, flue-cured tobacco, and tung estates which produced slightly more than half of the territory's exports by value and were the main employers of labor. Moreover, Europeans still outnumbered Africans in the senior posts of the civil service and held key positions in the police and army. Many of these white residents had come to think of Malawi as home and wished to remain there indefinitely. As the country advanced to independence under black rule, they pressed for constitutional arrangements which would enable them to protect their interests and make a continuing contribution to the country's economic development.

During the colonial period adjustments were repeatedly made in the structure of the legislature to reconcile growing African aspirations and persistent European apprehensions. For many years both communities were represented in the legislative council by Europeans whom the British governor invited to sit with a majority of colonial officials. Africans did not gain admission until 1949 when two were appointed. Elections were introduced by the 1955 constitution which established a legislature with six members chosen by voters under a franchise that excluded Africans, five Africans selected by the African provincial councils, and twelve officials.

In response to pressure from Dr. Banda, who returned to Nyasaland in 1958 to lead the nationalist movement, provision was made in 1960 for a majority of directly elected members—28 out of 33—and for the enfranchisement of about 100,000 Africans; but Europeans were guaranteed representation by a requirement that eight of the elected seats must be filled by voters on a separate roll with qualifications so high that less than 500 Africans could register on it. In the elections which followed, Dr. Banda's MCP won all twenty of the lower roll seats. Five of the higher roll seats were won by the European United Federal party (UFP) led by Mr. Michael H. Blackwood, one by an independent European, and two by the MCP.

A conference at London in 1962 and subsequent negotiations led to a reconstituted assembly containing 50 members elected by universal adult suffrage and, despite some objections in Nyasaland, three members elected by a special roll limited explicitly to Europeans. Only one candidate was nominated for each seat—by the MCP for all the general roll seats and by the Constitutional party (successor to the UFP) for all the special roll seats—and each was declared elected without ballots being cast. It was with this legislature that the Protectorate of Nyasaland became the independent constitutional monarchy of Malawi on July 6, 1964.

A little more than a year later, Dr. Banda announced that Malawi would become a republic on July 6, 1966, and appointed a ministerial committee to draft proposals for a new constitution. Its major tasks were to make provision for replacing the Westminster-style prime minister with a powerful president who would be both head of state and head of government and for establishing a one-party state de jure. The structure of Parliament was also open for reconsideration, however, and could now be determined by Malawians alone.

European representation seemed doomed, for the number of voters on the special roll now stood at only nine under the postindependence regulations which required citizenship for registration,

and Mr. Blackwood had informed Dr. Banda that he was not prepared to carry on with only two other European members since such
a small number could not cover the range of parliamentary business
satisfactorily. However, Dr. Banda expressed his personal view to the
chairman of the constitutional committee (and later publicly) that
it would be desirable to continue some kind of European representation and suggested that the president be authorized to appoint five
Europeans to the assembly. His suggestion was readily accepted, for
those ministers who had objected to seating Europeans earlier had
been dismissed or had resigned.

The committee submitted its draft to the annual convention of
the MCP in October 1965, and the delegates approved a resolution
proposing that the constitution "make provision for the President to
nominate not less than three nor more than five Europeans or other
representatives of minorities to represent their special interests."[1] A
slightly revised version of the proposal was included in a white paper
which Parliament endorsed the following month, and the constitutional bill was passed by that body on May 17, 1966. The explicit reference to Europeans and to a guaranteed minimum number of seats
for them which had appeared in the earlier discussions and drafts
was dropped from the final text. It read: "The President may appoint
as nominated members of the National Assembly such persons, not
exceeding five in number, as he considers desirable so to do in order
to enhance the representative character of the Assembly, or to represent particular minority or other special interests in the Republic."[2]
A later article specified that such a member must vacate his seat "if
the President so directs."[3]

It is clear that Dr. Banda was primarily responsible for including
five Europeans in the new republican parliament. Why did a man
who had fought long and hard against Europeans for a system of
government based on universal suffrage and majority rule now favor
an arrangement that allowed them privileged and disproportionate
representation, that smacked of colonialism and racialism, and that
struck some Europeans as well as many Africans as retrograde?

One explanation is that this seemed the democratic thing to do.

1. *Malawi News*, 19 October 1965.
2. Republic of Malawi (Constitution) Act 1966, Art. 20, *Malawi Gazette* Supple-
ment, 17 June 1966, p. 19.
3. Ibid., Art. 28, p. 24.

Dr. Banda told the MCP convention: "Since they are here paying tax and [in] many, many ways helping this country, they must be represented in Parliament."[4] "I am glad that you have agreed we must have Europeans in Parliament because we have about 8,000 to 10,000 Europeans in this country and they play a very, very important role in our economic life. Therefore, it is right and fair that somehow they should be represented in Parliament."[5]

The fact that almost all of the Europeans were merely residents was regarded as immaterial. "True, they are not citizens here," he said, "but they will be here for some years. Some of them might even decide to stay here."[6]

He recognized that if the European community were to be effectively represented, it would have to be by appointment rather than by election. The nine voters registered on the special roll were far too few to be permitted to elect members on their own, and the only kind of white man who could be expected to win election by the general roll would be one who identified himself so thoroughly with African interests that he could hardly be regarded as a proper spokesman for the Europeans. Dr. Banda explained later that he had wanted "a degree of true European representation . . . even those Europeans whom we know do not agree with us . . . so that . . . I can gauge the feelings of the Europeans." He asked, "if we put it to open vote, would one of these get in here?" and answered, "not a chance."[7]

The democratic nature of the arrangement was emphasized by two leading cabinet members. Mr. J. Z. U. Tembo, minister of finance, claimed that the Europeans' presence indicated the government's willingness to tolerate some sort of opposition while establishing a one-party state, saying, "It is nonsense to suggest that we are killing the opposition. In fact, contrary to this view, the Prime Minister decided to increase their membership."[8] Mr. R. B. Chidzanja, minister of home affairs and leader of the house, maintained that the require-

4. Speech by the Prime Minister, Ngwazi Dr. Kamuzu Banda, at the Republic Constitutional Conference at Lilongwe on Wednesday, 13 October 1965, Press Release No. 1021/65 (Blantyre: Ministry of Information), p. 6.

5. Speech by the Prime Minister, Ngwazi Dr. Kamuzu Banda, when closing the Republic Constitutional Conference at Lilongwe on Sunday, 17 October 1965, Press Release No. 1028/65 (Blantyre: Ministry of Information), p. 4.

6. Malawi Hansard, Official Verbatim Report of the Debates of Parliament, 7 October 1965, p. 198.

7. Ibid., 14 October 1968, p. 119.

8. Ibid., 9 November 1965, p. 234.

ments of democracy would be satisfied "as long as the individual has the right of freedom of expression," and argued that the provision for the appointment of Europeans "shows that we in Malawi are freely and willingly prepared to permit the voice of minority representatives to be heard in our Parliament."[9]

To appreciate this explanation, it is necessary to understand the special meaning which Dr. Banda gave to the concept of democracy. He frequently disparaged "academic" and "theoretical" democracy as unrealistic, and rejected the idea that the form which democracy had taken in Britain or the United States was applicable to Malawi. What he valued was "practical democracy"—democracy suited to local conditions, democracy which produced results and in particular improved the living conditions of the ordinary people and made them happy.

The one-party system was held to be democratic because the people had demonstrated in the elections of 1961 and 1964 that they wanted only MCP candidates and because the convention and the assembly had endorsed the new constitution which simply legalized a de facto situation. It was also justified on the "practical" grounds that Malawi could not afford wasteful disunity which threatened political stability and distracted the government from its efforts to promote economic development.

Democracy found expression within the single party, Dr. Banda maintained, for the rank-and-file members could play a part in the selection of legislators and the president and could petition for the removal of the former, and their delegates to the party convention, which he termed "the primary Parliament of this country,"[10] could question ministers and decide what the government should do.

No factions would be tolerated in the MCP, however; party members at all levels were frequently exhorted to adhere strictly to the "Four Cornerstones" of Unity, Loyalty, Obedience, and Discipline. Anyone who disturbed political stability would be detained, Dr. Banda warned, for stability was essential for economic development which would produce those benefits that were the true measure of democracy. In such a context, it is clear that the nomination of five Europeans to parliament could hardly be interpreted as striking a

9. Ibid., p. 238.
10. The President Speaks at the Closing Session of the Malawi Congress Party Annual Convention at the Kwacha National Cultural Centre in Blantyre on Saturday, 7 September 1969 (Blantyre: Department of Information), p. 2.

meaningful blow for democracy, as that concept is ordinarily understood in the West.

This arrangement did not signify respect for minorities generally, for the Europeans were regarded as a special case. All valid African interests were held to be embraced in the MCP and fully represented by its leaders; those Africans who dissented from party policy were by definition subversive and were not allowed freedom of expression. Europeans, as the only legitimate and acceptable minority, were formally relegated to a position outside the arena where policy was ostensibly made, for they were specifically denied membership in the party.

Nor did the provision for their separate representation in the Assembly signify the acceptance by Dr. Banda of the kind of parliamentary opposition which is associated with Western democracy. The nominations would be made by the president alone and would become effective without approval by anyone else. Dr. Banda assured the House that he would bring in "only those Europeans . . . who work with us, who are not coming here to cause trouble and be just a nuisance."[11] They would retain their seats at his pleasure, and there was good reason to believe that a frontal assault on the government would result in their speedy dismissal. Facing a tightly disciplined majority ten times their number, they stood no chance of defeating government policies in the legislature. There was no point in appealing beyond the walls of the House for support from the voters with a view to displacing the incumbents, for Dr. Banda controlled the nomination and electoral processes absolutely. Indeed, they must take care to do nothing which might be interpreted as interfering in the internal politics of Malawi, for it had been made clear that Europeans who cultivated anti-Banda sentiment would be promptly deported. Thus the so-called opposition presented no alternative to the present government. It simply had an opportunity to be heard, within severely defined limits, as a permanent minority.

This arrangement was, however, an expression of "practical democracy" in that Dr. Banda hoped that it would assist economic development and so benefit the people. He believed that Malawi still needed Europeans both in the public service and in the private sector of the economy. The abrupt departure of large numbers of white civil servants would imperil the efficiency of the government, he

11. Malawi Hansard, 7 October 1965, p. 198.

feared, and a wholesale flight of white planters and businessmen—
or of their capital—would throw the economy into grave disorder.
The five seats were a tangible expression of his regard for European
interests and would, he hoped, be a means of winning, or maintaining,
their confidence and persuading them to remain. White faces in the
Parliament would also help to project a favorable image of the Banda
regime abroad and so be a means also of attracting private foreign
investors and gaining good will in the United Kingdom (which was
supplying 40 percent of Malawi's annual recurrent revenue and a
larger proportion of its capital funds), South Africa (which was an
important trading partner, provided jobs for thousands of Malawians,
and seemed a likely source of financial and technical assistance),
and Portugal (which controlled Malawi's access to the sea through
Mozambique).

A second reason for giving five seats to Europeans was Dr. Banda's
desire to demonstrate the nonracialism of his government. Ever since
his return to Nyasaland in 1958, he had emphasized repeatedly that
his objective was not only to win independence but also to "bridge
the gulf of disunity between the races." He frequently proclaimed
that he was not anti-European, that he had not come back to fight
white people as such but to fight an unjust system of government
which benefitted and was supported by whites. The right kind of
Europeans—that is, those who obeyed the laws, who did not consider
themselves superior but understood that the African majority must
rule and were willing to accept the African way of doing things, and
who did not meddle in politics—were welcome, either as citizens or
as residents. He wanted them to feel secure and happy in Malawi,
and he urged his followers to treat them with justice and kindness.
"I am ready to build a state," he said following his first electoral victory, "not for the Africans of this country alone, but for all the people
who live in this territory or who intend to make this territory their
home." [12]

The provision for European representation was explicitly linked
with his nonracialism when he addressed a mass rally after the MCP
convention had approved the new constitution, as follows: "Now . . .
that we are free and independent, we have no quarrel with Europeans. Therefore, there is no need for us to hate Europeans—whether
they be settlers, farmers, businessmen, missionaries, civil servants.

12. Nyasaland Protectorate Proceedings of the Legislative Council, 29 November
1961, pp. 103–4.

That is why I want Europeans in Parliament."[13] Giving institutional expression to nonracialism in this fashion was no doubt based on sincerely held values, but was most likely motivated by pragmatic considerations as well, for Dr. Banda was convinced that interracial harmony was essential for Malawi's economic development.

A third important reason for his decision was that Mr. Blackwood and the other European members who had faced him since he entered the legislature in 1961 had conducted themselves in a fashion which impressed him very favorably. Dr. Banda characterized them from time to time as a sensible, cooperative, and responsible opposition, and expressed gratitude for their constructive contributions. When he told the assembly of his desire for European representation, he stated: "In fact, it may do us a great deal of good. Already these three gentlemen here have proved their worth in this House."[14] In making his appointments, Dr. Banda decided to retain the three Europeans who had been elected to the previous parliament and to invite their leader, Mr. Blackwood, to suggest possibilities for the other two seats.

Mr. Blackwood was born in England in 1917 and came to Nyasaland in 1946 to join a law firm. In the following years he built up a handsome legal practice and became a director of over thirty companies. He entered the legislature in 1954, strongly resisted Dr. Banda's effort to take Nyasaland out of the Central African Federation and gain self-government under black rule, and was instrumental in the British decision to detain the African leader in 1959. "He was," Dr. Banda said, "my bitterest opponent when I came here."[15] Since the MCP triumph in 1961, however, he had won Dr. Banda's respect; the latter described him as "a gentleman in the true tradition" for he had fought hard but had extended his hand in friendship once he was defeated and had not run away.[16]

Second in seniority among the white incumbents was Mr. Ernest C. Peterkins, who was born of British parents in Barbados in 1893. He came to Nyasaland in 1919, developed a large tobacco and tung farm, and became chairman of the Tung Board and a director of several companies. He had served in the legislature since 1958 and had made friends among the African members who called him "Uncle" and

13. The Prime Minister's Speech at the Mass Rally at Lilongwe on Sunday, 17 October 1965, Press Release No. 1030/65 (Blantyre: Ministry of Information), p. 7.
14. Malawi Hansard, 7 October 1965, p. 198.
15. Ibid., 1 November 1973, p. 248.
16. Ibid., 13 April 1965, p. 713.

frequently responded to his remarks with good-humored laughter and interjections.

Mr. E. M. Hendry was the junior European member. Born in England in 1893, he came to Nyasaland in 1920 and had worked as an engineer, a tobacco planter, and the manager of an agricultural grading station. When he entered the legislature in July 1965, the Leader of the House, who was from the same area, welcomed him as "a man of understanding . . . who cooperates with all of us," and added: "We agreed that in Lilongwe he was the only man who was acceptable to all."[17]

Mr. Blackwood suggested four candidates for the remaining seats—two tea planters and two tobacco planters—and discussed their qualifications at length with Dr. Banda. The latter interviewed all four in March 1966 and chose the two who were also Mr. Blackwood's first choices.

One of these was Mr. Christopher Barrow who was born in Nyasaland in 1930, the son of Sir Malcolm Barrow who had been one of Dr. Banda's principal enemies in the colonial period. Young Barrow went to work in his father's tea business and advanced to the position of joint managing director of the Naming'omba Tea Estates in 1961. He was also a director of several other tea estates and companies, a trustee of the Tea Research Foundation, and a director of the Tea Association of Central Africa.

The other was Mr. J. A. A. (Drew) Henderson. He was born in Nyasaland in 1931, began growing flue-cured tobacco in 1950, and had become chairman of the family company which owned the Chiwale Estates and a member of the Council of the Tobacco Association.

In analyzing the behavior of the European members of parliament one is struck by the extent to which the forms of a Westminster-style two-party system were retained despite the dissolution of Mr. Blackwood's party (as required by the constitution) and their repeated affirmation that they did not perceive themselves as an opposition and did not wish to be so regarded by others.

The Minority Group, as they were sometimes called, sat together on the Speaker's left, facing the African members. They organized themselves into a team with each one specializing in a limited range of matters, chose their own leader, deputy leader, and whip, and

17. Ibid., 14 July 1965, p. 101.

caucused separately from the Africans. Mr. Blackwood rose to speak on almost every bill or motion and raised numerous queries on the estimates, and the minister in charge took care to reply to him point by point before the vote was taken. The European representatives had no difficulty catching the Speaker's eye and the timetable seemed always to be arranged to allow them adequate opportunity to make their voices heard. Mr. Blackwood was named chairman of the Public Accounts Committee and served also on the Standing Orders Committee. His only complaint regarding the conduct of business was that bills were sometimes not published soon enough before the debate took place.

There were significant differences from the Westminster procedures, however. The Europeans asked no parliamentary questions until November 1972, when members on both sides were privately encouraged to make greater use of this device. Even then a total of only eight questions, plus six supplementaries, were put by the minority. They introduced only one motion beyond those moved by Mr. Blackwood which sought adoption of reports by the Public Accounts Committee. They moved amendments to only five bills and one motion, after having determined in each case that the government would accept it, and they called for the withdrawal of only two bills. There were never any divisions, and in the voice votes no's were heard from the European side on only two or three occasions.

The tone and substance of the debates were very unlike that of a two-party system. The Europeans refrained from attacking the government and its basic policies. They uttered no taunts. Their parliamentary questions were not contentious. Their single motion registered approval of the president's steps to develop friendly relations with neighboring states and of the progress made in economic development. They regularly welcomed the main budget proposals and expressed special appreciation for presidential statements regarding the tea, flue-cured tobacco, and tung industries. Ministers were congratulated on their performance, and the praise lavished on the president bordered on the extravagant. The only public servants whom they criticized were some in the Statistics Department, the Post Office, and the Ministry of Works.

The European members almost always accepted bills and motions in principle and restricted their criticism to a few technical flaws and matters of detail relating to means rather than ends. They supported without question or reservation 202 of the 274 bills on which they spoke. The remainder included some in which they spotted typographical errors, some with provisions they wished to have clarified, some which prompted requests for assurances as to how they would be implemented, and some which evoked mild complaints. They indicated that they would like to see substantive changes in only thirty-five bills, most often to remedy defects or to assure that the law would accomplish what was intended.

The measures to which they objected most strongly were those which threatened European interests most directly. They voiced concern over the extension of government controls of private enterprise, the development of state trading, and the acquisition by the government of land which was idle or was being farmed by tenants. They sought assurances that these policies did not herald nationalization and would be introduced gradually with due regard for the rights of those affected and in such a way as not to disrupt the existing patterns of commerce and agriculture.

The president and his ministers thanked the European members for their support, and generally undertook to answer their arguments cordially and fully. Only rarely did they appear irritated, abrupt, or evasive.

The president was persuaded to withdraw the Estate Duty Bill after Mr. Blackwood had explained how higher inheritance taxes would cause money to be diverted from investment in local development. In announcing this action, the minister of finance asserted: "We on this side have always made it clear that we listen to constructive argument about Bills or about any issue."[18] The government not only accepted amendments to five bills moved by Mr. Blackwood, but also moved amendments to 14 other bills to meet points raised by the Europeans in the debates. Ministers rejected European objections to 15 bills, but took note of the points made and promised that the laws would be administered fairly.

Some indication of the ground rules for criticism was provided in the debate on a bill which required the registration of building contractors and consultants to ensure that only those with proper qualifications would do business in Malawi. Mr. Blackwood's complaints about some of its provisions struck the president as altogether appropriate, although not convincing. "I do not at all blame the Honourable Member for taking a strong line here on anything," he stated.

18. Ibid., 21 December 1966, p. 246.

"That is what he is here for." He reacted sharply, however, to Mr. Blackwood's charges that the Ministry of Works was increasingly taking on jobs that could be done more economically by private contractors and was not making a proper cost accounting of its construction projects. He denied these charges with some heat and, in his only reprimand to the European representatives during their entire tenure, said that he felt "shocked" and "let down" and that Mr. Blackwood was "not now speaking as a responsible leader of a responsible Opposition."[19]

There were several reasons, apart from the constraints under which they operated, why the European members were so rarely critical. One was that they viewed Dr. Banda as their principal protector and considered his policies to be for the most part in their own interest. They deeply appreciated his antiracialism and were greatly impressed by how much more favorably Europeans were treated in Malawi than in other black-ruled states. His determination that Africanization should proceed slowly both in the government and in the economy and his frequent calls for racial harmony gave them a feeling of security. The summary deportation of a substantial number of white residents caused some uneasiness among those who remained, but evoked from the European members nothing more than a request that the reasons for such actions be publicized, for these measures were regarded by the latter as generally justified.

They welcomed his economic policies, for he was clearly committed to capitalist strategies for development. He was quite willing to provide the incentives and guarantees which encouraged local entrepeneurs and attracted foreign investors. He even named Mr. Blackwood chairman of a committee to review the country's tax structure, and agreed to alter the income tax in accordance with its recommendations. Although he favored state trading where private business was not doing the job to his satisfaction, as well as partnership arrangements under which government corporations acquired shares in certain privately owned firms, he repeatedly emphasized his opposition to nationalization of European companies and estates. Under his rule, business was good and Europeans were prospering.

They accepted his special brand of democracy because it provided law and order and political stability which permitted their enterprises to flourish. Freedom to attack the government, to form competing

19. Ibid., 14 October 1968, pp. 118, 123.

political parties, and to contest elections could not benefit Europeans for they would stand no chance of gaining power themselves and there was certainly no other African politician on the scene who could be expected to be more sympathetic to their interests. Indeed the dissidents whom Dr. Banda suppressed so harshly were typically anti-European and anticapitalist. The welfare of Europeans would obviously be best served by working with rather than against him.

The pages of Hansard do not tell the full story of the role of the European representatives in the legislative process. Actually, they were able to achieve a great deal behind the scenes as a result of direct contacts with the president, certain ministers, and some of the senior civil servants, particularly Mr. Brian Roberts who served as attorney general and permanent secretary to the president and the cabinet until May 1972. Mr. Blackwood enjoyed ready access to these levels of authority and was listened to respectfully. He was sometimes consulted on bills at the drafting stage and his suggestions were incorporated before they were published. On other occasions, he communicated his objections privately after a bill had been published but before the debate took place in the House, and the minister indicated when introducing the bill that he would move certain amendments at the committee stage—amendments which had been accepted to accommodate Mr. Blackwood's views, although this was not revealed in every case. Agreement was not always reached, of course, but Mr. Blackwood was able to accomplish so much through these private preliminary negotiations that there was less need for him to press European interests publicly. He understood that the government preferred for changes to be sought in this fashion since they could be made with less embarrassment, and he was quite willing to comply with its wishes since he was not out to score political points with the electorate.

This kind of "prenatal" activity cannot be fully documented and no precise estimate can be made of its frequency or effectiveness, but there are enough references in the published discussions to indicate that it was certainly not unusual. A striking example appeared in the debate on the Land Acquisition Bill which authorized the takeover of certain European-owned properties. When the minister introduced that measure he indicated that since its publication the government had received representations that the provisions regarding the assessment of compensation could give rise to "cases of real hardship or injustice," had reconsidered those provisions, and would

move amendments "designed to remove this possibility." Mr. Blackwood welcomed the amendments, saying: "Most of the real complaints which reached me ... are dealt with I think fairly."[20]

The rather cordial working relationship between the minority
group and the government had another aspect: the former served as
an important communication channel from the latter to the European community through which policy could be explained and support for it mobilized.

The president and the ministers frequently asked the European
members to assure those with whom they associated that they had
nothing to worry about so long as they obeyed the laws and refrained
from dishonest, arrogant, and subversive behavior. They were also
requested to encourage their acquaintances to invest their money in
Malawi, to invite local participation in their businesses, to develop
their property, etc. Dr. Banda called on Mr. Blackwood to "influence
his people ... to do things here that make sense," adding "It is your
job."[21] The minister of trade and industry spelled out the Europeans'
responsibility as follows: "They are in this House, not just because we
want to have some few Members of Parliament who do not look like
us. They are here in order to assist us. Some of us do not move in
their circles. ... They can help us more by giving the correct information to those people who are failing to do this or that."[22]

Mr. Blackwood and his colleagues conscientiously undertook to
perform this function. They promised to relay the messages and in
some cases indicated that they had already done so. Mr. Barrow re-
plied to the minister of trade and industry in these terms: "We do
go to very considerable lengths to assist you gentlemen in the front
bench and try to put the whys and wherefores and the reasons for
Government action. We do spend a very considerable time talking
to members of the private sector in industry and business. ... Where
we can give answers, we try to assure them and reassure them."[23]

In his speech opening the annual convention of the MCP on September 2, 1973, Dr. Banda asked the delegates to consider whether the
five Europeans should continue to sit in the national assembly. He
indicated that in his opinion the time had come for them to withdraw, whereupon the convention resolved to recommend the im-

20. Ibid., 29 July 1970, pp. 552–53.
21. Ibid., 23 April 1969, p. 368.
22. Ibid., 18 March 1970, p. 291.
23. Ibid., p. 295.

mediate abolition of European representation. The five members promptly submitted their resignations, but were prevailed upon by the president to serve through the next meeting, i.e., until November 1, 1973.

This move seemed quite abrupt, although Dr. Banda had told Mr. Blackwood in private shortly before the convention what he intended to do, and the reasons for it were not readily apparent. There had been no indication that the government had grown displeased with the Europeans' performance. Dr. Banda had reappointed them at the time of the April 1971 general election, and there had been no discernible change in the pattern of their behavior since then. Dr. Banda had, in fact, praised Mr. Blackwood warmly as recently as July 13, 1973, at the last meeting before the convention.

The official explanation offered by the president was that the arrangement was undemocratic since so few Europeans had become citizens of Malawi. At the convention he stated that when the decision was made to nominate European members "it was hoped that enough Europeans would register as citizens of Malawi to justify their being represented in Parliament." At that time there were twenty-three European citizens and since then, he reported, the number had not changed. "In any country," he argued, "representation and membership in Parliament is a privilege which is enjoyed by the citizens of that country."[24] He later told the national assembly that he had put the matter to the convention because it was unfair "by any democratic standards anywhere in the world" for twenty-three people to "have their own sectional representation, five at that."[25]

This argument was not consistent, however, with the case which had been made for European representation originally. There was no talk then of linking their seats to the number of citizens; the nominated members were designated as representatives of the important European economic interests and of the entire resident European community, and their retention of these seats was not made contingent on an increase in the number of European citizens. On several occasions Dr. Banda had emphasized that Europeans were welcome as citizens or residents and should feel no compulsion to become citizens.

The president and his ministers took great care to emphasize that

24. *Malawi News*, 7 September 1973.
25. Malawi Hansard, 1 November 1973, p. 244.

the abolition of European representation did not signify a change in the government's policy of racial tolerance. It seems likely, however, that racialism was not entirely absent from the decision.

There are those who believe that there was growing pressure on Dr. Banda to adopt policies which were less favorable to Europeans from some of his lieutenants, particularly Mr. Albert A. Muwalo, minister of state in the president's office, who had taken over the key position of secretary general of the MCP following the dismissal of Mr. Aleke Banda on March 9, 1973. Mr. Muwalo was said to dislike Europeans, and his speeches in parliament were certainly more anti-European than Mr. Aleke Banda's. Removing the European members may have been a concession to his demands, although Dr. Banda's power was such that this step would not have been taken unless he himself was convinced of its wisdom.

It is not unlikely that the president was growing fearful that the usefulness of Mr. Blackwood and his colleagues not only in the House but in any other capacity would be compromised if they remained much longer. They did serve as exposed targets for the African members who sat opposite them, and some felt that the remarks directed to them were becoming more pointed and more explicitly racialist in character. Mr. Blackwood said in his final speech that he had "no regrets" about leaving, not only for personal and financial reasons, but also because "we have felt from time to time, even recently, that our presence here has sometimes lent to a more racial approach than would otherwise have been the case."[26] Dr. Banda may very well have decided to remove them to reduce the "racial approach" and before racial confrontation sharpened to such an extent that the Europeans would be unacceptable for service on boards and commissions where he felt that their experience and skills were badly needed. Mr. Barrow, for example, might be expected to make a greater contribution to the development of Malawi in his capacity as chairman of the Electricity Supply Commission than as a nominated member of parliament, and his presence in the legislature might best be sacrificed if it jeopardized in any way his leadership of the commission. Moreover, Mr. Blackwood could continue to serve as a source of expert advice and as an effective link with the European community without being "on the firing line" in parliament.

26. Ibid., 31 October 1973, p. 220.

It can be said, in conclusion, that the arrangement for European representation proved useful as a temporary expedient in a critical transitional stage of Malawi's development.

The European members certainly made valuable contributions to the work of the House. This was particularly true of Mr. Blackwood who by virtue of his legal training, lengthy parliamentary experience, and keen critical mind was able to spot defects in bills which escaped others. He and his colleagues by virtue of their association with commerce, industry, and estate agriculture were able to bring to bear in the deliberations information and points of view which would not have been provided otherwise. Moreover, their speeches were carefully prepared and gracefully delivered; it was evident that they had given serious thought to the bills and motions before rising to comment on them. Thus they set a certain standard of debate for less experienced members to emulate. Dr. Banda and his ministers expressed appreciation for these contributions on several occasions. At the last meeting attended by the Europeans he told them with evident sincerity: "We have benefitted from your stay here."[27]

By causing ministers to explain and justify their policies and by securing assurances that laws which caused concern would be administered reasonably, they certainly assisted in building wider understanding and support among Europeans for the government and its works. Their ability to articulate European interests before final decisions were made assisted in creating a climate of confidence among businessmen and planters. Although the continuing large scale involvement of European capital and skills in the economic development of Malawi cannot be attributed to this arrangement alone, it is not unreasonable to regard it as a significant factor.

This experiment in communal representation was not, however, in origin, operation, or termination of such a nature as to signify that constitutional democracy was alive and well in Malawi or to generate confidence in its prospects.

It did not reflect a commitment to liberal democratic principles regarding rights of minorities and freedom of opposition. A particular— and unique—minority was given a voice in parliament primarily for reasons of expediency, and its representatives were responsible to the president alone. It is true that he selected individuals who were authentic leaders of the European community, that they were some-

27. Ibid., 1 November 1973, p. 248.

times critical, and that their suggestions were occasionally accepted. However, they had to operate cautiously and they could not provide the electorate with alternative policies or candidates. This proved to be somewhat less oppressive for them than might have been the case because they generally favored Dr. Banda's policies and because they were able to shape legislation to some extent prenatally.

The provision for nominated members in the republican constitution fell far short of guaranteeing continued representation for the white minority. The Europeans were told more than once that they were in parliament solely because Dr. Banda wanted them there; his magnanimity, not their rights, accounted for their presence. In fact, their status was doubly precarious. It was not simply the tenure of individual appointees which was subject to the president's pleasure; the same was true of the seats themselves. He was restrained from abolishing European representation altogether neither by the terms of the constitution nor by the political culture and popular will. Mr. Muwalo struck an ominous note when he asserted:

> Kamuzu [i.e., Dr. Banda] has asked us to maintain peace and law in this country. The man, therefore, who is our President is their [i.e., the Europeans'] insurance. If they are living in this country peaceably then they are only doing so because Kamuzu is here. To us what Kamuzu says is Law. To us, we say Kamuzu knows best.[28]

> These foreign guests must be grateful because their very existence and presence among us is made possible through the insurance . . . in one man, and that is His Excellency the Life President. If His Excellency the Life President let loose of us, I cannot tell you what the consequences will be.[29]

Although Dr. Banda was powerful enough to impose his will, he was not only mortal and already in his late sixties but was also capable of changing his mind on matters of fundamental importance. European representation was so weakly institutionalized that it not only stood no chance whatever of surviving Dr. Banda—especially since Mr. Muwalo was a leading contender for the succession—but also could be abruptly liquidated once he alone decided, as he did in August 1973, that it was no longer expedient.

28. Ibid., 1 December 1970, p. 737.
29. Ibid., 22 March 1973, p. 744.

At present Europeans are totally excluded from parliament. Those who have become Malawi citizens can vote, but they are not allowed to join the MCP which means not only that they cannot stand for election themselves but also that they cannot play a part in the nomination of candidates who are invariably elected without contest. The franchise therefore has no meaning for them. Moreover, Europeans do not consider the newly nominated African members as their representatives—nor does anyone else.

The abolition of communal representation is not such a serious loss to the Europeans, however, for the parliament is after all of very little significance in the policy-making process and their leaders, particularly Mr. Blackwood, still enjoy access to the president's office which is the real locus of power. So long as Dr. Banda continues to make personally the decisions that matter and to accord Europeans a sympathetic hearing, they need not despair. The current arrangement allows the white minority considerable influence and affords it protection from the black majority, momentarily at least. It further downgrades the role of parliament, however, and does not contribute to the development of a genuinely democratic system which requires competing interests to be articulated and reconciled openly in a representative assembly.

> Abandoned incorrigible people say ancient and present times were different in nature ... The Sage cannot be so deceived.
>
> — Hsün Tzǔ
> (trans. by H. H. Dubs)

> Footprints are made by shoes, but they are far from being shoes.
>
> — Lao Tzu
> (trans. by Arthur Waley)

Few phenomena have been subjected to more analysis in social science than the related concepts of social change and its inducement by transnational efforts. Components of such analysis undergird the extensive operations of both public and private foreign aid activities, the commerce of multinational corporations, and, in academic endeavors, much of the work in comparative studies. In this essay, I propose to develop somewhat new theoretical perspectives which have profound bearing on the closely allied concept of change which results from identification of cause within a context constantly being transformed.

I

In the forced but largely unsuccessful efforts at the reconstruction of political systems of developing countries during the last quarter century, we have been involved in the sometimes systematic but more usually idiosyncratic use of ideas, norms, or technologies of radiating (donor) political systems. I propose here a new intellectual posture which is not only more valid historically but far more replicative of real contemporary events leading to change. This new perspective requires the abandonment of terms encrusted with distracting connotations. We must use as substitutes either terms of new manufacture or those so old that their connotative encumbrances have sloughed off to reveal a useful pristinity. Thus we seek to discard the terms *transfer* and *transformation* of institutions or norms—terms in commonest use in referring to this phenomenon. The concept of transfer continues to have ethnocentric connotations, principally that of unidirectional movement from a radiating to a recipient society. The terms *diffusion* and *rediffusion* of technology, which are here proposed as alternative concepts, suggest a high degree of dynamic reciprocity rather than a flow in one direction.

The term *technology* is also more useful than institution, norm, or idea. By technology is meant a body of knowledge which incorporates a distinctive way of viewing the universe and has a relatively stable, or at least an identifiable doctrine, or paradigm, and which may include certain somatic skills. Such technologies may be divided into two general classes. The first may be called hard technologies, or those which are distinctive because somatic skill manipulation (arranged in an order of drill or sequence of actions) rather than complex intellectual doctrine predominates. Engineering and military affairs come to mind as examples. That is not to say that intellectual content or doctrine is totally absent, but rather that it is inoperative without the intervention of a heavy component of somatic skill manipulation. The second class can be called social technologies in which intellectual or doctrinal content predominates virtually to the exclusion of somatic skill manipulation. In this second class can be included such technologies as law, the judiciary, commerce, education, as well as both public and private administration and management.

Apart from the advantage of avoiding an unrealistic description of unidirectional, hence, ethnocentrically generated reconstruction, there is another reason for using the concepts of *diffusion* and *technology*. This involves the vexing problem of distinguishing between what we call loosely the indigenous and the imported. The dichotomy implied by these two words so common in the literature of reconstructing new political systems is too sharp and overdrawn. What is indigenous? In Asian systems with their own profound, ancient, and complex societies sustained by great bodies of canonical doctrine, both secular and sacerdotal, and ruled by Britain, the Netherlands, France, or the United States for significant periods, it is extremely difficult, if not impossible, to separate what is indigenous and what is not. Early mixtures of Taoism, Confucianism, Buddhism, Hinduism, Christianity, and Islam, and further European imperial rule, became wrought into a mosaic not always elegant, but certainly intricate and irreducible. The uncertain genesis and mixed evolution of complex social phenomena is illustrated by the more traceable evolution of language. The mixtures of European languages are well known. Even in Asia, largely as a consequence of British rule in the subcontinent and adjacent areas, we find linguistic diffusions so forceful that their earlier genesis is unknown and even denied.[1] If we think in terms of diffusion, we are less likely to be detoured into sterile intellectual argument with respect to the genesis of a particular norm, practice, or institution. Except for historiographic purposes, genesis for its own sake ought not unduly occupy our attention. Tracing the historical roots of most diffused phenomena is complicated by archeological findings which constantly require new periodizations and rearrangements of antecedent and postcedent phenomena.

What is now a concern for genesis should be replaced by a focus on what might be called the *transitory effervescence* of particular ideas or technologies at various locations on the globe. At given moments in history, a particular idiom, or a distinctive way of perceiving the universe or perceiving what is important may effervesce. The causes for such effervescence remain unknown. Superficially, they may appear to be related to the dynamics of modern communications technology with its supportive tissue of sustained liminal and subliminal indoctrination so well forecast in Orwell's *1984*. Yet often the causes of such effervescence are beguilingly simple. One brief visit to China by James Reston and his account of acupuncture in the *New York Times* gave this ancient practice global attention almost overnight without the apparatus of sustained, planned advertising or the dynamic intervention of profit-seeking international commerce. Probably one of the reasons for such transitory effervescence is the simple act of imitation. There is need to reconsider appreciatively earlier analyses of the power of extralogical forces which not infrequently result in the diffusion of technologies as in a "craze."[2] Equally useful is Allen's assertion that once the process of imitation

1. See the many intriguing examples in Henry Yule and A. C. Burnwell, *Hobson-Jobson: A Glossary of Colloquial Anglo-Indian Words* . . . , ed. William Crooke, new ed. (London, 1903).

2. Gabriel Tarde, *The Laws of Imitation*, trans. Elsie Crews Parsons from the 2d French ed. (New York, 1903).

is begun it goes "far beyond the stimuli of expediency and utility alone, and gathers momentum of its own motion." [3] He cites Maine's defense of the power of imitation and the manner in which the British constitution, once regarded as an "eccentric political oddity," spread over nearly all Europe in less than seventy years.[4] It may be that imitation is related to the global power and prestige of the political system in which it effervesces. Thus, the prestige of technologies may rise, fall, and be rejected. This is probably what we are now witnessing in Asia as the global position of the United States declines and the position of China and the Soviet Union rises.

When we consider the ancient systems of Asia, and to some extent, Africa, it is especially crucial that we consider the diffusion of transitorily effervescent technologies rather than the transfer of ideas if these systems are to recapture pride and dignity in their own cultural forms. The ethnocentric hubris of the Western world has too long distorted the significance of Asian systems. Thus, Macaulay's *Minute on Education* written for India in 1835 declared Sanskrit and Pali inferior to Latin and Greek. Nor did Tennyson's dictum, "Better fifty years of Europe than a cycle of Cathay" seem out of place for its time. Confucius, Lao Tzŭ, and Kautilya are rarely to be found in modern political theory volumes, although paradoxically, Janet devoted a chapter to the Sage in his *Histoire de la science politique . . .* in 1887.[5]

It is appropriate to cite four cases from administrative experience to illustrate that the diffusion of technologies is not necessarily from older to newer political systems. We have been conditioned to believe that we must reform Asian administrative systems by adapting Western technologies. But in truth, Western systems have been influenced by adaptation of Asian technologies. The beginnings of modern civil service can, for example, be traced to Confucian China. L. D. White suggested this in the first major text of public administration in the third edition of 1950 though he omitted it from the earlier editions of a quarter century before.[6] We now know that Lord McCartney based the Indian Civil Service on what he saw of the Chinese system. The

3. Carleton Kemp Allen, *Law in the Making*, 6th ed. (London, 1958), pp. 96 ff., esp. p. 106.

4. Henry Sumner Maine, *Dissertations on Early Law and Custom* (New York, 1883), p. 284.

5. Paul Janet, *Histoire de la science politique dans ses rapports avec la morale*, 3ième ed. 2 toms (Paris, 1887).

6. Leonard D. White, *Introduction to the Study of Public Administration*, 3d ed. (New York, 1950), p. 353.

Indian system in turn influenced the British and the Northcote-Trevelyan Act in Britain set the pattern for the Pendleton Act in the United States. Hansard's Debates of 1853 and the Congressional Record twenty years later record expressions of horror that Britain and the United States were copying the administrative forms of a barbaric, heathen land. This account of Chinese influence on Western civil service, first advanced in 1943 by Ssŭ-Tü Têng[7] must be a shocking revelation to those conditioned to believe that Asia depends exclusively on the West for patterns of "sound and efficient" government.

Somewhat less enthralling but still of corroborative value is Derk Bodde's discovery in 1945 that Henry Wallace, United States secretary of agriculture in the administration of Franklin Roosevelt in the 1930's, first learned about the idea of the ever-normal granary from reading a Columbia University doctoral dissertation by Chen Huan-chang entitled *The Economic Principles of Confucius and His School.* Wallace used the term in a series of editorials for *Wallace's Farmer* and the idea found statutory expression in the second Agricultural Adjustment Act of 1938.[8]

Consider for a moment that little known feature of Chinese government, the censorate, which ranked, along with the executive, legislative, judicial, and examination, as one of five coordinate branches of government which were the basis of the political reforms of Sun Yat-sen. Although the censorate existed in China in one form or another since 1000 B.C., political scientists had not been aware of it. Even when introduced to it by Richard L. Walker in 1947, and in 1951 by Charles O. Hucker,[9] scant attention was paid to it. We have known that a very similar institution called the council of censors existed in Vermont and Pennsylvania at the end of the Confederation and the beginning of the Republic. But, an otherwise thorough Syra-

7. Ssŭ-Yü Têng, "Chinese Influence on the Western Examination System," *Harvard Journal of Asiatic Studies* 7 (1943): 267–312. See also his "China's Examination System and the West," in Harley Farnsworth MacNair, ed., *China* (Berkeley, 1946) pp. 441–55. References to the Chinese system including a speech by T. B. Macaulay can be found in House of Commons, *Parliamentary Debates* 25 June 1853; 13 June 1853; 17 July 1863; 13 March 1854. References in the United States Congress to the Chinese system can be found in 43rd Cong., 1st Sess., (1873074) House Executive Documents, Document No. 221, *Report of the Civil Service Commission to the President,* 15 April 1874, p. 24.

8. Derk Bodde, "Henry A. Wallace and the Ever-Normal Granary," *The Far Eastern Quarterly,* August 1946, 411–26.

9. Richard L. Walker, "The Control System of the Chinese Government," *The Far Eastern Quarterly* VI (1947): 3–21, and Charles O. Hucker, "The Traditional Chinese Censorate and the New Peking Regime," *The American Political Science Review,* XLV (1951): 1041–58.

cuse University political science doctoral dissertation by Charlotte Cropley Brown on the Vermont and Pennsylvania censors, completed in 1946, traces the concept to Rome and makes no mention of the Chinese counterpart.[10] Yet the censorate is clearly the progenitor of the *ombudsman* which effervesced and was given its name in Scandinavian systems but has now spread to New Zealand, the United States, and Pakistan.

Finally, let us consider the currently popular idiom of participation—participatory democracy or participatory administration. A century ago, the participatory ethic effervesced in the United States in the form of the initiative, referendum, and recall as structural responses to widespread corruption in city and state government. Today, it emerges again as a regnant idiom as a response to distrust among racially and economically disparate groups in society. The evolution of the participatory ethic is far too complex to permit us to risk locating its genesis in time and space. Should it be traced to the early Scandinavian *folk moot*, to the social practice of obtaining consensus in the context of harmonious social relations so dominant in Asian society, to equivalent tribal practices in Africa or to the Westminster model of Britain?

We can frame our analysis of this first perspective and its implications for us in the following way. Developing systems of government in Asia and Africa must recover a sense of pride in their own manner of doing things. They must realize that there is not an inevitable and unilinear progression to Utopia which follows a route from West to East. If we think in terms of diffusion rather than transfer and of transitory effervescence rather than the inevitability of progression to a spurious modernity implying improvement, we can be better prepared to reassess the unique mode of each distinctive Asian or African system.

I do not mean to suggest antiquarianism, that is preserving what exists because of its aesthetically satisfying quaintness. On the contrary, it is incumbent upon every political system to seek out the advantages to itself of new technologies which arise almost at random at different places on the globe and at different times. Thus, it is morally imperative to adopt the technology consequent to Pasteur's germ theory of disease or the nutritional technology of protein-calorie malnutrition (PCM) or new technologies of administration. It is also

10. Charlotte Cropley Brown, *"The Vermont Council of Censors 1777–1870"* (Ph.D Diss., Syracuse University, 1946).

morally incumbent on the system in which this new knowledge arises, to facilitate although not to force, its global diffusion. On the other hand, it is a corresponding moral imperative for a system adapting a new technology to do so with extreme caution and only after assessing its own traditions for acculturated equivalents and using them whenever feasible. There is a moral responsibility to preserve man's psychic continuity with his past. This psychic continuity is typically fostered through religious and familial institutions which must be respected.

What I suggest is a new balance between the moral imperatives of change and psychic continuity. In one respect the forces of poverty and inertia have tipped the balance against change; indeed, this is the common complaint of modernizers. But in a more important respect, the balance has favored change simply because of the frightening momentum of change for its own sake, induced by the dynamic intervention of powerful radiating systems and transnational profit-seeking commerce. My plea here is for change in the context of profound comprehension of a system's cultural past and the psychic needs of its people. This context must embrace a new respect for the dignity and worth of unique cultures and a new suspicion, wariness, and even disdain for allegedly new social technologies dispensed by international traders who would feel at home in Jonathan Swift's Laputa and Balnibarbi where ignorance is concealed by a cloak of scientism and arrogance masked by a spurious humanism.

II

The recovery of pride in the culture of distinctive social systems is closely related to a principle which may be labelled "spiralling contextuality." Toffler, McLuhan, and Brzezinski have, in the perspectives of psychoanalysis, psychocommunications, and global power analysis, directed our attention to disparities in knowledge as well as in needs between newer political systems and those which are in a posttechnical (or technetronic) stage of development.[11] Despite rapid satellite communication, an enormous lag exists between postagrarian and technetronic nations. I do not refer here to the well-known problem of knowledge explosion. This expansion is a relatively simple problem, involving largely new criteria and techniques for rejection,

11. See Alvin Toffler, *Future Shock* (New York, 1970); Marshall McLuhan, *Understanding Media, The Extensions of Man* (New York, 1964); Zbigniew Brzezinski, *Between Two Ages: America's Role in the Technetronic Era* (New York, 1970).

selection, relating, and retrieval of segments of knowledge. Nor is the condition, as popular literature would have us believe, that developing nations simply lag behind or are backward. Rather, it is that rapid, almost revolutionary, changes in perceptions of knowledge resuscitate old notions which new countries may have discarded. New and old countries may be in a state of intellectual disequilibrium accepting and rejecting notions at an increasing rate of speed, thus promoting an instability in the order of knowledge bordering on intellectual disintegration. This is a complicated phenomenon which is elaborated below by three rather lengthy illustrations. The length is justified by the fact that this dimension of the problem of change is nowhere adequately treated in the relevant literature.

The designation "spiralling contextuality," inspired by Lasswell's treatment of contextual analysis, is used advisedly. By contextuality we mean a changing universe of referrents which are perceived as having an associational or perhaps even a causal relationship with an event or a segment of knowledge. The adjective "spiralling" is meant to convey an important perception. Context can expand or contract and it can move in either of two directions; hence the metaphor of the spiral, which also has these capabilities, seems to be of some explicative utility.

The context within which relationships are analyzed can change in at least three ways. The first can be called *episodic*; that is, a major discovery of new knowledge which substantially, dramatically and often immediately modifies a paradigm and hence the context. Such discoveries as Harvey's circulatory system of the living body, Pasteur's germ theory of disease, Watson's definition of the DNA molecule, Darwin's theory of evolution, Freud's exploration of the layers of the mind, Einstein's theory of relativity, Kirlian halophotography—to name but a few—are obvious examples by which contextuality was dramatically modified. A second determinant of change can be the result of *technological invention*. Such devices as the microscope and its electronic successors, x-ray, the computer, the space satellite are obvious examples which often create new knowledge and almost always enable new arrangements of knowledge, hence new perceptions. Space exploration, for example, not only revealed new knowledge but dramatically called our attention to the finite nature of the planet on which we live and the necessity for the recycling of resources on that planet. A third determinant of change may be characterized as being *reformulative*. In this category, we do not necessarily find dramatic new discoveries in knowledge. Rather an event or an episode either reformulates existing knowledge or directs attention to a different perception of relationships of existing knowledge. Such reformulation may set in motion a substantial change in contextuality. Illustrative of the latter would be Rachael Carson's *Silent Spring* which directed attention to ecological concerns. Other examples are Norbert Wiener's formulation of cybernetics, Lasswell and Lerner's formulation of policy sciences. Included in this third category are archeological discoveries which compel reformulations of existing knowledge, recast historical periodization, revise hypotheses of derivation and diffusion of cultural forms and of reciprocity in the relationship of civilizations, and expand the temporal and spatial dimensions of insights into man's behavior. Examples of this are the Egyptian excavations which made possible a scientific archeological system, discovery of the Rosetta Stone (1799) which made Egyptian hieroglyphics decipherable, Leakey's discovery of Rama [Kenya] pithecus (1968), the Mohenjodaro excavations of the Indus Valley civilization (1950), and the Xabis discoveries in Iran (1973) which may prove that true writing originated in Iran and moved westward into Mesopotamia instead of vice versa.

It cannot be said that any one of these determinants—*episodic, technological invention, reformulative*—acts in isolation of the others or that any one is more influential than the others in changing the contours of contextuality. Each class of determinant shades into the next class and each has effect on the others.

Change in contextuality produced by these three determinants occurs at two levels: in the perceptions of men and in the actions of institutions in consequence of changed perceptions. There is a reciprocal relationship between these two levels. Spiralling contextuality manifests itself spatially as when knowledge or technique from two distant points on the earth are associated together. Hence, the importance of global satellite communications which even now are in orbit over in India. There is also a temporal manifestation as when a reach into the past resurrects and reconsiders a doctrine once discarded (e.g., acupuncture, exorcism, and tribal medicine in the healing arts) and invests it with new validity. Before analyzing the significance of contextuality to change, it will be useful to give several illustrations to clarify the classification and generalizations made above. These illustrations are derived from the healing arts, social welfare, law, and nutrition.

In considering the first example drawn from the healing arts, it is essential to understand that we view the healing arts globally as embracing a variety of concepts and techniques. In this perspective, what is commonly but erroneously referred to as "Western," "scientific," or "modern" medicine is in reality but one small segment of the healing arts which we can designate as allopathy. Among other segments are homeopathy, osteopathy, naturopathy, chiropractic, Christian Science, unani and aryuvedic arts, herbalism, Persian, Arabic, witchcraft, voodoo, acupuncture, moxibustion, psychoanalysis, and clinical psychology. It is essential also to realize that there is perpetual change in status and acceptability across time and space among these perspectives. For example, homeopathy, founded by S. C. F. Hahnemann, has been absorbed by allopathy in part because the premises of *similia similibus curantur* were accepted and integrated into allopathy and in part because the M.D. degree awarded homeopaths had no separate identity. Osteopathy is in the process of being absorbed in a similar way and, indeed, in California complete structural integration of allopathy and osteopathy has occurred.

When we realize the spatial and temporal distinctions in modes of healing, we can view the spiralling movement of the context of healing with some clarity. At a given moment, a somatic disorder may be treated as a simple disturbance traced to a single source—perhaps a phase of the moon, bewitchment, or a blow on the head. Diagnostic, hence causal, inferences gradually expand to include such factors as skeletal arrangements, psychosomatic, interpersonal, chemical, and nutritional factors, and broadly environmental factors including the quality of air breathed. Other as yet unperceived factors may so expand as to once again embrace lunar causes and bewitchment though these may be perceived in different idioms, such as those of ionization and psychiatry. Expansion of the universe of causal referents to factors outside the afflicted person to include specific factors (e.g., water, air) and vague conditions (psychological) gives rise to "community" and "preventive" medicine and current efforts of "involved medical students" to appraise and rectify environmental sources of illness. One manifestation of this, directed towards analysis of the impact of tensions in family life on disease, is called social epidemiology. Indeed it has been said that the identification of behavioral and social factors in illness may become the most important skill of the physician as his diagnostic role is reduced and perhaps eventually displaced by computer technology.[12] In psychiatry a manifestation of the contextual principle is found in the controversial work of R. D. Laing at Kingsley Hall and the derivative "Network" movement in England, Europe, and America.[13] By removing the barrier between the "sane" physician and the "mad" patient, and by admitting the total context (psychic and physical) into diagnosis and therapy, psychiatric treatment becomes social rather than personal.

Spiralling contextuality includes not only spatial and essentially ethnocentric elements but temporal and transnational elements as well. Thus, there is a reconsideration of and a new deference accorded to ancient forms of healing, such as acupuncture, aryuvedic, and herbalism derivative from China, Persia, and tribal sources.[14] It is of no little significance that the training of new Navajo medicine men on the Rough Rock, Arizona, reservation was financed by the National Institute of Mental Health and that both the support and the program were praised by the American Psychiatric Association.[15] The changing nature of contextuality is reversible in its temporal dimensions as well as contractive and expansive in its spatial dimensions.

As a second example, similar expansion of context is evident in the social welfare profession, the emphasis of whose doctrine has changed from the individual to the community. One of that profession's leading scholars asserted that it is now commonplace for social work education to stress concern for the transformation of welfare agencies and of society as well as for change in individuals.[16] This doctrinal revolution has not gone unresisted within a profession so long dominated by the principle of the caseworker's help to the welfare re-

12. Ian Renwick McWhinney, "Beyond Diagnosis: Integration of Behavioral Science and Clinical Medicine," *The New England Journal of Medicine* 287 (1972): 384–88. On the role of computers in diagnosis see *The Wall Street Journal*, 9 July 1973, p. 24.

13. James S. Gordon, "Who is Mad? Who is Sane? R. D. Laing: In Search of a New Psychiatry," *The Atlantic* 227 (1971): 50–67. See also R. D. Laing, A. Esterson, *Sanity, Madness and the Family* (New York, 1970). See also Theodore R. Sarbin, "Schizophrenia is a Myth, Born of Metaphor, Meaningless," *Psychology Today* 6 (1972): 28–39.

14. For analysis consistent with this point of view, see Erwin H. Ackerknecht, "Primitive Medicine and Culture Pattern," *Bulletin of the History of Medicine* XII (1942): 545–74; Erwin H. Ackerknecht, "Problems of Primitive Medicine," ibid. XI (1941): 503–21; Ralph C. Croizier, "Medicine, Modernization, and Cultural Crisis in China and India," *Comparative Studies in Society and History* 12 (1970): 275–291.

15. *International Herald Tribune*, 12 July 1972, p. 16; E. Fuller Torrey, *The Mind Game* (New York, 1972). See also *Wall Street Journal*, 10 Jan. 1973, p. 14.

16. Robert Morris, "Overcoming Cultural and Professional Myopia in Education for Human Service," *Journal of Education for Social Work* 6 (1970): 46.

cipient as an individual. Indeed, Harry Specht said that the new ideological currents of "activism, anti-individualism, communalism, and environmental determinism" may bring the denouement of the social work profession.[17] The drastic change such a revolution in doctrine (context) requires of social work curricula is now a major theme in professional social work literature. Nor is this transformation limited to a single country; an analysis of global trends concludes that "[T]he boundaries of collective action for social welfare have been steadily expanded . . ."[18] and that social workers will play a more active part in bringing about planned change in society at large.

A third example may be taken from law whose universe of relevance has expanded significantly. Although our example is taken from one law school, the phenomenon is manifest in American legal education generally and to a lesser extent in legal practice.[19] Law students in the Duke University Law School have embarked on a program wherein they spend some time in North Carolina prisons and other correctional institutions as "inmates." This experience presumably enables them to learn about the rehabilitation needs of the prisoners after their release. They would then work through the institution of law to provide postrelease rehabilitative opportunities. Students expressed the view that the role of the lawyer in modern society is to go beyond the interpretation of statutes and the participation in litigation before courts; it must look after the rehabilitation of criminals who violate the law. A less extreme example in the law is the earlier establishment of legal aid clinics which provided the conceptual precedent for the "store-front" lawyer, and eventually for "curb-side judicare." We see first an expansion of the sphere of operational validity of traditional legal assistance to new groups formerly beyond the sphere of legal advice, then a transformation of the substantive content of legal aid given. This is an example par excellence of the concept of spiralling contextuality, especially in its spatial and its qualitative aspects. Here is the element of contextuality brought to bear on the psychological and sociological rehabilitative

17. Harry Specht, "The Deprofessionalization of Social Work," *Social Work* 17 (1972): 3.

18. Bernice Madison, "The Welfare State: Some Unanswered Questions for the 1970's," *The Social Service Review* 44 (1970): 434–51.

19. See, for example, Peter Vanderwicken, "The Angry Young Lawyers," *Fortune* LXXXIV (1971): Part 1, 74–77, 125–27; Part 2, "Towards the Socialization of Injury," ibid., 160–73 and Part 3, Robert H. Bork, "We Suddenly Feel that the Law is Vulnerable," ibid., 114–17. See also *The Wall Street Journal*, 13 Sept. 1971, p. 1.

mechanisms which are held necessary, and which presumably will be invoked after the law has been applied. This is drastic extension of traditional legal scholarship and practice to a conceptually and spatially unlimited context.

The foregoing three examples of spiralling contextuality illustrate an expansion of context from the individual to society. Just as often the spiral narrows from concern for society to the individual and even to successive layers of the individual's being. Thus, Freud's emphasis narrowed the spiral as it explored layers of the mind; yet the subsequent emphasis on the external (social) context of the mind's functioning expanded the spiral to society itself as manifest in the emphasis of R. D. Laing.

A comparable duality of movement from society to the individual is found in considering nutrition, our fourth and final example, and the development of political systems. Half a decade ago, our attention was directed to this problem[20] and more recently it has been given impetus by the World Bank's recognition of its importance.[21] Even earlier it was recognized in the Agency for International Development by establishment of an Office of Nutrition and by the AID-financed Southeast Asia Development Advisory Group's Nutrition Seminar.[22] We are not concerned here with the ancient and common problem of mere feeding of populations. Rather we are concerned with the quality of malnutrition and the strategic times in the life cycle when proper nutrition has maximum effect. We now know that protein-calorie malnutrition (PCM) during fetal and in the early years of postpartum growth profoundly and perhaps permanently affects the ability to reach full genetic potential.[23] Indeed we can legitimately raise the question that emphasis on raising living standards through "modernizing" societies may have minimal effect

20. Alan D. Berg, "Malnutrition and National Development," *Foreign Affairs* 46 (1967): 126–37; Alan Berg (portions with Robert J. Muscat), *The Nutrition Factor: Its Role in National Development* (Washington, D. C., 1973); See also Alan D. Berg, "Industry's Struggle with World Malnutrition," *Harvard Business Review*, January–February (1972): 130–41, esp. 139.

21. Robert McNamara, Annual Address to the World Bank Board of Governors, 27 Sept. 1971.

22. Southeast Asia Development Advisory Group "SEADAG Reports, Nutrition Workshop," 21–24 September 1970, Mimeographed (Ladyhill Hotel, Singapore), p. 10.

23. For general analysis see Nevin S. Scrimshaw and John E. Gordan, eds., *Malnutrition, Learning and Behavior* (Cambridge, Mass., 1968); Herbert G. Birch and Joan Dye Gussow, *Disadvantaged Children: Health, Nutrition and School Failure* (New York, 1970).

178 • *Ralph Braibanti*

so long as a population's intellectual, emotional, and physical capacities have already been determined by PCM. This example illustrates the ambivalence in determining whether the context is expanding or shrinking—hence the use of the more satisfactory term "spiralling." Certainly in terms of quality of depth of consideration, there is expansion from mere gross caloric intake to the protein ratio of such intake. Indeed the relationship between protein value and human behavior is even now being expanded beyond the syndrome (gross caloric intake—protein-calorie balance—timing of protein intake) suggested here. The chemical composition of protein is also important and this varies with the source of protein, i.e., animal or plant and even with the variety of plant, i.e., soybean or wheat.[24] Further, there is expansion from gross intake without regard to timing, to concern for fetal and three-year postpartum timing. Yet in another sense, the context contracts for it moves from large-scale activities to the individual and indeed, in the case of fetal growth, to very intimate aspects of the life cycles of both mother and child.

Such extension of the awareness of contextuality is one of the most important phenomena of contemporary life. Examples of this contraction and expansion of awareness need not be limited to the healing arts, social welfare, law, and nutrition as illustrated above. Further examples can be drawn from virtually all spheres of modern life. In education we have witnessed a steady deprivatizing of family to an expanding perception of public responsibility as organized schooling has stretched to embrace elementary, kindergarten, nursery, and prenursery levels. In the United States, in both Roman Catholic and Protestant varieties of organized Christianity, we find movements away from a focus on personal, spiritual regeneration emphasizing liturgy, meditation, and ecstatic phenomena to a concept of the social gospel expanded even to include revolutionary politics. The occasional retraction to personal regeneration induced by evangelism or by invigorated fundamentalist sects and more recently by interest in Oriental religions reveals the oscillating or reversible characteristic of this phenomenon which is not so clearly shown by other illustrations. In ethology, the work of Konrad Lorenz, Robert Ardrey, Lionel Tiger, and Robin Fox expands and deepens the context for analyzing man's behavior in a remarkable way.[25] It is probable that

24. See *Wall Street Journal*, 6 February 1973, p. 1.
25. Erich Fromm in *Anatomy of Human Destructiveness* (New York, 1973), p. 1., n. 1 asserts that long before Lorenz, John Stuart Mill used the term "ethology" de-

such new study of animal behavior will force a reclassification of instinctual and acculturated aspects of man's behavior. If what was formerly regarded as acculturated we now find to be instinctual simply because it is found in animal behavior never before observed, the monitoring, custodial and supportive roles of government with respect to these reclassified behaviors must be reinterpreted.

There are several significant connections between spiralling contextuality and our analysis of social change. The first of these is its relationship to the concept of causality. Transfer of the scientific method based on Descartes from the natural sciences to the social sciences carried with it an emphasis on identifying the causes of aspects of human behavior. A knowledge explosion, which greatly expanded the universe of referents in determining these causes, makes their isolation extremely difficult if not impossible. The cybernetic revolution which spawned computer technology gave new hope because of its capacity to classify and control data. But so extensive has been the spiralling of context, that it continues to outpace the capabilities of computer technology; hence, there has been a gradual shift away from an earlier hubris to a more recent modesty in identifying cause. What was once referred to as causality has given way to such relationships as probability, correspondence, association, correlation, and multivariate analysis.

The consequence of spiralling contextuality which results in the reduced utility of precise identification of cause converges with important strands of ancient Asian thought and more contemporary elements of Western thought.[26] The Lasswellian concept of the state as a manifold of events which, perhaps inspired by Whitehead, finds even more powerful support in the interrelatedness of all phenomena central to Freudian thought, precludes the division of events which would, by definition, make easy identification of cause possible. Here we find a remarkable congruence of Lasswell's interpretation of Whitehead's "emergence,"[27] Jung's "synchronicity" by which he so

---

noting science of character. Lorenz used it to refer to the study of behavior thus subsuming human under animal behavior. See also Robert Ardrey, *The Social Contract* (New York, 1970); Lionel Tiger and Robin Fox, *The Imperial Animal* (New York, 1971). Cf. Thomas Landon Thorson, *Biopolitics* (New York, 1970).

26. For relevant analysis, see F. S. C. Northrop, *The Meeting of East and West* (New York, 1946), pp. 315–46.

27. See Heinz Eulau, "The Maddening Methods of Harold D. Lasswell: Some Philosophical Underpinnings," in Arnold A. Rogow, ed., *Politics, Personality and Social Science in the Twentieth Century* (Chicago, 1969), pp. 21–22.

brilliantly explains Chinese thought,[28] and Niels Bohr's "complementarity" first advanced in physics in 1927 and subsequently expanded into a theory of knowledge.[29] With respect to the latter, it is of no small significance that Bohr when awarded the Danish Order of the Elephant in 1947 chose the symbol of *Yin-Yang* for the design of his coat of arms.

The concept of "rationality" overworked, misapplied, and widely misunderstood as a hallmark of "developed" systems must also be reconsidered in the light of spiralling contextuality. "Rationality" is premised on the isolation of causal factors and the ability to predict associations between such "causes" and outcomes. This syndrome is contorted by the spiralling of potential causes which defy identification. The concept of rationality, derivative from Weber's analysis of a bureaucratic model, "rationalized" in contrast to earlier religious, charismatic, and political forms of power, appears now to have reduced explanatory capacity.[30] Rational bureaucracy, i.e., formally structured and processually articulating with symmetry, elegance, efficiency, and in relative isolation, may exist concurrently with increasingly irrational behavior in society at large and within the bureaucracy. Further, the paralysis induced by clientele relations—interest-group liberalism, as Lowi calls it—vitiates the effectiveness of an architectonic polity and lessens the "rationality" which Weber described in his ideal type. The salient issue now appears to be not a goal of "rationality" but rather the achievement of a structure of interrelatedness to accommodate recognized nonrational as well as

28. C. G. Jung, "Foreword," *The I Ching or Book of Changes*, The Richard Wilhelm Translation (Princeton, 1969), 3d ed., p. xxiv.

29. See Gerald Holton, "The Roots of Complementarity," *Daedalus* (Fall 1970: The Making of Modern Science: Biographical Studies): 1015–56. Not only Freudian thought, but structural anthropology as developed by Lévi-Strauss strengthens the concept of "emergence" by its emphasis on the structure of relationships between patterns of recurrences. Claude Lévi-Strauss, *Structural Anthropology* (New York, 1967), esp. pp. 31 and 57. See also David Goddard, "Lévi-Strauss and the Anthropologists," *Social Research* 37 (1970): 366–79.

30. This is implicit in the analysis by Theodore Lowi in *The End of Liberalism* (New York, 1969), and his *The Politics of Disorder* (New York, 1971), and explicit in Anton C. Zijderveld, "Rationality and Irrationality in Pluralistic Society," *Social Research* 37 (1970): 23–47. See also Parsons' exposition of his concern with this issue: Talcott Parsons, "On Building Social System Theory: A Personal History," *Daedalus* (1970): 870–73. Exploring another dimension of this problem Jacobs substitutes the term "objectivity" for "rationality" on the ground that Asians do not comprehend the latter concept. Norman Jacobs, *Modernization Without Development* (New York, 1971), p. 9. This semantic substitution is not comparable to our rejection of "rationality" in this essay. Here rationality is rejected as a goal (a) because it is ethnocentric, (b) resists operational definition, and (c) may or may not emerge from reconstruction based primarily on each individual national culture.

"rational" components of thought. Classification into these categories will vary from one political system to another. In sum, the always permeable wall separating bureaucracy from politics has weakened and interpermeation of norms has made the two processes less distinguishable.

The nature of spiralling contextuality casts doubt on the utility both to theory-construction and to practice of the scholastic exercise "structural-functionalism" which, as introduced into political science by its interpreters from the then deeper well of Parsonian sociological waters, primed the political science pump for two decades only to produce a flow too gushing to bottle and too muddy to drink. Indeed Parsons asserts that recent developments "have made the designation 'structural-functional' increasingly less appropriate." Our perspective puts emphasis on structure, but function is subsumed in the consideration of process which must be constantly articulated to "spiralling contextuality." This appears, quite by chance, to be consonant with Parsons' latest emphasis.[31]

The inadequacy of a notion which assumes that cause can be precisely specified will have an important effect on the relations between countries giving and those receiving development assistance. A much less aggressive and interventionist posture is likely to result from the humility induced by an awareness of the complexity of context. The acceptance of an acausal principle thus assists in articulating change to indigenous culture.

Another important consequence of this analysis of context is that spiralling contextuality occurs at different rates in different political systems. The extremely rapid expansion and contraction of contextuality in the United States and elsewhere, for example, produces the condition which Toffler has aptly called *Future Shock*. In consequence, a radiating system is likely to induce change derivative from its own rapidly changing context with minimal awareness of the nature of contextual change in the recipient system. All sorts of anomalies occur. Thus indigenous medicine such as unani, aryuvedic, and voodoo is abandoned as being primitive in some countries while in the United States these practices are being explored with sympathy. Midwifery and paramedical techniques are discouraged in developing countries while they reemerge in the United States. Perhaps there is no better example than the spread of "sensitivity train-

31. Talcott Parsons, "On Building Social System Theory: A Personal History," *Daedalus* (Fall, 1970: The Making of Modern Science: Biographical Studies): 849.

ing" techniques to administration in such countries as Saudi Arabia, Pakistan, and the Philippines even while the American Medical Association warned against such techniques in the United States.[32]

The contextual disparities between agrarian (recipient) and technetronic (radiating) societies is aggravated by the communications and distributive technologies of the latter. The premium put on novelty in the technetronic society, and the diffusion of novelty with secularized messianic zeal easily overwhelms the agrarian society which doubts its own cultural integrity and lacks the structural apparatus to resist such cultural invasions.

III

The first requisite in this view of context, change, and cause is to adopt an intellectual posture—a way of perceiving ourselves, our historical consciousness, and the universe around us. The posture is one which views human development, hence national development, in circular rather than linear terms. Growth consists in reformulating and reconstructing the past in terms of new perceptions of the present and future. In this perspective we must think not in terms of the new and the old, or the modern and the outdated. We must think in terms of perennial reconstruction of elemental truths slightly changed by new applications. Such a nonlinear view requires us to regard knowledge as being diffused and effervescent in given places and at given times in history. Developing states can then reassess themselves and the nations of which they are a part, not as recipients of a superior technology, but as equal participants in an endless circular process of global sharing of ideas.

This posture, followed by profound understanding of the nature of spiralling contextuality, will ultimately move us to reconsider the philosophy, life-style, psychic values, and structures of government in Asia and Africa in a new context of respect and even admiration. If we view the colonial experience as embracing stages of political then economic dependence, it may be said that the nations of Asia and Africa in this recovery of their distinctive identities are emancipating themselves from a third and final stage of colonialism—that of dependence on ideas and cultures incompatible with local contexts.

32. See "Report of the Council on Mental Health of the American Medical Association," *Journal of the American Medical Association* 217 (27 Sept. 1971): 1853–54.

Emmette S. Redford • Watergate: A Test of
Constitutional Democracy

Watergate constitutes, among other things, a test of a particular system of constitutional democracy. To show the gravity and import of the test we will look at the bases and nature of the political system and its uniqueness in democratic government, next the nature of the test, then its resolution and significance for democracy, and finally some problems for the future.

The American system of government was constructed on the principles of rule of law and consent of the people. The latter was the basis of republicanism and later, with the expansion of the suffrage, of democracy. The former was the basis of constitutionalism, whereby all officials of government would be restrained by established mechanisms. These had as their purpose the protection of the liberty and security of the subject. The primary means in the minds of many of the constitutional fathers of the eighteenth century was to divide the powers of government among institutions deriving their selection from independent sources and serving as checks on each other, thus establishing in the words of James Madison a "constitutional equilibrium."[1] Experience in the colonial period had made them distrustful of executives, and in the revolutionary period, of legislatures. Their answer was the "constitutional equilibrium" and through it the maintenance of the rule of law. The weak instrument in the equilibrium appeared to be the judiciary;[2] but Marshall, by basing judicial review on the supreme law of the Constitution, was able to establish a foundation for judicial strength in the equilibrium.

The system, combined with the pluralism of society and its political forces and with the other institutional mechanisms (federalism, local government, and administrative delegations) has made positive government difficult in the United States, for it requires decision by concurrent consents. To make the system viable in a period of demands for positive government, the nation came increasingly to rely on executive leadership for both executive and legislative branches, par-

1. *The Federalist*, No. 49.
2. In *The Federalist*, No. 78, Alexander Hamilton wrote: "the judiciary is beyond comparison the weakest of the three departments of power."

ticularly the latter. As the tribune of the people since Jackson's presidency and with the status, powers, and influence developed in his office, the president has been expected in the twentieth century to provide policy leadership to the political parts of the government. The Congress—bicameral, its leadership decentralized to committees, its parties weak in their control of members—has found it difficult to legislate without presidential policy proposals. And by Nixon's presidency the threat of the judiciary to political decision in the combined action of the other two branches was not deemed to be formidable.

While there were dissenting voices, the dominant views about this development seemed to be summarized by two eminent political scientists. "What is good for the country is good for the President, and *vice versa*," wrote Richard Neustadt in 1960.[3] "The power of the President moves as a mighty host only with the grain of liberty and morality," wrote Clinton Rossiter in 1956.[4] In sum, a strong president and national welfare were interdependent, and the arbitrary or immoral exercise of presidential power was not to be feared.

The American system, like other constitutional democracies, has moved toward unity in executive-legislative action through executive leadership. Yet its basic feature of distributed power among independent centers is unique in a world where democracy—if it exists— usually is parliamentary democracy.[5] It establishes no single channel of representation, through which on the one hand an executive can be brought down promptly, or, on the other, can obtain solid support for his policies. Americans sometimes look with envy at parliamentary governments, at least those with two-party systems, because of the union of responsibility and of capability for viable government. Still, they have a system, and it has in its own confusing way both given and checked leadership, been based on consent, and maintained the rule of law through the constitutional equilibrium, including judicial review of legislative and executive actions.

Threat to the System

In a narrow sense, Watergate was an event—the break-in of Democratic party headquarters by emissaries of the Republican party; but

3. Richard E. Neustadt, *Presidential Power: The Politics of Leadership* (New York: John Wiley & Sons, Inc., 1960), p. 185.
4. Clinton Rossiter, *The American Presidency* (New York: The New American Library, 1956), p. 53.
5. One scholar, tracing its origins, has characterized it as "significantly medieval in

to look no further would be to miss its much more serious threat to the unique features of the American system. Broadly the word has encompassed a set of events that threatened Americans' ideal of constitutional democracy. In their entirety these events symbolized personal and immoral dominance of the government by the executive, the Machiavellian Prince overriding the restraints and supplanting the spirit of the constitutional system. What was "good for the United States" had become what was essential for firming the personal power of the Prince; government moved contrary to "the grain of liberty and morality."

In its broader sense Watergate included a number of specific activities that challenged the concept that government was limited for the security of the citizen by the spirit and mechanisms of constitutionalism. These activities, occurring either within or under the aegis of the Nixon presidency, included the following:

1. Espionage, including a break-in and a burglary of private premises, and also the search of public files containing information on private persons that was legally protected except for specific purposes.

2. Use of the investigatory and enforcement powers of agencies in the executive branch of the government against political enemies of the administration.

3. "Cover up" of violations of law, in disobedience of specific requirements of criminal law and the general constitutional duty of the president "to take care that the laws be faithfully executed."

4. Refusal to provide evidence to the courts and grand juries, thus indicating further violation of the "take care" provision of the Constitution.

5. Refusal to supply information to the Congress in aid to its investigatory function.

6. Use of the claim of national security to support excessive secrecy in government.

7. Violation of various laws on campaign contributions, including particularly soliciting or receiving such contributions with express or implied promises of public favor, and coercion through fear of loss of public favor on corporate executives to make illegal contributions.

---

character." Samuel P. Huntington, *Political Order in Changing Societies* (New Haven and London, 1968), p. 96.

8. Suspension of law by impounding funds appropriated through constitutional process.

9. Concentration of the powers of the executive branch in the White House staff, which became the center of illegal or immoral influence.

10. Conduct of acts of war without approval of the Congress, and false reporting on military activities to Congress.

The System's Remedy

The constitutional remedy that can be used against all civil officers is impeachment. For Watergate offenses an additional legal remedy was the prosecution of officers of government, other than the president,[6] and agents of the Republican political organization for specific violations of the criminal law. Those who violated the criminal law could not claim immunity because they acted on direction of a superior, including even the president. There were indictments and trials against a range of persons—from those in low stations to cabinet officers and White House staff. A parallel occurrence was resignations from cabinet members, White House staff, and agency heads. These occurred before convictions in criminal trials; they were a response to the unwritten rule that persons in such positions under grave suspicion of illegal or immoral acts should not remain in office.

But were there legal or political remedies that could operate effectively against the president himself? Resignation would apparently have been a prompt cure in a parliamentary system, for it seems inconceivable that a chief of government could have maintained his position if he had been subjected to the immediate confrontation and questioning of a representative body, and forced to assume responsibility for the acts of government. But the American system contained no precedent for presidential resignation, no provision for direct confrontation, and no fixed standard of complete presidential responsibility for the acts of subordinates.

The obvious remedy was the constitutionally prescribed process of impeachment—charge by the House of Representatives, trial in the Senate. Yet there were three complications in the use of this process. The first was the issue of grounds for impeachment. The Constitution provided for impeachment for "treason, bribery, other

6. Whether the president can be criminally prosecuted, prior to removal from office by an impeachment conviction, is an unresolved question. The question was not tested in Watergate proceedings.

high crimes and misdemeanors." By a narrow and legalistic interpretation of the words "high crimes and misdemeanors" the president would need to be convicted of a preexisting statutory or common law offense. A broader interpretation, and ultimately that accepted by the majority of the House judiciary committee, gave the provision a political meaning. Alexander Hamilton in the *Federalist*, Number 65, had defined the subjects of impeachment as being "those offences which proceed from the misconduct of public men, or, in other words, from the abuse or violation of some public trust" and had said that these were of a nature denominated *"Political."* This interpretation had support in preceding English uses of impeachment, other statements of founding fathers, and in precedents in impeachments in this country. It also made the impeachment provision meaningful in a system of constitutional checks designed to prevent abuse of power and protect the security of citizens.[7]

A second, and related, complication was the issue of the guilt of the president. Whether the charge was criminal acts or abuse of public power, the existence, and the discovery, of facts sufficient to sustain the charge in the House of Representatives and a conviction of the president in the Senate was requisite for application of the constitutional remedy.

A third factor was the time required for impeachment. The gamut of events would include a resolution in the House of Representatives to direct an inquiry by a committee (in this case, the Committee on the Judiciary), an investigation and report by this committee, the passage of an impeachment resolution in the House, arrangements for prosecution in the Senate, and a long trial and verdict by that body. In the meantime, it could be assumed that the president would remain in office, as did President Johnson in his impeachment trial in 1868. Yet a charge of impeachment would impair the leadership of the president and thus the functioning of the government; it would also raise the spectre of dangerous, even mad, action by a president seeking to divert attention from the trial and to sustain his power.[8]

7. For full analysis of the issue see *Constitutional Grounds for Presidential Impeachment*, Report of the Staff of the Impeachment Inquiry, Committee on the Judiciary, House of Representatives, 93d Congress, 2d Session, February 1974. Also, *Impeachment of Richard M. Nixon, President of the United States*, Report of the Committee on the Judiciary, House of Representatives, 93d Congress, 2d Session, 1974. Secondary sources on the issue are listed in the first of these publications.

8. The Twenty-fifth Amendment to the Constitution contains provisions for devolvement of duties on the Vice President whenever the President "is unable to discharge the powers and duties of his office." The applicability of these provisions to a situation

The search for facts both within and without the judiciary committee proceeded without prior resolution of the legal issue on grounds of impeachment. As was appropriate for a government resting on rule of law and consent of the people, the processes of search and deliberation on Watergate, whether related to guilt of the president or otherwise, were both legal and political. They included these main interacting and complementary elements:

1. Discovery by law officers of the break-in of Democratic headquarters, an obviously illegal act.

2. Relentless inquiry and fearless publicity by the mass communication media—making Watergate the nation's trauma, and creating citizens' concern that in turn led to a multitude of communications to their representatives in Congress.

3. Alertness in an opposition political party that had a majority in both houses of Congress, and thus was in a position to press committee action—a reflection of the way party development could support the independent position of the parts of the government contemplated by the framers of the Constitution.

4. Investigation by a committee of the Senate—wide-ranging and revealing and televised to the nation at hours when most of the television audience would be observing.

5. The appointment of a special prosecutor in the Department of Justice, independent of presidential control, to uncover and prosecute violations of law, and who ultimately would be able to move even against the president's claims of executive privilege to retain information—developments that reflected the strength of commitment in the nation to the rule of law.

6. A grand jury investigation of probable guilt followed by trial of the indicted.

7. Inquiry into the grounds for impeachment and the facts relating to guilt or innocence of the president by a committee in the House of Representatives.

8. The referendum to the sense of the people—taken through polls, the multiple other modes of public expression, and the sensitive ears of congressmen. For example, 800,000 letters were sent to the chairman of the House Judiciary Committee.

9. A Supreme Court ruling, by an 8 to 0 vote, that the president's

---

created by impeachment of a President seems unlikely unless the President himself invoked the amendment.

assertion of executive privilege on the ground of a public interest in confidentiality could not be sustained when it was interposed as a basis for withholding relevant and necessary evidence in a criminal trial. This ruling, of course, was the result of processes through which the Court acts as an independent check upon the executive.

These processes led eventually to a voting of impeachment charges in the House Judiciary Committee on July 27, 29, and 30, 1974. A first charge, based solely on criminal conduct of the president, was sustained by a vote of 27 to 11 (21 Democrats and 6 Republicans in the majority, 11 Republicans in the minority). A second charge based largely on abuse of public power was sustained by 28 to 10 (21 Democrats and 7 Republicans against 10 Republicans). A third charge was based on failure to supply information in response to subpoena to the House subcommittee. It was approved by 21 over 17 votes (19 Democrats and 2 Republicans over 2 Democrats and 15 Republicans).

Next, following the Supreme Court decision on July 24, the president in compliance with the Court's decision, yielded the tapes that were in his possession. The yielded evidence clearly revealed criminal action of the president to cover up evidence of criminal activity, and all members of the House committee then registered their vote for approval of the first charge in the impeachment articles. On August 9 the president resigned.

Four factors of significance in the events that had occurred can be justifiably emphasized. First, the president surrendered. A president who had stretched his powers to the limit, and whose supporters had used every resource to maintain his personal occupancy, was defenseless against an approaching conviction in the Senate on impeachment charges. A student from a country without confirmed democratic practices asked me in class months before Nixon's resignation, "If he is impeached, will he not use military power to stay in office?" My confident answer was, "He couldn't do it." The resignation was confirmation of three other significant things.

Second, as the saying goes in the nation, "the system worked." Grand juries and courts and congressional committees with independent positions had brought down a president. The institutional system created by the framers had been vindicated. It was victory for a system of "separated institutions sharing powers."[9]

9. Neustadt, *Presidential Power*, p. 33.

Third, law ruled. Courts carried on their procedures, committees sought legality in all their processes, the Supreme Court remained arbiter of constitutional conflict.

Fourth, the people gave consent. While nothing was decided either "in the streets" or by popular ballot, the light under which the struggle for legality moved forward was that of an open society. Press and commentators kept the light bright and the political representatives in Congress were responsive to an informed public.

If Watergate was trauma for constitutional democracy, it was also victory for it!

The Future

Yet, despite current victory, one may ask these questions: What will be the effects of Watergate on American government? Can Watergate supply confidence to Americans in the future of their form of constitutional democracy?

It can be suggested, first, that the succession of events that brought down President Nixon in 1974 are so exceptional that they provide no certainty of capability in the system to correct future abuse in the office of the president. There was chance discovery of the break-in, unusual vigor in a special prosecutor, tenacity and independence in a trial judge, persistence in the press, a majority in the opposition party in Congress, and the existence of taped conversation in the White House—through which the president convicted himself. There was, moreover, in this instance blatancy in offense, foolishness in the acts of the president's men, and naïveté in the president's behavior; in a future instance, a threat to constitutional democracy could be conducted with more subtlety, wisdom, and finesse.

Certainly no victory of the present assures victory in the future. As Thomas Jefferson said, "Eternal vigilance is the price of liberty." What offers hope against abuse in the future is the revelation of alertness and vigor in diverse centers of power and influence, and the allegiance in the public to the morality of the constitutional system.

It can be noted, secondly, that problems in the use of the constitutional remedy of impeachment remain unsolved. The issue on grounds of impeachment was not settled in a conviction in the Senate. Without a constitutional amendment to make abuse of power a basis for impeachment, there can be no certainty that a "constitutional equilibrium" exists. Nevertheless, powerful precedent is contained in article II of the impeachment charges, and the strength of the precedent is increased by the historical evidence gathered by the staff of the House committee on impeachment.

Moreover, the nation was spared the experience of a president in office, and an administration immobilized or acting dangerously, during a prolonged impeachment trial. There is consequently no public sense of need to consider whether the president should be suspended from office and an acting incumbency created for the period between a House vote for impeachment and the termination of a Senate trial.

There is the further question whether Watergate has weakened the presidency for the functions required of it in the American system. While the eighteenth-century purpose to avoid such concentration of power that its abuse could threaten the liberty and security of persons is preserved and strengthened by Watergate, the twentieth-century necessity for leadership to produce viable government toward positive ends calls for a strong president. It is probable, however, that Watergate will have no negative effects on presidential leadership; rather, that it will only emphasize the qualities that must exist in that leadership: that it can, as Rossiter said, "move as a mighty host only with the grain of liberty and morality."

It seems likely the severest tests of the American form of democracy in the future will be, not the prevention of abuse, but the capacity for governance. Yet the satisfaction of the American people now is in the ability of the system to restrain abuse; they see no need for radical change in the form of constitutional democracy to meet either this objective or the needs for viable government. Watergate has produced no sustained discussion of adoption of the alternate of parliamentary government. It is unlikely that Watergate will lead to any constitutional reforms that are designed to alter in any radical way the legal and political balances that have created government by concurrent consents made possible by presidential leadership, or impossible because such leadership does not exist.

Watergate has, however, produced a desire for reform within the system and a consciousness of issues with respect to its improved operation. The most notable focus of the reform movement is in the effort toward cleansing government from the deleterious effects of campaign financing. The revelations resulting from Watergate and associated incidents led to passage by Congress of the Federal Election Campaign Act Amendments of 1974. The new law provides limitations on the amounts that can be contributed to candidates for national offices by individuals or special interest groups and political committees; it also sets spending limits for the candidates for these offices. The law further provides a radical change in financing of presidential campaigns: it provides for public financing for presidential election campaigns and a mix of public and private financing for qualified candidates seeking a party nomination for president.

Watergate has, for the moment at least, made political officeholders more conscious of the need for rectitude in all matters of campaign financing and expenditures, and indeed, in all financial relationships with private interests. It has similarly heightened the public awareness of the corruptibility of government through private money, and it is possible that public interest lobbies will be able to sustain a movement for further reforms.

Watergate has also concentrated attention on numerous problems in the exercise of presidential powers and the conduct of the executive branch of the government.[10] Reference may be made to some of these that will have the attention of future presidents and may be the subjects of legislation. One is the separation of the political functions of campaign management from public officeholding. Although public officials in high policy positions have engaged in party activities in the past, and some political participation—such as speaking in defense of an administration—may be inevitable and appropriate on their part, Watergate revealed forms of partisan political participation that may be regarded as inacceptable in the future. Cabinet officers headed election committees and raised campaign funds, and White House staff devoted some of their time to the reelection campaign for the president. A prominent Senator has suggested, as one reform need, a legislative prohibition against any executive official soliciting or receiving campaign funds. Perhaps this and additional legislation will be considered and a presumption will develop that public executives should limit their energies to public duties.

Another problem is the relation of the president to law enforcement agencies of the government. The Constitution delegates to the president the responsibility "to take care that the laws be faithfully executed," and this requires that he be concerned with law enforce-

---

10. For full discussion of these problems, see the following report prepared and published by the National Academy of Public Administration: *Watergate: Its Implications for Responsible Government* (1974).

ment policy that will protect the public interest. But, law enforcement, whether civil or criminal, cannot be said to protect the public interest if used selectively to single out political opponents or political dissidents. The "take care" power was debased when it was used to direct tax collecting and other enforcement agencies to investigate "enemies" of the administration. Watergate should lead to a greater consciousness by presidents and other executive officers of the appropriate means and limits of presidential exercise of the "take care" provision. The distinctions between policy direction and policy application to individuals, between action that is necessary for public interests and that which is directed against particular persons or firms, may be difficult to draw in instant cases; but more caution in the exercise of presidential power and increased attention to procedural and structural safeguards that insure evenhanded administration of law can be expected as a consequence of the revelation of the gross misuses of presidential power in the Nixon administration.

Watergate has also renewed attention to the respective roles of White House aides and departmental executives in the conduct of the executive branch of the government. Departmental executives have visibility and legal responsibility; they are persons whose trustworthiness for high public position is partially insured through the processes of senatorial confirmation; they are men with personal achievements and reputations which they will desire to enhance through service in their posts. White House aides are less visible; they are fully dependent on the president and their achievement is through service to his needs.

Both types of public servants are essential to the president and the performance of public business. Likewise, Watergate revealed that public trust in either type could be misplaced. Nevertheless, Watergate exhibited an unhealthy enlargement in the number of staff aides to the president, and an unhealthy extension of their activities. In the end these aides were interposed between the president and the department heads, creating a centralization of government in aides who lacked public visibility and legal responsibility.

The problems in obtaining a balance between the service of the two kinds of officials are complex and numerous. President Nixon sought resolution, in part, through a departmental reorganization that would facilitate coordination and direction at the department level, but Congress did not act on his proposal. This illustrates only one aspect of the problems in presidential use and supervision of assistants.

With respect to these problems, the significance of Watergate is that it has illuminated hazards that will engage attention in future deliberations and decisions.

Watergate has also emphasized the need for a cooperative and open presidency. The constitutional system was devised for cooperation as well as check between branches of government. The "take care" provision implies an obligation of the executive to assist the courts. The Supreme Court's decision limiting executive privilege when interposed against subpoenas for evidence in criminal trials supports this obligation. The issues on support of congressional investigation were not similarly decided and may be at rest.

Also, a proposed article of impeachment alleging that the president had "authorized, ordered, and ratified the concealment from the Congress of the facts and the submission to the Congress of false and misleading statements" on bomb operations in Cambodia was voted down (26 to 12) in the House committee considering impeachment. This does not mean, however, that the broader issues on cooperation and openness are at rest. Watergate has made the nation more conscious of excessive claims for secrecy in matters affecting national security, and of the importance of accurate reporting to Congress and the public on military and other operations. Future presidents may be warned that credibility before Congress and the public is a test of their responsibility and that openness, honesty, and accuracy are the routes to achieving it.

Changes in campaign financing, improvements in the operation of the executive branch, and heightened consciousness of the need for a cooperative and open presidency will not by themselves establish confidence in the future of the constitutional system. There must be confidence also in the ability of Congress to perform its functions. The Congress has, in comparison with other parliamentary structures, unique roles in checking abuses and carrying forward the process of government. Most observers will probably conclude that with respect to Watergate, the checking function of Congress was performed satisfactorily, but that—as was shown at the first of this section— there are uncertainties on the adequacy of its remedy for future situations. Perhaps, however, the more important questions relate to the ability of Congress to maintain the continuous checks on the executive revealed to be needed by Watergate but not rising to the level requiring removal of a president. Can Congress effectively penetrate the secrecy that exists on matters of national security? Can it effectively prevent executive actions that commit it to support war? Can it maintain, even in domestic affairs, oversight of the executive branch that prevents favoritism, unequal enforcement of law, and diversion of purpose expressed in law?

The primary answer that has evolved in the American system is a committee structure through which constant oversight of the executive is exercised. This institutional arrangement is supplemented by the practice of presidents of conferring with leaders of the Congress on critical issues of policy, particularly in crisis situations. The solutions to Congress's problem can be sought in the improvement of its internal processes and its interrelationships with the president.

Information—adequate and timely—is the need. It is probably unavoidable that presidents will take some actions on which congressional information and executive-congressional consultation are inadequate, and congressional consent anticipated by the rules of the constitutional system is not obtained, at least if prompt national security decisions seem to be required. It may be doubted, however, whether provision for questioning cabinet members on the floor of the Houses or other techniques not now employed, would be more conducive to producing congressional information than committee oversight and executive-congressional consultations.

Congressional oversight over the exercise of executive power will not be enough to maintain an effective equilibrium of power. Even though a strong presidency is required, and may not have been threatened by Watergate, the excessive concentration of power in that office in response to the need for viable government can be prevented only by the existence of a strong coactive Congress in the development of the policy of the nation. Part of the lesson of Watergate is that the maintenance of the constitutional system requires concern, not only with the operation of the executive branch, but also with the capability of Congress for sharing the active force of government. There is movement in Congress toward assertion of its position, revealed particularly in efforts to equip itself for effective budgetary control and to insure its participation in decisions on engaging in war. There is also continued movement within Congress toward improving its organization. But in exempting congressional candidacies from the public financing provisions of the Campaign Act Amendments, Congress showed more concern for purity in the executive than in the Congress. Also, the reign of an opposition party in Congress, frequent in the twentieth century, can create readiness to apply constitutional checks against the executive but makes difficult congressional cooperation with the executive in developing policy. Nevertheless, Watergate was a good thing for the Congress, for it has alerted its members and the public to the need for congressional effectiveness.

One other factor that affects the expectations for the future is the role of the press. Watergate demonstrated the capabilities for effectiveness of the press as the fourth branch of government. In a sense the victory of Watergate was a victory for the press. It uncovered facts; it enlightened the public; it kept the issues alive. It must be noted, however, that as with Watergate in its totality, the action of the press was "by the skin of the teeth." The White House correspondents did not uncover Watergate. Reporters from the *Washington Post*, ordinarily assigned to local and suburban news, discovered and pursued the Watergate facts; many other newspapers, particularly in the smaller cities, tended to ignore or abbreviate the *Post* stories, especially during the first year. Nevertheless, the nation's faith in its bloodhounds of the press is supported. It should be noted, also, that this branch of the government, too, may be more effective as a means of checking power than as a contributor to viable government. The press, it has been said, is the natural enemy of the president; it may indeed be true that the press's effectiveness as critic of the president and its concentration on failures rather than successes in government undermine the leadership of any president. And thus the nation may pay some price for the addition of the press to the equilibrium of powers.

Does Watergate, then, supply confidence in the future of constitutional democracy in the United States? Nothing can be certain for long in these changing and tempestuous times. Events may overwhelm any constitutional system. But despite the chance nature of the events and the unresolved problems of the future, Watergate supplies strong support for confidence in the American form of constitutional democracy. It has demonstrated that when evil men in high positions, even the president, abuse the public trust placed in them, the multiple checks in a government of divided powers can bring such men down—indeed, it may not be too much to say that this can be expected. Watergate has left a powerful warning to those who govern in the future on the potency of legal and popular checks on the exercise of power. It has vindicated the view that a president can use power successfully only if he "moves with the grain of liberty and morality" in the nation, and supported the conviction that the grain of liberty and morality is rule of law and popular consent.

For the present, Watergate has had other consequences. Undoubtedly, it has lowered the faith of the people in government and the politicians who serve in it. Yet this lack of faith is traditional and a healthy degree of skepticism has positive as well as negative effects. Watergate has, on the other hand, educated the present generation of Americans on the nature of their constitutional system. It has increased awareness of the public and its leaders to problems in the operation of the system that need to be faced. It has even generated reform activity directed toward increased morality in gaining and using power, legal and open use of executive power, and maintenance of the constitutional equilibrium. These immediate consequences may have a long-run effect of substantially strengthening the system of constitutional democracy.